DATE DUE

FAULT TOLERANT
AND
FAULT TESTABLE
HARDWARE DESIGN

FAULT TOLERANT
AND
FAULT TESTABLE
HARDWARE DESIGN

Parag K. Lala

formerly of the
Department of Computer Science
University of York, UK

currently
Associate Professor
Dept of Electrical and Computer Engineering
Syracuse University
New York, USA

Prentice/Hall International

Englewood Cliffs, New Jersey   London   New Delhi   Rio de Janeiro
Singapore   Sydney   Tokyo   Toronto   Wellington

Library of Congress Cataloging in Publication Data

Lala, Parag K., 1948–
  Fault tolerant and fault testable hardware design.

Bibliography: p.
  Includes index.
    1. Electronic digital computers—Reliability. 2. Fault-
tolerant computing. I. Title
TK 7888.3.L27 1985   621.3819′583   84-8316
ISBN 0-13-308248-2 (case)

British Library Cataloguing in Publication Data

Lala, Parag, K.
  Fault tolerant and fault testable hardware
  design.
  1. Fault-tolerant computing
  I. Title
  001.64   QA 76.9.F38

  ISBN 0-13-308248-2

0-13-308248 2

Prentice-Hall International, Inc., *London*
Prentice-Hall of Australia Pty Ltd., *Sydney*
Prentice-Hall Canada Inc., *Toronto*
Prentice-Hall of India Private Ltd., *New Delhi*
Prentice-Hall of Japan, Inc., *Tokyo*
Prentice-Hall of Southeast Asia Pte Ltd., *Singapore*
Prentice-Hall, Inc., *Englewood Cliffs, New Jersey*
Prentice-Hall do Brasil Ltda, *Rio de Janeiro*
Whitehall Books Ltd., *Wellington, New Zealand*

10 9 8 7 6 5 4 3 2

Typeset by Pintail Studios Ltd., Ringwood, Hampshire, England

Printed in the United States of America

To my mother Madhuri and the memory of my father Benoyendra Nath

In the thick of a teeming snowfall
I saw my shadow on snow.
I turned and looked back up at the sky,
Where we still look to ask the why
Of everything below.

Robert Frost   *Afterflakes*

CONTENTS

4   FAULT TOLERANT DESIGN OF DIGITAL SYSTEMS

PREFACE

Fault tolerance and testability have the common objective of improving the reliability of computer hardware. Fault tolerance is concerned with masking or recovering from the effects of faults once they have been detected, whereas testability involves a design approach aimed at easing the detection of faults. It is the relative cost which determines whether for a certain application one approach is more desirable than the other. Much work has been done recently in both areas. Such efforts have resulted in certain design philosophies and techniques. Unfortunately many engineers are not familiar with these; consequently there is an urgent need for university courses and textbooks to provide engineers with both general and specific directions on designing for fault tolerance and testability.

This book has been written mainly as a reference volume for postgraduate students in electrical engineering and computer science; it will also be suitable as a text for final-year options in undergraduate courses, provided that the readers have some background in switching theory and logic design. The book will prove equally useful for practicing engineers who require familiarity with recent research on reliable hardware design; a list of references on which I have drawn is provided at the end of each chapter.

Chapter 1 deals with the basics of reliability theory. Common terms used in reliability measure, such as mean-time-between-failures and availability, are defined and the importance of maintainability is emphasized.

Chapter 2 covers most of the important faults that can be found in digital circuits. The classical stuck-at-1, stuck-at-0 logic faults are discussed and then non-classical faults, such as bridging and stuck-open faults, are introduced. The difference between intermittent and transient faults is also considered and various models for intermittent faults are described.

Chapter 3 covers fault detection in combinational and sequential logic circuits. The basic testing techniques for detecting fault conditions in combinational circuits are explained with examples; the problem created by the presence of multiple faults is also considered. The testing of sequential circuits still remains a major problem, for which no generally accepted solution has been found. In this chapter the state-table verification technique for testing sequential circuits is discussed in detail. Next some non-conventional yet extremely effective techniques for testing logic circuits, such as random and transition count testing, are introduced. Finally the signature testing of logic circuits using linear shift registers is presented in detail with examples of signature formats and their generation.

Chapter 4 discusses in detail many classes of hardware fault tolerance techniques including a detailed examination of fault detection and recovery methods. The use of error-correcting codes in the design of fault tolerant sequential circuits and computer memory systems have also been dealt with. In addition software and time redundancy techniques are outlined. The concept of "fail-soft" operation is introduced and several fault tolerant systems are described. Finally a scheme for fault tolerant design of VLSI chips is given.

Chapter 5 presents recent developments in the area of self-checking and fail-safe circuit design. The design of a specific circuit type, self-checking checkers, is examined for various error-detecting codes which are likely to be used in hardware design. Self-checking and fail-safe design of sequential circuits are also considered. The last section deals with the work done so far on the design of self-checking programmable logic arrays (PLA).

Chapter 6 focuses on the various design techniques which can be used to enhance the testability of combinational and sequential logic circuits. A number of design methods, proposed for improving the testability of VLSI chips, are described. The concepts of built-in-tests and autonomous self-tests are explained. In addition several techniques are considered to improve the testability of logic boards designed without due consideration to their testing.

Chapter 7 discusses the current research issues in reliable computing systems design.

The appendix is included to provide an introduction to Markov models, which have been widely applied to the study of temporary faults. An annotated bibliography of conference proceedings and books for further reading, is also given.

I am grateful to my colleagues Professor I. C. Pyle and Mr D. G. Burnett-Hall, who helped me, directly or indirectly, in the preparation of certain sections of the manuscript. I also thank the reviewers of the manuscript for their constructive criticism, which has helped in making this a better book than it would have been otherwise. My special thanks go to Dr J. I. Missen of the City University, London, who first introduced me to the subject. I am also indebted to Angela Fairclough, who typed parts of the manuscript.

Lastly I acknowledge the support of my wife, Meena, with typing, editing and retyping to bring this text into reality; without her help and encouragement I should still be working on the manuscript.

PARAG K. LALA

FAULT TOLERANT
AND
FAULT TESTABLE
HARDWARE DESIGN

1 BASIC CONCEPTS OF RELIABILITY

1.1 THE DEFINITION OF RELIABILITY

In recent years the complexity of digital systems has increased dramatically. Although semiconductor manufacturers try to ensure that their products are reliable, it is almost impossible not to have faults somewhere in a system at any given time. As a result, reliability has become a topic of major concern to both system designers and users [1.1, 1.2]. A fundamental problem in estimating reliability is whether a system will function in a prescribed manner in a given environment for a given period of time. This, of course, depends on many factors such as the design of the system, the parts and components used, and the environment. Performance of a given system, under given conditions, for a given period of time can be considered as a chance event—i.e. the outcome of the event is unknown until it has actually occurred. Hence it is natural to consider the reliability of a system as an unknown parameter which is defined to be the probability that the given system will perform its required function under specified conditions for a specified period of time.

The reliability of a system can be increased by employing the method of worst case design, using high-quality components and imposing strict quality control procedures during the assembly phase. However such measures can increase the cost of a system significantly. An alternative approach to reliable system design is to incorporate "redundancy" (i.e. additional resources) into a system with the aim of masking the effects of faults. This approach does not necessitate the use of high-quality components; instead standard components can be used in a redundant and reconfigurable architecture (see Chap. 4). In view of the decreasing cost of hardware components it is certainly less expensive to use the second approach to design reliable systems.

1

1.2   RELIABILITY AND THE FAILURE RATE

Let us consider the degradation of a sample of N identical components under "stress conditions" (temperature, humidity, etc.). Let $S(t)$ be the number of surviving components, i.e. the number of components still operating at time t after the beginning of the "ageing experiment", and $F(t)$ the number of components that have failed up to time t. Then the probability of survival of the components, also known as the *reliability* $R(t)$, is

$$R(t) = \frac{S(t)}{N}$$

The probability of failure of the components, also known as the *unreliability* $Q(t)$, is

$$Q(t) = \frac{F(t)}{N}$$

Since $S(t) + F(t) = N$, we must have

$$R(t) + Q(t) = 1$$

The failure rate, also known as the "hazard rate", $Z(t)$ is defined to be the number of failures per unit time compared with the number of surviving components:

$$Z(t) = \frac{1}{S(t)} \frac{dF(t)}{dt} \tag{1.1}$$

Study of electronic components show that under normal conditions the failure rate varies as indicated in Fig. 1.1. There is an initial period of high failure because in any large collection of components there are usually components with defects and these fail, i.e. they do not work as intended, after they are put into operation. For this reason, the first period is called the "burn-in" period of defective components. The middle phase is the "useful life" period when the failure rate is relatively constant; in this phase failures are random in time. The

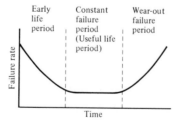

Fig. 1.1   Variation of failure rate with time.

final phase is the "wear out" period, when the failure rate begins to increase rapidly with time. The curve of Fig. 1.1 is often called the "bath-tub" curve because of its shape.

In the "useful life" period the failure rate is constant, and therefore

$$Z(t) = \lambda \text{ (say)} \tag{1.2}$$

With the previous nomenclature,

$$R(t) = \frac{S(t)}{N} = \frac{N - F(t)}{N} = 1 - \frac{F(t)}{N}$$

Therefore

$$\frac{dR(t)}{dt} = -\frac{1}{N} \cdot \frac{dF(t)}{dt}$$

or

$$\frac{dF(t)}{dt} = -N \frac{dR(t)}{dt} \tag{1.3}$$

Substituting equations (1.2) and (1.3) in equation (1.1)

$$\lambda = -\frac{N}{S(t)} \cdot \frac{dR(t)}{dt}$$

$$= -\frac{1}{R(t)} \cdot \frac{dR(t)}{dt} \quad \text{since} \quad R(t) = \frac{S(t)}{N}$$

or

$$\lambda \cdot dt = -\frac{dR(t)}{R(t)}$$

The above expression may be integrated giving

$$\lambda \int_0^t dt = -\int_1^{R(t)} \frac{dR(t)}{dt}$$

The limits of the integration are chosen in the following manner: $R(t)$ is 1 at $t = 0$, and at time t by definition the reliability is $R(t)$. Integrating, then

$$\lambda |t|_0^t = |\log_e R(t)|_1^{R(t)}$$

$$\lambda t = -|\log_e R(t) - \log_e 1|$$

$$-\lambda t = \log_e R(t)$$

Therefore

$$R(t) = \exp(-\lambda t) \qquad (1.4)$$

The above relationship is generally known as the *exponential failure law*; λ is usually expressed as percentage failures per 1000 hours or as failures per hour. When the product λt is small,

$$R(t) = 1 - \lambda t \qquad (1.5)$$

System failures, like component failures, can also be categorized into three periods of operation. The early system failures such as wiring errors, dry joints, faulty interconnections, etc., are normally eliminated by the manufacturer's test procedures. System failures occurring during the useful life period are entirely due to component failures.

If a system contains k types of component, each with failure rate λ_k, then the system failure rate, λ_{ov}, is

$$\lambda_{ov} = \sum_{1}^{k} N_k \lambda_k$$

where there are N_k of each type of component.

1.3   RELATION BETWEEN RELIABILITY AND MEAN-TIME-BETWEEN-FAILURES

Reliability $R(t)$ gives different values for different operating times. Since the probability that a system will perform successfully depends upon the conditions under which it is operating and the time of operation, the reliability figure is not the ideal for practical use. More useful to the user is the average time a system will run between failures; this time is known as the *mean-time-between-failures* (MTBF). The MTBF of a system is usually expressed in hours and is given by $\int_0^{\infty} R(t)\,dt$, i.e. it is the area underneath the reliability curve $R(t)$ plotted versus t; this result is true for any failure distribution. For the exponential failure law,

$$MTBF = \int_0^{\infty} \exp(-\lambda t)\,dt$$

$$= -\frac{1}{\lambda} |\exp(-\lambda t)|_0^t = \frac{1}{\lambda} \qquad (1.6)$$

In other words, the MTBF of a system is the reciprocal of the failure rate. If λ is the number of failures per hour, the MTBF is expressed in hours. If, for example, we have 4000 components with a failure rate of 0.02% per 1000 hours, the average number of failures per hour is:

$$\frac{0.02}{100} \times \frac{1}{1000} \times 4000 = 8 \times 10^{-4} \text{ failures/hour}$$

The MTBF of the system is therefore equal to $1/(8 \times 10^{-4})$ or $1/8 \times 10^{4} = 1250$ hours. Substituting equation (1.6) in the reliability expression equation (1.4) gives

$$R(t) = \exp(-\lambda t)$$

$$= \exp(-t/\text{MTBF}) \qquad (1.7)$$

A graph of reliability against time is shown in Fig. 1.2. As time increases the reliability decreases and when $t = \text{MTBF}$, the reliability is only 36.8%. Thus a system with an MTBF of say 100 hours has only a 36.8% chance of running 100 hours without failure.

By combining equations (1.5) and (1.6), we have

$$R(t) = 1 - \lambda t$$

$$= 1 - \frac{t}{\text{MTBF}}$$

Therefore

$$\text{MTBF} = \frac{t}{1 - R(t)}$$

Example   A first-generation computer contains 10 000 thermionic valves each with $\lambda = 0.5\%/(1000 \text{ hours})$. What is the period of 99% reliability?

$$\text{MTBF} = \frac{t}{1 - 0.99}$$

$$t = \text{MTBF} \times 0.01$$

$$= \frac{0.01}{\lambda_{\text{ov}}} \qquad (1.8)$$

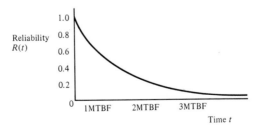

Reliability $R(t)$

Fig. 1.2   Reliability curve.

$$N = \text{No. of valves} = 10\ 000$$

$$\lambda = \text{failure rate of valves} = 0.5\%/(1000 \text{ hours})$$

$$= 0.005/(1000 \text{ hours})$$

$$= 5 \times 10^{-6}/\text{hour}$$

Therefore

$$\lambda_{ov} = N\lambda = 10^4 \times 5 \times 10^{-6} = 5 \times 10^{-2}/\text{hour}$$

From equation (1.8),

$$t = \frac{0.01}{5 \times 10^{-2}} = \frac{10^{-2}}{5 \times 10^{-2}} = 0.2 \text{ hour} = 12 \text{ minutes}$$

This figure was often typical!

1.4 MAINTAINABILITY

When a system fails, repair action is normally carried out to restore the system to operational effectiveness. The probability that a failed system will be restored to working order within a specified time is called the *maintainability* of the system. In other words maintainability is the probability of isolating and repairing a "fault" (see Chap. 2) in a system within a given time. There is therefore a relationship between maintainability and repair rate μ and hence with mean-time-to-repair (MTTR). MTTR and μ are always related [1.3]:

$$\mu = \frac{1}{\text{MTTR}}$$

MTTR and μ are related to maintainability $M(t)$ as follows:

$$M(t) = 1 - \exp(-\mu t) = 1 - \exp\left(-\frac{t}{\text{MTTR}}\right)$$

where t is the permissible time constraint for the maintenance action.

In order to design and manufacture a maintainable system, it is necessary to predict the MTTR for various fault conditions that could occur in the system. Such predictions are generally based on the past experiences of designers and the expertise available to handle repair work.

The system repair time consists of two separate intervals—passive repair time and active repair time [1.3]. The passive repair time is mainly determined by the time taken by service engineers to travel to the customer site. In many cases the cost of travel time exceeds the cost of the actual repair. The active repair time is directly affected by the system design and may be subdivided as follows:

1. The time between the occurrence of a failure and the system user becoming aware that it has occurred.
2. The time needed to detect a fault and isolate the replaceable component(s) responsible.
3. The time needed to replace the faulty component(s).
4. The time needed to verify that the fault has been removed and the system is fully operational.

The active repair time can be improved significantly by designing the system so that faults may be detected and quickly isolated. As more complex systems are designed, it becomes more difficult to isolate the faults. However if adequate self-test features are incorporated into the replaceable components of a system, it becomes easier to detect and isolate faults, which facilitates repair |1.4|.

1.5 AVAILABILITY

The availability of a system is the probability that the system will be "up", i.e. functioning according to expectations at any time during its scheduled working period |1.3|.

$$\text{Availability} = \frac{\text{System up-time}}{\text{System up-time} + \text{System down-time}}$$

$$= \frac{\text{System up-time}}{\text{System up-time} + (\text{No. of failures} \times \text{MTTR})}$$

$$= \frac{\text{System up-time}}{\text{System up-time} + (\text{System up-time} \times \lambda \times \text{MTTR})}$$

$$= \frac{1}{1 + (\lambda \times \text{MTTR})}$$

$$= \frac{\text{MTBF}}{\text{MTBF} + \text{MTTR}} \quad \text{since} \quad \lambda = \frac{1}{\text{MTBF}}$$

If the MTTR can be reduced, availability will increase and the system will be more economical. A system where faults are rapidly diagnosed is more desirable than a system which has a lower failure rate but where the cause of a failure takes a long time to locate, and consequently a lengthy system down-time is needed for repair.

1.6   SERIES AND PARALLEL SYSTEMS

The reliability of a system can be derived in terms of the reliabilities or the failure rates of the subsystems used to build it. Two limiting cases of system design are frequently met in practice:

1. Systems in which each subsystem must function if the system as a whole is to function.
2. Systems in which the correct operation of just one subsystem is sufficient for the system to function satisfactorily. In other words the system consists of redundant subsystems and will fail only if all subsystems fail.

Case 1   Let us consider a system in which a failure of any subsystem would cause a system failure. This can be modelled as a series system as shown in Fig. 1.3. If the subsystem failures are independent and R_i is the reliability of subsystem i, then the overall system reliability is

$$R_{ov} = \prod_{i=1}^{N} R_i$$

In the constant failure rate case where $R_i = \exp(-\lambda_i t)$

$$R_{ov} = \prod_{i=1}^{N} \exp(-\lambda_i t)$$

$$= \exp\left(\sum_{i=1}^{N} \lambda_i t \right)$$

Therefore the failure rate of the system is just the sum of the failure rates of the subsystems.

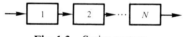

Fig. 1.3   Series system.

If the N subsystems have identical failure rates $\lambda_i = \lambda$, then $R_i = R$. Hence the overall system reliability is

$$R_{ov} = \exp(-N\lambda t)$$

$$= R^N$$

and

$$MTBF = \frac{1}{N\lambda}$$

Note that the overall reliability is decreased N-fold while the MTBF is $1/N$ of that of the subsystem. For example if each subsystem has 99% reliability after a year, a system consisting of 10 subsystems will have a reliability of 0.99^{10} or about 0.9. Consequently in a series system high reliability can be achieved only if the individual subsystems have very high reliability.

Case 2   In this case system failure can occur only when all subsystems have failed. This can be modelled as a parallel system, as shown in Fig. 1.4. If the failures are independent and R_i is the reliability of subsystem i, then the overall reliability of the system is

$$R_{ov} = 1 - \prod_{i=1}^{N} (1 - R_i)$$

If all the subsystems are identical, each with a constant failure rate λ, then

$$R_{ov} = 1 - (1 - R)^N$$
$$= 1 - |1 - \exp(-\lambda t)|^N$$

For example, if a system consists of 10 mutually redundant subsystems, each having only 0.75 reliability, the overall reliability of the system will be

$$R_{ov} = 1 - (1 - 0.75)^{10}$$
$$\approx 0.9999$$

In general the MTBF of a parallel system with N identical subsystems is $\sum_{j=1}^{N} 1/j$ times better than that of a single subsystem. For example if a parallel system consists of two subsystems, then

$$R_{ov} = 1 - |1 - \exp(-\lambda t)|^2$$
$$= 2 \exp(-\lambda t) - \exp(-2\lambda t)$$

Therefore the MTBF of the system is

$$= \int_0^\infty |2 \exp(-\lambda t) - \exp(-2\lambda t)| \, dt$$
$$= 3/2\lambda$$

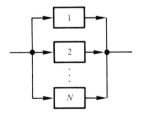

Fig. 1.4   Parallel system.

In practice a system normally consists of a combination of series and parallel subsystems. Figure 1.5 depicts two different interconnections of four subsystems. These systems are useful when short-circuits or open-circuits are the most commonly expected faults. The parallel-to-series network of Fig. 1.5(a) is used when the primary failure mode is an open-circuit, whereas the series-to-parallel network of Fig. 1.5(b) is used when the primary mode is a short-circuit [1.5].

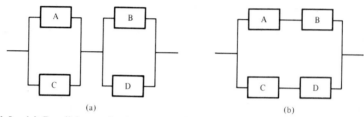

(a)   (b)

Fig. 1.5   (a) Parallel-to-series interconnection scheme; (b) series-to-parallel interconnection scheme.

If subsystems A and C are processors and subsystems B and D are memories, the system of Fig. 1.5(a) can operate if (A, D) or (C, B) or (A, B) or (C, D) works, whereas the system of Fig. 1.5(b) can operate only if either (A, B) or (C, D) works. In this situation the reliability of the parallel-to-series system is

$$R_{PS} = [1 - (1 - R_A)(1 - R_C)][1 - (1 - R_B)(1 - R_D)]$$

and the reliability of the series-to-parallel system is

$$R_{SP} = [1 - (1 - R_A R_B)(1 - R_C R_D)]$$

where R_A, R_B, R_C and R_D are the reliabilities of subsystems A, B, C and D respectively. Assuming

$$R_A = R_B = R_C = R_D = R$$

Then

$$R_{PS} = R^4 - 4R^3 + 4R^2$$

and

$$R_{SP} = 2R^2 - R^4$$

Some indication of the effectiveness of the series-to-parallel and parallel-to-series schemes is shown by assigning a range of values to R, as in Table 1.1. The figures in the table show clearly that $R_{PS} > R_{SP}$.

R	0.7	0.8	0.9	0.95
R_{PS}	0.828	0.921	0.980	0.995
R_{SP}	0.739	0.870	0.963	0.991

Table 1.1   Comparison of R_{PS} and R_{SP}

1.7   REFERENCES

1.1 Champine, G. A., "What makes a system reliable?", *Datamation*, 195–206 (September 1978).

1.2 *IEEE Spectrum*, Special issue on Reliability (October 1981).

1.3 Smith, D. J., *Reliability Engineering*, Pitman (1972).

1.4 Thomas, J. L., "Modular maintenance design concept", *Proc. IEEE Micro-Delcon*, 98–103 (1979).

1.5 McConnel, S. and D. P. Siewiorek, "Evaluation criteria", Chap. 5 of *The Theory and Practice of Reliable System Design* (Edited by D. P. Siewiorek and R. S. Swarz), Digital Press (1982).

2 FAULTS IN DIGITAL CIRCUITS

2.1 FAILURES AND FAULTS

A *failure* is said to have occurred in a circuit or system if it deviates from its specified behavior |2.1|. A *fault* on the other hand is a physical defect which may or may not cause a failure. A fault is characterized by its nature, value, extent and duration |2.2|. The "nature" of a fault can be classified as logical and non-logical. A *logical* fault causes the logic value at a point in a circuit to become opposite to the specified value. *Non-logical* faults include the rest of the faults such as the malfunction of the clock signal, power failure, etc. The "value" of a logical fault at a point in the circuit indicates whether the fault creates fixed or varying erroneous logical values. The "extent" of a fault specifies whether the effect of the fault is localized or distributed. A local fault affects only a single variable whereas a distributed fault affects more than one. A logical fault, for example, is a local fault while the malfunction of the clock is a distributed fault. The "duration" of a fault refers to whether the fault is permanent or temporary.

2.2 MODELLING OF FAULTS

Faults in a circuit may occur due to defective components, breaks in signal lines, lines shorted to ground or power supply, short-circuiting of signal lines, excessive delays, etc. Besides errors or ambiguities in design specifications, design rule violations, etc., also result in faults. Faulkner *et al.* |2.3| have found that specification faults and design rule violations accounted for 10% of the total faults encountered during the commissioning of subsystems of a mid-range mainframe computer which was implemented using MSI; however, during the system validation such faults constituted 44% of the total. Poor designs may also result in hazards, races or metastable flip-flop behavior in a circuit; such faults manifest themselves as "intermittents" throughout the life of the circuit.

In general the effect of a fault is represented by means of a model, which represents the change the fault produces in circuit signals. The fault models in use today are:

1. Stuck-at fault.
2. Bridging fault.
3. Stuck-open fault.

2.2.1   Stuck-at Faults

The most common model used for logical faults is the "single stuck-at fault". It assumes that a fault in a logic gate results in one of its inputs or the output being fixed to either a logic 0 (stuck-at-0) or a logic 1 (stuck-at-1). Stuck-at-0 and stuck-at-1 faults are often abbreviated to s-a-0 and s-a-1 respectively, and the abbreviations will be adopted here.

Let us consider a NAND gate with input A s-a-1 (Fig. 2.1). The NAND gate perceives the input A as a 1 irrespective of the logic value placed on the input. The output of the NAND gate in Fig. 2.1 is 0 for the input pattern shown, when the s-a-1 fault is present. The fault-free gate has an output of 1. Therefore, the pattern shown in Fig. 2.1 can be used as a "test" for the A input s-a-1, since there is a difference between the output of the fault-free and the faulty gate.

The stuck-at fault model, often referred to as the "classical" fault model, offers good representation for the most common types of failures, e.g. short-circuits ("shorts") and open-circuits ("opens") in many technologies. Figure 2.2 illustrates the transistor–transistor (TTL) realization of a NAND gate, the numbers 1, 2, 3 indicating places where opens may principally occur, while 4 and 5 indicate the basic types of shorts |2.4|.

1. Signal line open (fault 1)   This fault prevents the sink current I_s from flowing through the emitter of the input transistor T1 into the output of the preceding gate. Thus, the input appears to be connected to a constant level 1, i.e. s-a-1.

2. Supply voltage open (fault 2)   In this case the gate is deprived of its supply voltage and thus neither the current I_s, which would switch the transistor T1 on, nor the current I_r, which may excite T3, can flow. Both output transistors

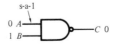

Fig. 2.1   NAND gate with input A s-a-1.

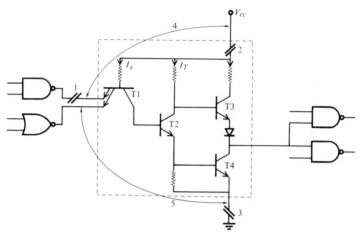

Fig. 2.2   Schematic diagram of a NAND gate (*courtesy of Digital Processes*).

are cut off and the output appears to be open. The fault can be interpreted as the gate output s-a-1.

3. Ground open (fault 3)   This fault prevents transistors T2 and T4 from conducting and thus the current I_T continually switches transistor T3 on. The output has the value of a normal logic 1, i.e. the fault may be interpreted as output s-a-1.

4. Signal line and V_{cc} short-circuited (fault 4)   This fault is of the s-a-1 type, but the transistor T4 of the preceding gate is overloaded. Thus a secondary fault can be caused.

5. Signal line and ground short-circuited (fault 5)   A fault of this type may be interpreted as s-a-0.

The "stuck-at" model is also used to represent multiple faults in circuits. In a "multiple stuck-at fault" it is assumed that more than one signal line in the circuit are stuck-at logic 1 or logic 0; in other words a group of stuck-at faults exist in the circuit at the same time. A variation of the multiple fault is the "unidirectional fault". A multiple fault is unidirectional if all of its constituent faults are either s-a-0 or s-a-1 but not both simultaneously. The stuck-at model has gained wide acceptance in the past mainly because of its relative success with small scale integration. However, it is not very effective in accounting for all faults in present day LSI/VLSI chips, which mainly use MOS technology |2.5|. Faults in MOS circuits do not necessarily produce logical faults that can be described as stuck-at faults |2.6, 2.7|. This can be illustrated by an example.

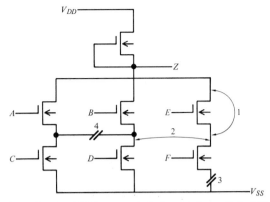

Fig. 2.3   An MOS network (*adapted from Ref. 2.6*).

Figure 2.3 represents the MOS logic implementation of the Boolean function

$$Z = \overline{(A + B)(C + D) + EF}$$

Two possible shorts numbered 1 and 2 and two possible opens numbered 3 and 4 are indicated in the diagram. Short number 1 can be modelled by s-a-1 of input E; open number 3 can be modelled by s-a-0 of input E or input F or both. On the other hand short number 2 and open number 4 cannot be modelled by any stuck-at fault because they involve a modification of the network function. For example, in the presence of short number 2 the network function will change to

$$Z = \overline{(A + B + E)(C + D + F)}$$

and open number 4 will change the function to

$$Z = \overline{AC + BD + EF}$$

For the same reason, a short between the outputs of two gates (Fig. 2.4)

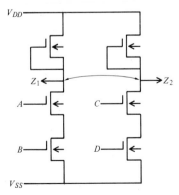

Fig. 2.4   An MOS network of two gates (*adapted from Ref. 2.6*).

cannot be modelled by any stuck-at fault. Without a short the outputs of gates Z_1 and Z_2 are

$$Z_1 = \overline{AB} \quad \text{and} \quad Z_2 = \overline{CD}$$

whereas with a short

$$Z_1 = Z_2 = \overline{AB + CD}$$

2.2.2   Bridging (Short-circuit) Faults

Bridging faults form an important class of permanent faults which cannot be modelled as stuck-at faults. A bridging fault occurs when two leads in a logic network are connected accidentally and "wired logic" is performed at the connection. Depending on whether positive or negative logic is being used the faults have the effect, respectively, of ANDing or ORing the signals involved, as shown in Fig. 2.5 |2.8|.

With stuck-at faults, if there are n lines in the circuit, there are $2n$ possible single stuck-at faults, and $(3^n - 1)$ possible multiple stuck-at faults. With bridging faults, if bridging between any s lines in a circuit are considered, the number of single bridging faults alone will be $\binom{n}{s}!$ and the number of multiple bridging faults will be very much larger |2.9|.

Bridging faults inside an integrated circuit chip may arise if the insulation between adjacent layers of metallization inside the chip breaks down or two conductors in the same layer are shorted due to improper masking or etching. At the printed circuit level bridging faults occur due to defective printed circuit traces, feedthroughs, loose or excess bare wires, shorting of the pins of a chip, etc. |2.10|.

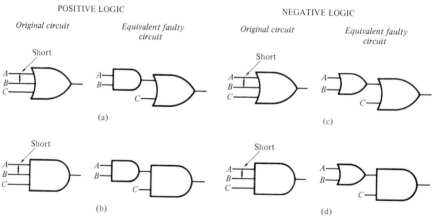

Fig. 2.5   Examples of bridging faults (*courtesy of IEEE,* © *1974*).

Bridging faults may be classified into two types |2.11|:

1. Input bridging.
2. Feedback bridging.

Let us consider a combinational circuit implementing $F(x_1, x_2, \ldots, x_n)$. If there is bridging among s input lines of the circuit, it has an input bridging fault of multiplicity s. A feedback bridging fault of multiplicity s results if there is bridging among the output of the circuit and s input lines. Figures 2.6 and 2.7 show the logical models of input and feedback bridging respectively. With the feedback bridging fault between the primary output and s input lines, the faulty primary output Y_e is equal to the AND function of the original output of the circuit and $x_1, x_2, \ldots, x_s$.

The presence of a feedback bridging fault can cause a circuit to oscillate or convert it to a sequential circuit. Under feedback bridging $(Yx_1, x_2, \ldots, x_s)$ any circuit N implementing $F(x_1, x_2, \ldots, x_n)$ oscillates if the input combination $(x_1 \ldots x_n)$ satisfies the following condition

$$x_1 x_2 \ldots x_s F(0, 0, \ldots, 0, x_{s+1}, \ldots, x_n) \bar{F}(1, 1, \ldots, 1, x_{s+1}, \ldots, x_n) = 1$$

$$(2.1)$$

The network will behave like an asynchronous sequential circuit if

$$x_1 x_2 \ldots x_s \bar{F}(0, 0, \ldots, 0, x_{s+1}, \ldots, x_n) F(1, 1, 1, x_{s+1}, \ldots, x_n) = 1 \quad (2.2)$$

For example, if the network of Fig. 2.8(a) has the feedback bridging fault $Yx_1 x_2$ (Fig. 2.8(b)), it will oscillate for the input combination

$$(x_1, x_2, x_3, x_4, x_5, x_6) = (1, 1, 1, 1, 0, 0)$$

since condition (2.1) is satisfied for this input pattern.

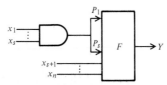

Fig. 2.6   Logical model of input bridging $(x_1, \ldots, x_s)$ *(courtesy of IEEE, © 1980)*.

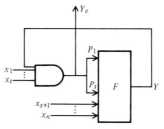

Fig. 2.7   Logical model of feedback bridging $(Yx_1, \ldots, x_s)$ *(courtesy of IEEE, © 1980)*.

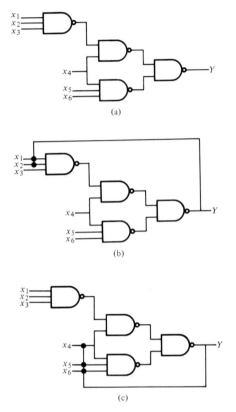

(a)

(b)

(c)

Fig. 2.8   A network with feedback bridging faults (*courtesy of IEEE,* © *1980*): (a) A NAND network, $Y = \overline{x_1 x_2 x_3} x_4 + x_4 x_5 x_6$; (b) Feedback bridging $Y x_1 x_2$; (c) Feedback bridging $Y x_4 x_5 x_6$.

The network will show asynchronous behavior if the input combination $x_4 = x_5 = x_6 = 1$ is applied in presence of the bridging $Y x_4 x_5 x_6$ (Fig. 2.8(c)); since

$$F(x_1, x_2, x_3, 0, 0, 0) = 0$$

and

$$F(x_1, x_2, x_3, 1, 1, 1) = 1$$

condition (2.2) is satisfied.

2.2.3   Stuck-open Faults

A certain type of logic fault associated with a digital circuit depends upon the particular semiconductor technology chosen to realize the circuit. "Stuck-open (s-op)" faults are a peculiarity of CMOS digital integrated circuits; they are not

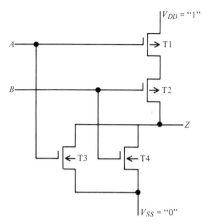

Fig. 2.9   A two-input CMOS NOR gate.

equivalent to classical stuck-at faults. The major difference between the classical and the s-op faults is that the former leave the faulty gate as a combinational circuit, but the s-op faults turn it into a sequential circuit.

CMOS technology uses MOSFET devices of both p-channel and n-channel transistors. Figure 2.9 shows a two-input CMOS NOR gate. The two p-channel transistors are pull-up transistors; they are turned on when both inputs are zero, i.e. $A = B = 0$. The n-channel transistors are pull-down transistors; they connect the output to ground if either A or $B = 1$.

A stuck-open fault causes the output to be connected neither to V_{SS} nor to V_{DD}. If, for example, transistor T2 is open-circuited, then for input $AB = 00$, the pull-up circuit will not be active and there will be no change in the output voltage. In fact, the output retains its previous logic state; however, the length of time the state is retained is determined by the leakage current at the output node. Table 2.1 shows the truth table for the two-input CMOS NOR gate. The fault-free output is shown in column Z; the other three columns represent the outputs in presence of the three s-op faults. The first, Asop, is caused by any input, drain or source missing connection, to the pull-down FET T3. The second, Bsop, is caused by any input, drain or source missing connection to the

A	B	Z	Z (Asop)	Z (Bsop)	Z (V_{DD}sop)
0	0	1	1	1	Z_t
0	1	0	0	Z_t	0
1	0	0	Z_t	0	0
1	1	0	0	0	0

Table 2.1   Truth table for two-input CMOS NOR gate

pull-down FET T4. The third, V_{DD}sop, is caused by an open anywhere in the series, p-channel pull-up connection to V_{DD}. The symbol Z_l is used to indicate that the output state retains the previous logic value. The modelling of the stuck-open faults has been proposed by Wadsack |2.12|.

2.3   TEMPORARY FAULTS

A major portion of digital system malfunctions are caused by temporary faults |2.13, 2.14|. These faults have also been found to account for more than 90% of the total maintenance expense, because they are difficult to detect and isolate |2.15, 2.16|.

In the literature temporary faults have often been referred to as "intermittent" or "transient" faults with the same meaning. It is only recently that a distinction between the two types of faults has been made |2.17|.

Transient faults are non-recurring temporary faults. They are usually caused by α-particle radiation or power supply fluctuation, and they are not repairable because there is no physical damage to the hardware. They are the major source of failures in semiconductor memory chips (see Sec. 4.9).

Intermittent faults are recurring faults that reappear on a regular basis. Such faults can occur due to loose connections, partially defective components or poor designs. Intermittent faults occurring due to deteriorating or ageing components may eventually become permanent. Some intermittent faults also occur due to environmental conditions such as temperature, humidity, vibration, etc. The likelihood of such intermittents depends on how well the system is protected from its physical environment through shielding, filtering, cooling, etc. An intermittent fault in a circuit causes a malfunction of the circuit only if it is active; if it is inactive the circuit operates correctly. A circuit is said to be in a *fault active state* if a fault present in the circuit is active, and it is said to be in the *fault not-active state* if a fault is present but inactive |2.18|.

Since intermittent faults are random, they can be modelled only by using probabilistic methods. Several probabilistic models for representing the behavior of intermittent faults have been presented in literature. The first model is a two-state first-order Markov model (see Appendix) presented by Breuer for a specific class of intermittent faults, which are "well behaved" and "signal independent" |2.19|. An intermittent fault is "well behaved" if, during an application of a test pattern, the circuit under test behaves as if either it is fault-free or a permanent fault exists. An intermittent fault is "signal independent" if its being active does not depend on the inputs or the present state of a circuit. Figure 2.10 shows the fault model proposed by Breuer. It assumes that the fault oscillates between the fault-active state (FA) and the fault-not-active state (FN). The transition probabilities indicated in Fig. 2.10 depend on a selected time-step; they have to be changed if this time-step is changed. Lala and Hopkins |2.20| used an adaptation of the Breuer's model which characterizes

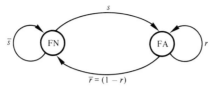

Fig. 2.10   Two-state Markov model.

the transition between the fault-active state and the fault-not-active state by two parameters α and δ, referred to as frequencies of transition. The ratio α/δ is called the *latency factor*; the higher the latency factor the lower is the probability of the fault being active.

Kamal and Page |2.21| introduced a zero-order Markov model for intermittent faults, and suggested a procedure for the detection of a single, well-behaved, signal-independent, intermittent fault in non-redundant combinational circuits. The model assumes prior estimation of the probability that a circuit possesses an intermittent fault and the conditional probability of a fault being active, given that it is present. The fault detection procedure employs the repeated application of tests that are generated to detect permanent faults. After applying a test, the probability of detection of a given intermittent fault is calculated using Bayes' rule |2.22|. This probability approaches 1 if the test is repeated an infinite number of times. However, a finite number of repetitions can be found by using one of the two decision rules. One decision rule is to terminate repetition when the posterior probability (i.e. the probability of a given intermittent fault being present in a circuit after the application of the test) goes below a certain value. The other decision rule is to stop the application of the test when the "likelihood ratio" (which is a function of the posterior probabilities) becomes less than a threshold number. Usually the number of repetitions required is still very large. The zero-order Markov model has also been used by Savir |2.23|, and by Koren and Kohavi |2.24| for describing the behavior of intermittent faults.

Su *et al.* |2.25| have presented a continuous-parameter Markov model for intermittent faults; this is a generalization of the discrete-parameter model proposed by Breuer. In this model shown in Fig. 2.11, the transition probabilities depend linearly on the time-step Δt. For example, if a circuit is in

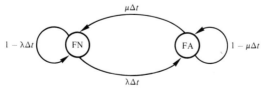

Fig. 2.11   Continuous-parameter Markov model (*courtesy of IEEE, © 1978*).

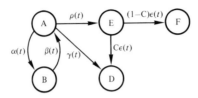

Fig. 2.12   Intermittent fault model (*courtesy of IEEE, © 1980*).

the fault-not-active (FN) state at time t, the probability that it will go to the fault-active (FA) state at time $t + \Delta t$ is proportional to Δt. If a constant of proportionality λ is assumed, then this probability is given by $\lambda \Delta t$. Similarly the probability for going from FA state at time t to FN state at time $t + \Delta t$ is $\mu \Delta t$. The time-period during which a circuit stays in state FA(FN) is exponentially distributed with mean $1/\mu(1/\lambda)$. When the time-step Δt is very large, the continuous Markov model reduces to the discrete zero-order Markov model in which case the probability of the fault being active is given by $\lambda/(\lambda + \mu)$.

The major problem with the intermittent fault models discussed so far is that it is very hard to obtain the statistical data needed to verify their validity. The model proposed by Stifler |2.26| goes a long way to alleviate this problem. It consists of five states (Fig. 2.12). States A and B are the fault-active and the benign state respectively. If a fault occurs the error state E is entered. D is a fault-detected state and F is a failed state resulting from the propagation of an undetected error. $\alpha(t)$ represents the probability of transition from the fault-active to the benign state. $\beta(t)$ is the rate of occurrence of the transition from the benign state to the fault-active state. $\rho(t)$, $\gamma(t)$ and $\varepsilon(t)$ denote respectively the rates of occurrence of error generation, fault detection and error propagation. Each of these transition functions is a function only of the time t, spent in the source state. The parameter C represents the "coverage" probability, which is the probability of detecting an error before it causes any damage.

Considerable work has been done in recent years on the "diagnosis" of permanent faults in hardware (see Chap. 3); however, the "diagnosis" of temporary faults as yet remains a major problem. Currently two types of technique are used in order to prevent temporary faults from causing system failures: fault masking and concurrent fault detection. The fault-masking techniques tolerate the presence of faults and provide continuous system operation (see Chap. 4). Concurrent fault detection techniques use "totally self-checking circuits" (see Chap. 5) to signal the presence of faults but not mask them.

2.4   REFERENCES

2.1 Anderson, T. and P. Lee, *Fault-tolerance: Principles and Practice*, Prentice-Hall International (1981).

2.2 Avizienis, A., "Fault-tolerant systems", *IEEE Trans. Comput.*, 1304–1311 (December 1976).

2.3 Faulkner, T. L., C. W. Bartlett and M. Small, "Hardware design faults: a classification and some measurements", *ICL Technical Jour.*, 218–228 (November 1982).

2.4 Hlavicka, J. and E. Kotteck, "Fault model for TTL circuits", *Digital Processes*, **2**, 169–180 (1976).

2.5 Nickel, V. V., "VLSI—the inadequacy of the stuck-at fault model", *Proc. IEEE Test Conf.*, 378–381 (1980).

2.6 Galiay, J., Y. Crouzet and M. Vergnianlt, "Physical versus logical fault models in MOS LSI circuits, impact in their testability", *Proc. Int. Symp. Fault-tolerant Computing*, 195–202 (1979).

2.7 Mangir, T. E. and A. Avizienis, "Failure modes for VLSI and their effect on chip design", *Proc. IEEE Int. Conf. Circuits and Computers*, 685–688 (1980).

2.8 Friedman, A. D., "Diagnosis of short-circuit faults in combinational circuits", *IEEE Trans. Comput.*, 746–752 (July 1974).

2.9 Mei, K. C. Y., "Bridging and stuck-at faults", *ibid.*, 720–727.

2.10 Karpovsky, M. and S. Y. H. Su, "Detecting bridging and stuck-at faults at the input and output pins of standard digital components", *Proc. 17th Design Automation Conf.*, 494–505 (1980).

2.11 Karpovsky, M. and S. Y. H. Su, "Detection and location of input and feedback bridging faults among input and output lines", *IEEE Trans. Comput.*, 523–527 (1980).

2.12 Wadsack, R. L., "Fault modelling and logic simulation of CMOS and MOS integrated circuits", *Bell Syst. Tech. Jour.*, 1149–1475 (May–June 1978).

2.13 Ball, M. and F. Hardie, "Effects and detection of intermittent failures in digital systems", *Proc. Fall Joint Computer Conf.*, 329–335 (1969).

2.14 Tasar, O. and V. Tasar, "A study of intermittent faults in digital computers", *AFIPS Conf. Proc.*, 807–811 (1977).

2.15 Clary, J. B. and R. A. Sacane, "Self-testing computers", *IEEE Computer*, 49–59 (October 1979).

2.16 Lala, P. K. and J. I. Missen, "Method for the diagnosis of a single intermittent fault in combinatorial logic circuits", *IEEE Jour. Computers and Digital Techniques*, 187–190 (October 1979).

2.17 McCluskey, E. J. and J. F. Wakerly, "A circuit for detecting and analyzing temporary failures", *Proc. COMPCON*, 317–321 (1981).

2.18 Malaiya, Y. K. and S. Y. H. Su, "A survey of methods for intermittent fault analysis", *Proc. Nat. Comput. Conf.*, 577–584 (1979).

2.19 Breuer, M. A., "Testing for intermittent faults in digital circuits", *IEEE Trans. Comput.*, 241–245 (March 1973).

2.20 Lala, J. H. and A. L. Hopkins, "Survival and dispatch probability models for the FTMP computer", *Proc. Int. Symp. Fault-tolerant Computing*, 37–43 (1978).

2.21 Kamal, S. and C. V. Page, "Intermittent faults: a model and a detection procedure", *IEEE Trans. Comput.*, 241–245 (July 1974).

2.22 Smith, D. J., *Reliability Engineering*, Pitman (1972).

2.23 Savir, J., "Optimal random testing of single intermittent failures in combinational circuits", *Proc. Int. Symp. Fault-tolerant Computing*, 180–185 (1977).

2.24 Koren, I. and Z. Kohavi, "Diagnosis of intermittent faults in combinational networks", *IEEE Trans. Comput.*, 1154–1158 (November 1977).

2.25 Su, S. Y. H., I. Koren and Y. K. Malaiya, "A continuous parameter Markov model and detection procedures for intermittent faults", *IEEE Trans. Comput.*, 567–569 (June 1978).

2.26 Stifler, J. I., "Robust detection of intermittent faults", *Proc. Int. Symp. Fault-tolerant Computing*, 216–218 (1980).

3 TEST GENERATION

3.1 FAULT DIAGNOSIS OF DIGITAL SYSTEMS

Digital systems, even when designed with highly reliable components, do not operate for ever without developing some faults. When a system ultimately does develop a fault it has to be detected and located so that its effect can be removed. *Fault detection* means the discovery of something wrong in a digital system or circuit. *Fault location* means the identification of the faults with components, functional modules or subsystems, depending on the requirements. *Fault diagnosis* includes both fault detection and fault location.

Fault detection in a logic circuit is carried out by applying a sequence of test inputs and observing the resulting outputs. Therefore the cost of testing includes the generation of test sequences and their application. One of the main objectives in testing is to minimize the length of the test sequence. Any fault in a non-redundant* n-input combinational circuit can be completely tested by applying all 2^n input combinations to it; however 2^n increases very rapidly as n increases. For a sequential circuit with n inputs and m flip-flops the total number of input combinations necessary to test the circuit exhaustively is $2^n \times 2^m = 2^{m+n}$. If, for example, $n = 20$, $m = 40$, there would be 2^{60} tests. At a rate of 10 000 tests per second, the total test time for the circuit would be about $3\frac{1}{2}$ million years! Fortunately a complete truth-table exercise of a logic circuit is not necessary—only the number of input combinations which detect most of the faults in the circuit is required. In order to determine which faults have been detected by a set of test patterns, a process known as "fault-simulation" is performed [3.1]. For example, if a circuit has x stuck-at faults, then fault simulation is the process of applying every test pattern to the fault-free circuit, and to each of the x copies of the circuit containing exactly one stuck-at fault.

---

* A circuit is said to be non-redundant if the function realized by the circuit is not the same as the function realized by the circuit in the presence of a fault.

When all test patterns have been simulated against all the faults x, the detected faults f are used to compute the "test coverage (t_c)", which is defined as

$$t_c = \frac{f}{x}$$

Instead of simulating one fault at a time, the method of "parallel simulation", which uses the word size N of a host computer to process N faults at a time, can be employed. Another approach is to utilize the "deductive simulation" method, which allows simulation of all faults simultaneously but is much harder to implement and requires enormous memory capacity for larger circuits.

It has been shown that the time required to compute test patterns for a combinational circuit grows in proportion to the square of the number of gates in the circuit |3.2|. Hence for circuits of VLSI complexity the computation time required for test generation will be prohibitive.

3.2   TEST GENERATION FOR COMBINATIONAL LOGIC CIRCUITS

There are several methods available for deriving tests for combinational circuits. All these methods are based on the assumption that the circuit under test is non-redundant and only a single stuck-at fault is present at any time. In this section we discuss each method in some detail.

3.2.1   One-dimensional Path Sensitization

The basic principle involved in "path sensitizing" is to choose some path from the origin of the failure to the circuit output. The path is said to be "sensitized" if the inputs to the gates along the path are assigned values so as to propagate the fault along the chosen path to the output |3.3|.

The method can be illustrated with an example. Let us consider the circuit shown in Fig. 3.1 and suppose that the fault is line X_3 s-a-1. To test X_3 for s-a-1, X_5 and G_2 must be set at 1 and X_3 set at 0 so that $G_5 = 1$ if the fault is

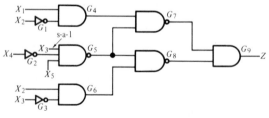

Fig. 3.1

absent. We now have a choice of propagating the fault from G_5 to the circuit output Z via a path through G_7G_9 or through G_8G_9. To propagate through G_7G_9 requires the output of G_4 and G_8 to be 1. If $G_4 = 1$, the output of G_7 depends on the output of G_5 and similarly if $G_8 = 1$, the circuit output depends on G_7 only. This process of propagating the effect of the fault from its original location to the circuit output is known as the "forward trace". The next phase of the method is the "backward trace", in which the necessary gate conditions to propagate the fault along the sensitized path are established. For example, to set G_4 at 1 both X_1 and G_1 must be set at 1; $G_1 = 1$ implies $X_2 = 0$. In order for G_2 to be 1, X_4 must be set at 0. For G_8 to be 1, G_6 must be 0, which requires either $X_2 = 0$ or $G_3 = 0$. Since X_2 has already been specified as 0, the output of G_6 will be 0. It is worth noting that G_6 cannot be set at 0 by making $G_3 = 0$, since this would imply $X_3 = 0$, which is inconsistent with the previous assignment of X_3. Therefore the test $X_1X_2X_3X_4X_5 = 10001$ detects the fault X_3 s-a-1, since the output of Z will be 0 for the fault-free circuit and 1 for the circuit having the fault.

In general, the input combination generated by the path-sensitization procedure for propagating a fault to the output may not be unique. For example, the X_3 s-a-1 fault in the circuit of Fig. 3.1 can also be detected by the test $X_1X_2X_3X_4X_5 = -1001$; this is done by sensitizing the path $G_5G_8G_9$. X_1 has an unspecified value in this test, i.e. the test is independent of input X_1.

The flaw in the one-dimensional path sensitization technique is that only one path is sensitized at a time. The following example shows the inadequacy of this procedure |3.4|.

Let us try to derive a test for the fault G_2 s-a-0 in Fig. 3.2 by sensitizing the path $G_2G_6G_8$. We set $X_2 = X_3 = 0$ so as to propagate the effect of the fault through gate G_2. Setting $X_4 = 0$ propagates it through gate G_6. In order to propagate it through gate G_8, we require $G_4 = G_5 = G_7 = 0$. Since X_2 and X_4 have already been set to 0, we have $G_3 = 1$, which makes $G_7 = 0$. To make $G_5 = 0$, X_1 must be set to 1; consequently $G_1 = 0$, which with $X_2 = 0$, would

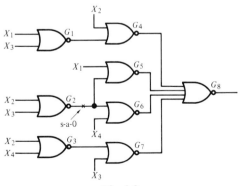

Fig. 3.2

make $G_4 = 1$. Therefore we are unable to propagate through G_8. Similarly, we can show that it is impossible to sensitize the single path $G_2 G_5 G_8$. However, we note that $X_1 = X_4 = 0$ sensitizes the two paths simultaneously and also makes $G_4 = G_7 = 0$. Thus, two inputs to G_8 change from 0 to 1 as a result of the fault G_2 s-a-0, while the remaining two inputs remain fixed at 0. The fault will cause the output of G_8 to change from 1 to 0 and $\bar{X}_1 \bar{X}_2 \bar{X}_3 \bar{X}_4$ is a test for G_8 s-a-0.

The above example shows the necessity of sensitizing more than one path, in deriving tests for certain faults. This is the principal idea behind the D-algorithm (see Sec. 3.2.3).

3.2.2 Boolean Difference

The basic principle of the Boolean difference is to derive two Boolean expressions—one of which represents normal fault-free behavior of the circuit, and the other represents the logical behavior under an assumed single s-a-1 or s-a-0 fault condition. These two expressions are then exclusive-ORed; if the result is 1 a fault is indicated [3.5].

Let $F(X) = F(x_1, \ldots, x_n)$ be a logic function of n variables. If one of the inputs to the logic function, e.g. input x_i, is faulty, then the output would be $F(x_1, \ldots, \bar{x}_i, \ldots, x_n)$. The Boolean difference of $F(X)$ with respect to x_i is defined as

$$\frac{dF(x_1, \ldots, x_i, \ldots, x_n)}{dx_i} = \frac{dF(X)}{dx_i}$$

$$= F(x_1, \ldots, x_i, \ldots, x_n) \oplus F(x_1, \ldots, \bar{x}_i, \ldots, x_n)$$

The function $dF(X)/dx_i$ is called the Boolean difference of $F(X)$ with respect to x_i.

It is easy to see that when $F(x_1, \ldots, x_i, \ldots, x_n) \neq F(x_1, \ldots, \bar{x}_i, \ldots, x_n)$, $dF(X)/dx_i = 1$ and that when $F(x_1, \ldots, x_i, \ldots, x_n) = F(x_1, \ldots, \bar{x}_i, \ldots, x_n)$, $dF(X)/dx_i = 0$. To detect a fault on x_i, it is necessary to find input combinations (tests) so that whenever x_i changes to $\bar{x}_i$ (due to a fault), $F(x_1, \ldots, x_i, \ldots, x_n)$ will be different from $F(x_1, \ldots, \bar{x}_i, \ldots, x_n)$. In other words, the aim is to find input combinations for each fault occurring on x_i such that $dF(X)/dx_i = 1$.

Some useful properties of the Boolean difference are:

1. $\dfrac{d\overline{F(X)}}{dx_i} = \dfrac{dF(X)}{dx_i}$; $\overline{F(X)}$ denotes the complement of $F(X)$.

2. $\dfrac{dF(X)}{dx_i} = \dfrac{dF(X)}{d\bar{x}_i}$

3. $\dfrac{d}{dx_i} \cdot \dfrac{dF(X)}{dx_j} = \dfrac{d}{dx_j} \dfrac{dF(X)}{dx_i}$

4. $\dfrac{d|F(X)G(X)|}{dx_i} = F(X)\dfrac{dG(X)}{dx_i} \oplus G(X)\dfrac{dF(X)}{dx_i} \oplus \dfrac{dF(X)}{dx_i} \cdot \dfrac{dG(X)}{dx_i}$

5. $\dfrac{d|F(X) + G(X)|}{dx_i} = \overline{F(X)}\dfrac{dG(X)}{dx_i} \oplus \overline{G(X)}\dfrac{dF(X)}{dx_i} \oplus \dfrac{dF(X)}{dx_i} \cdot \dfrac{dG(X)}{dx_i}$

A Boolean function $F(X)$ is said to be *independent of* x_i if and only if $F(X)$ is logically invariant under complementation of x_i, i.e. if

$$F(x_1, \ldots, x_i, \ldots, x_n) = F(x_1, \ldots, \bar{x}_i, \ldots, x_n)$$

This implies that a fault in x_i will not affect the final output $F(X)$ and $dF(x)/dx_i = 0$. Some additional properties can now be added to the original set (1–5):

6. $\dfrac{dF(X)}{dx_i} = 0$ if $F(X)$ is independent of x_i

7. $\dfrac{dF(X)}{dx_i} = 1$ if $F(X)$ depends only on x_i

8. $\dfrac{d|F(X)G(X)|}{dx_i} = F(X)\dfrac{dG(X)}{dx_i}$ if $F(X)$ is independent of x_i

9. $\dfrac{d|F(X) + G(X)|}{dx_i} = \overline{F(X)}\dfrac{dG(X)}{dx_i}$ if $F(X)$ is independent of x_i

To illustrate how the Boolean difference is used, two examples are given.

Example 1   Consider the logic circuit shown in Fig. 3.3(a). Find the Boolean difference with respect to x_3. We have:

$$\dfrac{dF(X)}{dx_3} = \dfrac{d(x_1x_2 + x_3x_4)}{dx_3}$$

$$= \overline{x_1x_2}\dfrac{d(x_3x_4)}{dx_3} \oplus \overline{x_3x_4}\dfrac{d(x_1x_2)}{dx_3} \oplus \dfrac{d(x_1x_2)}{dx_3} \cdot \dfrac{d(x_3x_4)}{dx_3}$$

(By property 5)

$$= \overline{x_1x_2}\dfrac{d(x_3x_4)}{dx_3}$$

(By property 6)

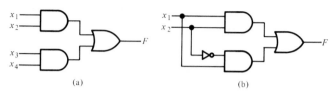

(a)   (b)

Fig. 3.3   Circuit examples.

$$= \overline{x_1 x_2} \left(x_3 \frac{dx_4}{dx_3} \oplus x_4 \frac{dx_3}{dx_3} \oplus \frac{dx_3}{dx_3} \cdot \frac{dx_4}{dx_3} \right) \qquad \text{(By property 4)}$$

$$= \overline{x_1 x_2} x_4 \qquad \qquad \text{(By properties 6 and 7)}$$

This means that a fault on x_3 will cause the output to be in error only if $\overline{x_1 x_2} x_4 = 1$, i.e. if x_1 or x_2 (or both) are equal to 0 and x_4 equal to 1. This can be verified by inspection of Fig. 3.3(a).

Example 2   Consider the logic circuit shown in Fig. 3.3(b). Find the Boolean difference with respect to x_2. We have:

$$\frac{dF(X)}{dx_2} = \frac{d(x_1 x_2 + x_1 \bar{x}_2)}{dx_2}$$

$$= \overline{x_1 x_2} \frac{d(x_1 \bar{x}_2)}{dx_2} \oplus \overline{x_1 \bar{x}_2} \frac{d(x_1 x_2)}{dx_2} \oplus \frac{d(x_1 x_2)}{dx_2} \cdot \frac{d(x_1 \bar{x}_2)}{dx_2}$$

$$\text{(By property 5)}$$

$$= \overline{x_1 x_2} x_1 \oplus \overline{x_1 \bar{x}_2} \cdot x_1 \oplus x_1 \qquad \text{(By properties 1, 7 and 8)}$$

$$= x_1 (\overline{x_1 x_2} \oplus \overline{x_1 \bar{x}_2}) \oplus x_1$$

$$= x_1 (\overline{x_1 x_2} \cdot x_1 \bar{x}_2 + \overline{x_1 \bar{x}_2} \cdot x_1 x_2) \oplus x_1$$

$$= x_1 [(\bar{x}_1 + \bar{x}_2) x_1 \bar{x}_2 + (\bar{x}_1 + x_2) x_1 x_2] \oplus x_1$$

$$= x_1 [x_1 \bar{x}_2 + x_1 x_2] \oplus x_1$$

$$= x_1 \oplus x_1$$

$$= 0$$

This means that a fault in x_2 will not cause the output to be in error, which indicates that the circuit is not really a function of x_2; this can be verified by noting that the original output $F(X) = x_1 \cdot x_2 + x_1 \cdot \bar{x}_2 = x_1$.

So far the Boolean difference method has been applied to derive tests for input line faults, but it can also be used for faults on lines which are internal to the circuit.

Let a combinational circuit realize the function $F(X)$ and let h be an internal wire in the circuit. Tests for h can be found by expressing F as a function of h, $F(x_1, x_2, \ldots, x_n\ h)$, and h as a function of the inputs $h(x_1, x_2, \ldots, x_n)$.

As an example consider the circuit of Fig. 3.4 and find tests to detect s-a-0 and s-a-1 faults on h.

$$F = x_1 x_2 + x_3 x_4 + \overline{x_2 x_4}$$

$$= \quad h + \underbrace{(x_3 x_4 + \overline{x_2 x_4})}_{G}$$

$$\frac{dF}{dh} = \bar{G}\,\frac{dh}{dh} \oplus \bar{h}\,\frac{dG}{dh} \oplus \frac{dG}{dh} \cdot \frac{dh}{dh}$$

$$= \overline{(x_3 x_4 + \overline{x_2 x_4})} \cdot \frac{dh}{dh} \oplus \bar{h} \cdot \frac{d(x_3 x_4 + \overline{x_2 x_4})}{dh} \oplus \frac{d(x_3 x_4 + \overline{x_2 x_4})}{dh} \cdot \frac{dh}{dh}$$

$$= \overline{(x_3 x_4 + \overline{x_2 x_4})} \oplus 0 \oplus 0$$

$$= \overline{x_3 x_4} \cdot x_2 x_4 = (\bar{x}_3 + \bar{x}_4)x_2 x_4 = x_2 \bar{x}_3 x_4$$

Tests for h s-a-0 are given by

$$h \cdot \frac{dF}{dh} = x_1 x_2 \cdot x_2 \bar{x}_3 x_4 = x_1 x_2 \bar{x}_3 x_4$$

and h s-a-1 by

$$\bar{h} \cdot \frac{dF}{dh} = \overline{x_1 x_2} \cdot x_2 \bar{x}_3 x_4 = (\bar{x}_1 + \bar{x}_2)x_2 \bar{x}_3 x_4 = \bar{x}_1 x_2 \bar{x}_3 x_4$$

In general the conventional Boolean difference is not capable of deriving tests for all the internal nodes of a logic network. This is illustrated by the following example.

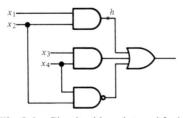

Fig. 3.4   Circuit with an internal fault.

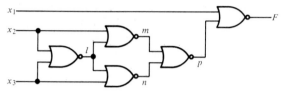

Fig. 3.5   A network implementation for $F = \bar{x}_1 x_2 \bar{x}_3 + \bar{x}_1 \bar{x}_2 x_3$.

Example   Given the logic network of Fig. 3.5, determine the tests for checking all single-node faults.

The network function is given by

$$F = \bar{x}_1 x_2 \bar{x}_3 + \bar{x}_1 \bar{x}_2 x_3$$

The conventional Boolean differences of F with respect to x_1, x_2 and x_3 are:

$$\frac{dF}{dx_1} = x_2 \bar{x}_3 + \bar{x}_2 x_3$$

$$\frac{dF}{dx_2} = \bar{x}_1 \bar{x}_3 + \bar{x}_1 x_3$$

$$\frac{dF}{dx_3} = \bar{x}_1 x_2 + \bar{x}_1 \bar{x}_2$$

The test inputs resulting from these Boolean differences will check all input-line faults and are as follows:

x_1 (s-a-0)	1 1 0 or	1 0 1
x_1 (s-a-1)	0 1 0 or	0 0 1
x_2 (s-a-0)	0 1 0 or	0 1 1
x_2 (s-a-1)	0 0 0 or	0 0 1
x_3 (s-a-0)	0 1 1 or	0 1 0
x_3 (s-a-1)	0 0 1 or	0 0 0

One may select the test set (110, 010, 001) as the set of tests capable of detecting the faults on primary input lines. However, this test set may or may not be sufficient to detect all internal-node faults. In order to develop a complete set of tests which will detect both input-line and internal-node faults, it is necessary to find tests which will exercise completely each and every path connecting a primary input to the primary output. This can be carried out by using the "partial" Boolean difference technique |3.6|.

In general a conventional Boolean difference expression may be formed by concatenating individual Boolean differences. For example, if $Z = f(y)$ and $y = f(x)$, then

$$\frac{dZ}{dx} = \frac{dZ}{dy} \cdot \frac{dy}{dx}$$

where dZ/dx is termed the partial Boolean difference with respect to x. The partial Boolean difference associated with the path x_2-l-n-p-F in Fig. 3.5 is given by

$$\frac{dF}{dx_2} = \frac{dF}{dp} \cdot \frac{dp}{dn} \cdot \frac{dn}{dl} \cdot \frac{dl}{dx_2}$$

Since

$$\frac{dF}{dp} = \frac{d}{dp}(\bar{x}_1 \cdot \bar{p}) = \bar{x}_1$$

$$\frac{dp}{dn} = \frac{d}{dn}(\bar{m} \cdot \bar{n}) = \bar{m} = x_2 + l = x_2 + \bar{x}_2 \cdot \bar{x}_3$$

$$\frac{dn}{dl} = \frac{d}{dl}(\bar{l}\bar{x}_3) = \bar{x}_3$$

$$\frac{dl}{dx_2} = \frac{d}{dx_2}(\bar{x}_2 \cdot \bar{x}_3) = \bar{x}_3$$

$$\frac{dF}{dx_2} = \bar{x}_1 \cdot (x_2 + \bar{x}_2\bar{x}_3) \cdot \bar{x}_3 \cdot \bar{x}_3$$

$$= \bar{x}_1 x_2 \cdot \bar{x}_3 + \bar{x}_1\bar{x}_2\bar{x}_3 = \bar{x}_1\bar{x}_3$$

Therefore the tests which will exercise the path x_2-l-n-p-F, are

$$\bar{x}_1 \cdot x_2 \cdot \bar{x}_3 \quad \text{or} \quad (0\ 1\ 0)$$

and

$$\bar{x}_1 \cdot \bar{x}_2 \cdot \bar{x}_3 \quad \text{or} \quad (0\ 0\ 0)$$

Proceeding in a similar manner, the partial Boolean difference associated with path $x_3 - n - p - F$ is given by

$$\frac{dF}{dx_3} = \frac{dF}{dp} \cdot \frac{dp}{dn} \cdot \frac{dn}{dx_3}$$

$$= \bar{x}_1 \cdot \bar{m} \cdot \bar{l}$$

$$= \bar{x}_1 \cdot (x_2 + \bar{x}_2\bar{x}_3) \cdot (x_2 + x_3)$$

$$= \bar{x}_1 x_2$$

which yields the tests

$$\bar{x}_1 x_2 \bar{x}_3 \quad (0 \ 1 \ 0)$$

and

$$\bar{x}_1 x_2 x_3 \quad (0 \ 1 \ 1)$$

The Boolean difference method generates all tests for every fault in a circuit. It is a complete algorithm and does not require any trial and error. However, the method is costly in terms of computation time and memory requirements.

3.2.3 D-Algorithm

The D-algorithm is the first algorithmic method for generating tests for non-redundant combinational circuits |3.7|. If a test exists for detecting a fault then the D-algorithm is guaranteed to find this test. Before the D-algorithm can be discussed in detail, certain new terms must be defined.

Singular cover The singular cover of a logic gate is basically a compact version of the truth table. Figure 3.6 shows the singular cover for a two-input NOR gate; Xs or blanks are used to denote that the position may be either 0 or 1. Each row in the singular cover is termed a "singular cube". The singular cover of a network is just the set of singular covers of each of its gates on separate rows in the table. This is illustrated by the example in Fig. 3.7.

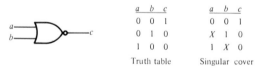

a	b	c
0	0	1
0	1	0
1	0	0

Truth table

a	b	c
0	0	1
X	1	0
1	X	0

Singular cover

Fig. 3.6

Propagation D-cubes D-cubes represent the input–output behavior of the good and the faulty circuit. The symbol D may assume only one value 0 or 1; $\bar{D}$ takes on the value opposite to D, i.e. if $D = 1$, $\bar{D} = 0$ and if $D = 0$, $\bar{D} = 1$. The definitions of D and $\bar{D}$ could be interchanged but they should be consistent

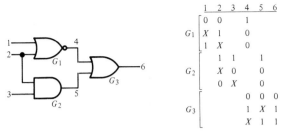

Fig. 3.7

throughout the circuit. Thus all Ds in a circuit imply the same value (0 or 1) and all $\bar{D}$s will have the opposite value.

The "propagation D-cubes" of a gate are those that cause the output of the gate to depend only on one or more of its specified inputs (and hence to propagate a fault on these inputs to the output). The propagation D-cubes for a two-input NOR gate are:

a	b	c
0	D	$\bar{D}$
D	0	$\bar{D}$
D	D	$\bar{D}$

The propagation D-cubes $0D\bar{D}$ and $D0\bar{D}$ indicate that if one of the inputs of the NOR gate is 0, the output is the complement of the other input; $DD\bar{D}$ propagates multiple-input changes through the NOR gate.

Propagation D-cubes can be derived from the singular cover, or by inspection. To systematically construct propagation D-cubes, cubes with different output values in a gate's singular cover are intersected, using the following algebraic rules:

$$0 \cap 0 = 0 \cap X = X \cap 0 = 0$$

$$1 \cap 1 = 1 \cap X = X \cap 1 = 1$$

$$X \cap X = X$$

$$1 \cap 0 = D$$

$$0 \cap 1 = \bar{D}$$

For example, the propagation D-cubes of the two-input NAND gate can be formed from its singular covers, as shown in Fig. 3.8.

Primitive D-cube of a fault The primitive D-cube of a fault is used to specify the existence of a given fault. It consists of an input pattern which brings the

	a	b	c
C_1	1	1	0
C_2	X	0	1
C_3	0	X	1

(a) Singular covers of the NAND gate

	a	b	c
$C_1 \cap C_2$	1	D	$\bar{D}$
$C_1 \cap C_3$	D	1	$\bar{D}$

(b) Propagation D-cubes of the NAND gate

Fig. 3.8

influence of a fault to the output of the gate. For example, if the output of the NOR gate shown in Fig. 3.6 is s-a-0, the corresponding primitive D-cube of a fault is:

$$a \quad b \quad c$$

$$0 \quad 0 \quad D$$

Here, the D is interpreted as being a 1 if the circuit is fault-free and a 0 if the fault is present. The primitive D-cubes for the NOR gate output s-a-1 are:

$$a \quad b \quad c$$

$$1 \quad X \quad \bar{D}$$
$$X \quad 1 \quad \bar{D}$$

The primitive D-cube of any fault in a gate be obtained obtained from the singular covers of the normal and the faulty gates in the following manner:

1. Form the singular covers of the fault-free and the faulty gate. Let α_0 and α_1 be sets of cubes in the singular covers of the fault-free gate whose output coordinates are 0 and 1 respectively, and let β_0 and β_1 be the corresponding sets in the singular covers of the faulty gate.
2. Intersect members of α_1 with members of β_0, and members of α_0 with members of β_1. The intersection rules are similar to those used for propagation D-cubes.

The primitive D-cubes of faults obtained from $\alpha_1 \cap \beta_0$ correspond to those inputs that produce a 1 output from the fault-free gate and a 0 output from the faulty gate. The primitive D-cubes of faults obtained from $\alpha_0 \cap \beta_1$ correspond to those inputs which produce a 0 output from the fault-free gate and a 1 output from the faulty gate.

Example Consider a three-input NAND gate with input lines a, b and c, and output line d. The singular cover for the NAND gate is:

	a	b	c	d	
C_{1g}	0	X	X	1	⎫
C_{2g}	X	0	X	1	⎬ α_1
C_{3g}	X	X	0	1	⎭
C_{4g}	1	1	1	0	⎬ α_0

Assuming the input line b is s-a-1, the singular cover for the faulty NAND gate is:

$$
\begin{array}{c c c c c}
 & a & b & c & d \\
\hline
C_{1'} & 0 & X & X & 1 \\
C_{2'} & X & X & 0 & 1 \\
C_{3'} & 1 & X & 1 & 0 \\
\end{array}
\begin{array}{l}
\left.\begin{array}{l}\\ \\ \end{array}\right\} \beta_1 \\
\} \beta_0
\end{array}
$$

Therefore

$$C_{1g} \cap C_{3f} = \bar{D} \quad X \quad 1 \quad \bar{D} \qquad C_{4g} \cap C_{1f} = D \quad 1 \quad 1 \quad \bar{D}$$

$$C_{2g} \cap C_{3f} = 1 \quad 0 \quad 1 \quad D \qquad C_{4g} \cap C_{2f} = 1 \quad 1 \quad D \quad \bar{D}$$

$$C_{3g} \cap C_{3f} = 1 \quad X \quad \bar{D} \quad D$$

The primitive D-cube of the b s-a-1 fault is $101D$. The primitive D-cubes of all stuck-at faults for the three-input NAND gate is shown below:

a	b	c	d	fault
0	X	X	D	d s-a-0
X	0	X	D	d s-a-0
X	X	0	D	d s-a-0
1	1	1	$\bar{D}$	d s-a-1
0	1	1	D	a s-a-1
1	0	1	D	b s-a-1
1	1	0	D	c s-a-1

D-intersection   Finally we need to consider the concept of D-intersection which provides the tool for building sensitized paths. This is first explained by a simple example. Consider the simple circuit shown in Fig. 3.9. We attempt to generate a test for the 2 s-a-0 fault, described by the D-cube of the fault:

$$
\begin{array}{c c c}
1 & 2 & 4 \\
\hline
0 & 1 & \bar{D}
\end{array}
$$

To transmit the $\bar{D}$ on line 4 through G_2, we must try and match, i.e. intersect,

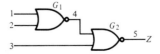

Fig. 3.9   Circuit to illustrate D-intersection.

the $\bar{D}$ specification with one of the propagation D-cubes for G_2. Such a match is possible if we use the propagation D-cube:

3	4	5
0	$\bar{D}$	D

This produces a full circuit D-cube:

1	2	3	4	5
0	1	0	$\bar{D}$	D

Thus, setting $X_1 = 0$, $X_2 = 1$, $X_3 = 0$ will sensitize a path from line 2 through line 4 to line 5, and will therefore test for inverse polarity faults on these connections.

It is worth noting that intersection of the D-cube of the fault with the other single D-input propagation cube ($\bar{D}0\bar{D}$) would not be successful, because in the first cube the status of line 4 is $\bar{D}$, whereas, in the second cube, it is required to be set at 0. This is incompatible with the requirement. The full set of rules for the D-cube intersection is as follows |3.8|:

Let $A = (a_1, a_2, \ldots, a_n)$ and $B = (b_1, b_2, \ldots, b_n)$ be D-cubes where a_i and b_j equal 0, 1, X, D or $\bar{D}$ for $i, j = 1, 2, \ldots, n$. The D-intersection, denoted by $A \cap B$, is given by:

1. $X \cap a_i = a_i$
2. If $a_i \neq X$ and $b_i \neq X$ then

$$a_i \cap b_i = \begin{cases} a_i & \text{if } b_i = a_i \\ \emptyset & \text{otherwise} \end{cases}$$

Finally $A \cap B = \emptyset$, i.e. the empty cube, if for any i, $a_i \cap b_i = \emptyset$; otherwise

$$A \cap B = a_i \cap b_i, \ldots, a_n \cap b_n$$

For example,

$$(1X1D0) \cap (X\bar{D}1D0) = 1\bar{D}1D0$$

$$(01\bar{D}X1) \cap (00XD1) = 0\emptyset\bar{D}D1 = \emptyset$$

Now that singular cubes, primitive D-cubes of a fault, propagation D-cubes and D-intersections have been defined, we shall discuss the D-algorithm in detail.

The first stage of the D-algorithm consists of choosing a primitive D-cube of the fault under consideration. The next step is to sensitize all possible paths from the faulty gate to a primary output of the circuit; this is done by successive intersection of the primitive D-cube of the fault with the propagation D-cubes of successor gates. The procedure is called the "D-drive". The D-drive is continued until a primary output has a D or $\bar{D}$. The final step is the consistency operation which is performed to develop a consistent set of primary input values that will account for all lines set to 0 or 1 during the D-drive.

The application of the D-algorithm is demonstrated in Table 3.1 by deriving a test for detecting the fault 6 s-a-0 in the circuit of Fig. 3.10. The test for line 6 s-a-0 is 1010.

Fortunately, no inconsistencies were encountered in the above example. When they are, one must seek a different path for propagating the fault to the

G_1			G_2			G_3			G_4			G_5		
1	2	5	3	4	6	3	5	7	2	6	8	7	8	9
X	1	0	1	0	D	0	X	1	0	D	$\bar{D}$	1	D	$\bar{D}$
1	X	0	0	1	D	X	0	1	D	0	$\bar{D}$	0	1	$\bar{D}$
0	0	1	1	1	$\bar{D}$	1	1	0	D	D	$\bar{D}$	D	D	$\bar{D}$
Singular cover			Primitive D-cube of fault			Singular cover			Propagation D-cube			Propagation D-cube		

	1	2	3	4	5	6	7	8	9
D-drive operation									
1. Select *pdcf* for 6 s-a-0				1	0	D			
2. Intersect with Gate 4 propagation D-cube			0	1	0	D		$\bar{D}$	
3. Intersect with Gate 5 propagation D-cube (N.B. G_5 D-cube: polarity inverted) End of D-drive			0	1	0	D	*1*	$\bar{D}$	D
Consistency operation									
1. Check line 7 is at 1 from G_3 singular cover Set line 5 at 0		0	1	0	0	D	*1*	$\bar{D}$	D
2. Check line 5 is at 0 from G_1 singular cover: set primary input 1 at 1	1	0	1	0	0	D	*1*	$\bar{D}$	D

End of Consistency

Table 3.1

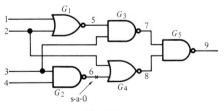

Fig. 3.10

output. This is illustrated by deriving the test for 5 s-a-1 in the circuit diagram of Fig. 3.11.

The singular covers and the propagation D-cube of the circuit are shown in Tables 3.2 and 3.3 respectively. The blanks in the tables are treated as Xs while performing intersections. The D-drive along lines 5–8–9 and the consistency operations are shown in Table 3.4. Any D-cube which represents a partially formed test during the D-drive is called a "test cube" and is represented by tc and a superscript denoting the step at which it is obtained. The primitive D-cube of the fault is chosen as the initial test cube tc^0.

As can be seen from the table the consistency operation terminates unsuccessfully due to the null intersection tc^5. If j is chosen instead of i, tc^3 becomes undefined. We now attempt to D-drive along lines 5–7–9; this is shown in Table 3.5 with the consistency operations. It can be seen from Table

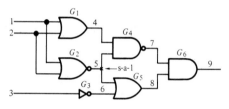

Fig. 3.11

		1	2	3	4	5	6	7	8	9
Gate 1	a	X	1		1					
	b	1	X		1					
	c	0	0		0					
Gate 2	d	X	1			0				
	e	1	X			0				
	f	0	0			1				
Gate 3	g			0			1			
	h			1			0			
Gate 4	i				0	X		1		
	j				X	0		1		
	k				1	1		0		
Gate 5	l					X	1		1	
	m					1	X		1	
	n					0	0		0	
Gate 6	o							X	0	0
	p							0	X	0
	q							1	1	1

Table 3.2   Singular cover

		1	2	3	4	5	6	7	8	9
Gate 1	a_d	0	D		D					
	b_d	D	0		D					
Gate 2	c_d	0	D			$\bar{D}$				
	d_d	D	0			$\bar{D}$				
Gate 3	e_d			D			$\bar{D}$			
Gate 4	f_d					1	D		$\bar{D}$	
	g_d					D	1		$\bar{D}$	
Gate 5	h_d						0	D	D	
	i_d						D	0	D	
Gate 6	j_d							D	1	D
	k_d							1	D	D

Table 3.3 Propagation D-cubes

	1	2	3	4	5	6	7	8	9
D-drive									
tc^0	1	0			$\bar{D}$				
$tc^1 = tc^0 \cap i_d$	1	0			$\bar{D}$	0		$\bar{D}$	
$tc^2 = tc^1 \cap k_d$	1	0			$\bar{D}$	0	1	$\bar{D}$	$\bar{D}$
Consistency									
$tc^3 = tc^2 \cap i$	1	0		0	$\bar{D}$	0	1	$\bar{D}$	$\bar{D}$
$tc^4 = tc^3 \cap h$	1	0	1	0	$\bar{D}$	0	1	$\bar{D}$	$\bar{D}$
$tc^5 = tc^4 \cap c$	$\emptyset$	0	1	0	$\bar{D}$	0	1	$\bar{D}$	$\bar{D}$

Table 3.4 D-drive along lines 5–8–9 and consistency operations

	1	2	3	4	5	6	7	8	9
D-drive									
tc^0	1	0			$\bar{D}$				
$tc^1 = tc^0 \cap f_d$	1	0		1	$\bar{D}$		D		
$tc^2 = tc^1 \cap j_d$	1	0		1	$\bar{D}$		D	1	D
Consistency									
$tc^3 = tc^2 \cap l$	1	0		1	$\bar{D}$	1	D	1	D
$tc^4 = tc^3 \cap g$	1	0	0	1	$\bar{D}$	1	D	1	D

Table 3.5 D-drive along lines 5–7–9 and consistency

3.5 that the final test cube is tc^4. Thus 100 is a test for detecting the fault 5 s-a-1.

The D-algorithm generates a test for every fault in a circuit, if such a test exists. It uses less computation time and less memory space, and hence is more efficient than the Boolean difference method. It can also identify redundant faults by "proving" that no corresponding tests exist.

A modified version of the D-algorithm, the LASAR (Logic Automated Stimulus and Response) system, is currently widely employed for automatic test generation |3.9|. The test generation algorithm of the LASAR is similar to the line justification part of the D-algorithm |3.10|.

3.2.4 PODEM

PODEM (path oriented decision making) is a new test generation algorithm for combinational logic circuits. It has been found to be more efficient than the D-algorithm, particularly in generating tests for ECAT (error correction and translation) type circuits |3.11|. It is very similar in principle to the D-algorithm and uses five-valued logic ($0, 1, X, D, \bar{D}$) for test generation. The PODEM algorithm consists of the following steps:

1. Assign a logic level 0 or 1 to a primary input; all primary inputs are initially assumed to have undefined values, i.e. Xs.

   An initial assignment of either 0 or 1 to a primary input is recorded as a node in a decision tree. If the initial assignment has been rejected and the alternative is being tried, a node is "flagged". When both assignment choices at a node are rejected, the node is removed from the decision tree and its predecessor node's assignment is set to X.

2. Determine whether the current combination of values on the primary inputs, assigned or unassigned, constitutes a test. If a test is found, stop.

3. Check if it would be possible to generate a test by assigning 0 or 1 to the remaining unassigned primary inputs. Go to step 1 if such a possibility exists.

4. Determine if there is an input pattern which has not been examined as a possible test. Go to step 2 if there is such a pattern, otherwise the fault is untestable.

A more detailed algorithm description of the PODEM algorithm is shown in Fig. 3.12. Given a fault, an empty decision tree and all primary inputs at X, the algorithm will find a test for the fault provided it is detectable. The proper choice of a primary input and its logic level assignment saves a lot of effort during test generation.

A two-step procedure is used by PODEM to choose a primary input and logic level for initial assignment:

1. Determine an "initial objective", the aim of which is to set up D or $\bar{D}$ at the output of the gate under test (G.U.T.).

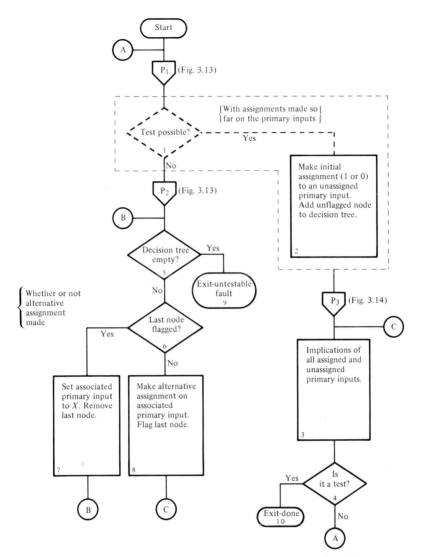

Fig. 3.12   Basic PODEM algorithm (*courtesy of IEEE,* © *1981*).

2.   Choose a primary input and assign a logic value to it so that D or $\bar{D}$ at the output of the G.U.T. can be propagated through another level of logic to the primary output.

A procedure for determining initial objectives is shown in Fig. 3.13. An objective is defined by a logic level 0 or 1 that is referred to as the *objective logic level,* and an *objective net* is the circuit net on which the objective logic level is required.

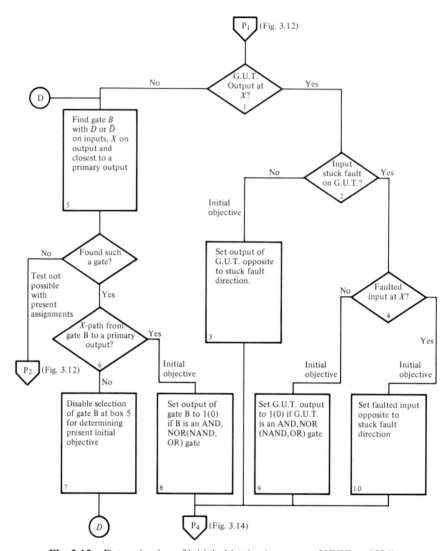

Fig. 3.13   Determination of initial objective (*courtesy of IEEE,* © *1981*).

The procedure for obtaining a primary input assignment given an initial objective is shown in Fig. 3.14; this is known as *backtrace*. The backtrace procedure traces a signal path from the objective net backwards to a primary input. When a primary input is reached, an input pattern is formed with a new value on this primary input; all other primary input assignments remain unchanged. This pattern is checked to determine whether it is a test for the given fault.

Let us demonstrate the application of the **PODEM** algorithm by deriving a

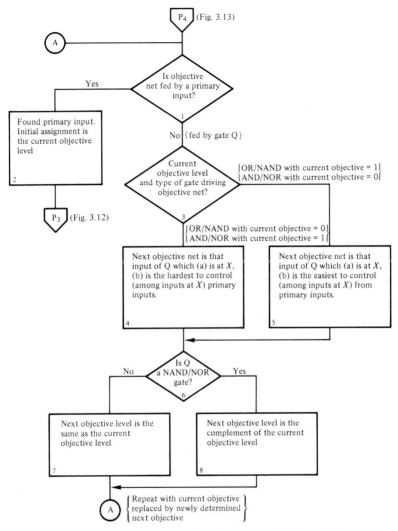

Fig. 3.14   Backtrace procedure (*courtesy of IEEE, © 1981*).

test for detecting the fault α s-a-0 in the circuit of Fig. 3.15. The initial objective is to set the output of gate A to logic 1, i.e. the objective logic level is 1 on net 5 (Box 3 in Fig. 3.13). By going through the backtrace procedure, it can be determined that the next objective net is 1 (or 2) and the objective logic level is 0. Since net 1 is fed by the primary input x_1, the current objective logic level, i.e. logic 0, is assigned to the primary input x_1 as shown below:

1	2	3	4	5	6	7	8	9	10	11	12
0	X	X	X	X	X	X	X	X	X	X	X

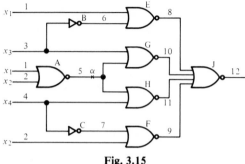

Fig. 3.15

Since $x_1x_2x_3x_4 = 0XXX$ is not a test for the fault, a second pass through the algorithm results in the assignment of primary input x_2, which sets up D as the output of gate A

1	2	3	4	5	6	7	8	9	10	11	12
0	0	X	X	D	X	X	X	X	X	X	X

Since the output of gate A, i.e. net 5, is not X, it is necessary to find a gate with D as its input, X as its output and closer to the primary output (Box 5, Fig. 3.13). Both gates G and H satisfy the requirements. The selection of gate G and the subsequent initial objective (Box 8, Fig. 3.13) result in the assignment of primary input x_3

1	2	3	4	5	6	7	8	9	10	11	12
0	0	0	X	D	1	X	0	X	$\bar{D}$	X	X

$x_1x_2x_3x_4 = 000X$ is not a test for the fault because the primary output is X. Gate J has $\bar{D}$ on input net 10 and Xs on input nets 9 and 11. The initial objective is to set the objective net 12 to logic 1. The selection of net 9 as the next objective results in the assignment of primary input x_4:

1	2	3	4	5	6	7	8	9	10	11	12
0	0	0	0	D	1	1	0	0	$\bar{D}$	$\bar{D}$	D

Thus the test for the fault α s-a-0 is $x_1x_2x_3x_4 = 0000$. The same test could be found for the fault by applying the D-algorithm; however, the D-algorithm requires substantial trial and error before the test is found. This is because of the variety of propagation paths and the attendant consistency operations that are required. For example, α s-a-0 has to be simultaneously propagated to the output via the paths AGJ and AHJ; propagation along either path individually will lead to inconsistency. This feature of the D-algorithm can lead to a waste of effort if a given fault is untestable.

The PODEM is more efficient than the D-algorithm in terms of computer time required to generate tests for combinational circuits. It has been preferred to the D-algorithm as the stuck-at fault test pattern generator in the PODEM-X test system |3.12|. The PODEM-X system is used to generate tests for VLSI logic structures of up to 50 000 gates, designed using the LSSD (level sensitive scan design) technique (see Sec. 6.6).

3.3   DETECTION OF MULTIPLE FAULTS IN COMBINATIONAL LOGIC CIRCUITS

One of the assumptions normally made in test generation schemes is that only a single fault is present in the circuit under test. This assumption is valid only if the circuit is frequently tested, when the probability of more than one fault occurring is small. However, this is not true when a newly manufactured circuit is tested for the first time. Multiple-fault assumption is also more realistic in an LSI/VLSI environment, where faults which occur during manufacture frequently affect several parts of a circuit. Some statistical studies have shown that multiple faults, composed of at least six single faults, must be tested in an LSI chip to establish its reliability |3.13|.

Designing multiple-fault detection tests for a logic network is difficult because of the extremely large number of faults that have to be considered. In a circuit having k lines there are $2k$ possible single faults but a total of $(3^k - 1)$ multiple faults |3.14|. Hence test generation for all possible multiple faults is impractical even for small networks.

One approach which reduces the number of faults that need be tested in a network is "fault collapsing", which uses the concept of "equivalent faults" |3.15, 3.16|. For example, an x-input logic gate can have $(2x + 2)$ possible faults; however, for certain input faults, a gate output would be forced into a state which is indistinguishable from one of the s-a-0/s-a-1 output faults. Thus, for an AND gate any input s-a-0 fault is indistinguishable from the output s-a-0 fault, and for an OR gate any input s-a-1 fault is indistinguishable for the output s-a-1 fault. Such faults are said to be equivalent. For a NAND(NOR) gate, the set of input s-a-0 (s-a-1) faults and the set of output faults s-a-1 (s-a-0) are equivalent. Thus, an x-input gate has to be tested for $(x + 2)$ logically distinct faults.

A systematic approach which reduces the number of faults that have to be considered in test generation is the process of "fault folding" |3.17|. The central idea behind the process is to form fault equivalence classes for a given circuit by folding faults towards the primary inputs. For non-reconvergent fan-out circuits the folding operation produces a set of faults on primary inputs, and this set test covers all faults in the circuit. For reconvergent fan-out circuits, the set of faults at the primary inputs, fan-out origins and fan-out branches test cover all faults in the circuit.

Another approach which results in a significant reduction in the number of faults to be tested uses the concept of "prime faults" |3.18|. The set of prime faults for a network can be generated by the following procedure:

1. Assign a fault to every gate input line if that is a primary input line or a
    fan-out branch line. The fault is s-a-1 for AND/NAND gate inputs, and
    s-a-0 for OR/NOR gate inputs. Treat an inverter as a single input
    NAND/NOR gate if its output is a primary output, otherwise no fault
    value should be assigned to an inverter input line.
2. Identify every gate, that has faults assigned to all its input line, as a "prime
    gate". Assign a fault to the output line of every prime gate that does not
    fan out. The fault is s-a-0 for AND/NOR gate outputs, and s-a-1 for
    OR/NAND gate outputs.

The number of prime faults in a network is significantly fewer than the
number of single faults, since many single faults can be represented by
equivalent multiple prime faults.

In general, test sets derived under the single-fault assumption are capable of
detecting a large number of multiple faults. However, there is no guarantee that
a multiple fault will be detected by a single-fault-detecting test set, although all
the single-fault components of the multiple fault may be individually detected;
this is due to masking relations between faults [3.19].

Schertz et al. [3.20] have shown that for a "restricted fan-out free" network,
every single fault detection test set is also a multiple-fault detection test set.
Any network which does not contain the network of Fig. 3.16 (or its
equivalent) as a subnetwork is called a "restricted fan-out free" network. It has
been proved that the network of Fig. 3.16 is the smallest fan-out free network
that can contain multiple faults which are not detected by every single-fault
detection test set [3.14].

Bossen and Hong [3.21] have shown that any multiple fault in a network
can be represented by an equivalent fault, whose components are faults on
certain "checkpoints" in the network. Checkpoints are associated with each
fan-out point and each primary input.

Agarwal and Fung [3.22] have recently shown that the commonly used
hypothesis about testing multiple faults by single-fault tests is not correct for
reconvergent fan-out circuits. They suggested that the only way to test for
multiple faults in LSI/VLSI chips is to design them so that they will be easily
testable for multiple faults.

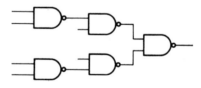

Fig. 3.16   Multi-level fan-out free network.

3.4   TEST GENERATION FOR SEQUENTIAL LOGIC CIRCUITS

While the D-algorithm and other test generation methods are well able to handle purely combinational logic circuits, the testing of sequential circuits still remains as a major problem. The behavior of a sequential circuit depends not only on the present values of the inputs but also on the set of past inputs, and there lies the difficulty in testing. It takes an entire sequence of inputs to detect many of the possible faults in a sequential network.

There are two distinctly different approaches to the problem of finding tests for sequential circuits:

1.   By converting a given synchronous sequential circuit into a one-dimensional array of identical combinational circuits. Most techniques for generating tests for combinational circuits can then be applied.
2.   By verifying whether or not a given circuit is operating in accordance with its state table.

3.4.1   Testing of Sequential Circuits as Iterative Combinational Circuits

A general model of *synchronous sequential circuits*, also known as *sequential* or *finite state machines*, is shown in Fig. 3.17(a). The output is determined by the present state of the flip-flops and the input. If there are n copies of the same sequential circuit and these are so interconnected that the state of the first copy is communicated to the second, that the state of the second copy is communicated to the third, etc., the resulting diagram will be as shown in Fig. 3.17(b). In the diagram $x(i)$, $y(i)$ and $z(i)$, associated with the ith copy of the circuit, correspond to the input, the next state and the output of the sequential circuit at the ith instant of time.

The circuit of Fig. 3.17(b) is a combinational network since it consists of a cascade of identical "cells", with each cell having a pair of inputs (to receive input signals and information from its neighbor on the left) and a pair of outputs (to supply information to its neighbor on the right and to the network outputs). Thus the transformation indicated in Fig. 3.17(b) replaces the problem of testing synchronous sequential circuits by the problem of finding tests for the iterative combinational network.

Each fault in the sequential network leads to n identical faults in the iterative network, so the problem of fault detection in a synchronous sequential circuit can be treated as the problem of multiple-fault detection in a combinational network. The increased number of faults to be considered and the extra complexity of the replicated logic make this technique unrealistic for complex circuits. Moreover, it is necessary to derive test sequences which should be able to detect a fault independently of the initial state of a circuit. This requires derivation of test sequences for all possible initial states, and then constructing

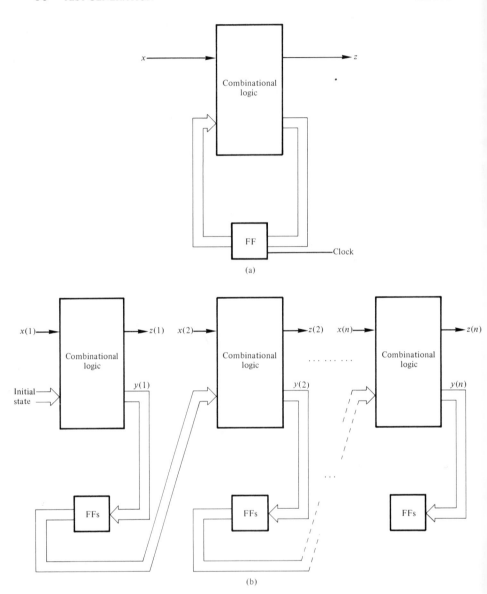

Fig. 3.17   (a) Sequential network; (b) iterative model of the sequential network.

a sequence which will detect the fault in all cases. However, this may not be computationally feasible.

3.4.2   State Table Verification

In this approach a sequential machine is tested by performing an "experiment" on it, i.e. by applying an input signal and observing the output |3.23, 3.24|.

Hence, the testing problem may be stated as follows: given the state table of a sequential machine, find an input/output sequence pair (X, Z) such that the response of the machine to X will be Z if and only if the machine is operating correctly. The application of this input sequence X and the observation of the response, to see if it is Z, is called a "checking experiment"; the sequence pair (X, Z) is referred to as a "checking sequence".

Checking experiments are classified either as "adaptive" or "preset". In "adaptive" experiments the choice of the input symbols is based on the output symbols produced by a machine earlier in the experiment. In "preset" experiments the entire input sequence is completely specified in advance. A measure of efficiency of an experiment is its "length", which is the total number of input symbols applied to the machine during the execution of an experiment. The derivation of "checking sequence" is based on the following assumptions:

1. The network is fully specified and deterministic. In a deterministic machine the next state is determined uniquely by the present state and the present input.
2. The network is strongly connected, i.e. for every pair of states q_i and q_j of the network, there exists an input sequence that takes the network from q_i to q_j.
3. The network in the presence of faults has no more states than those listed in its specification. In other words, no fault will increase the number of states.

In order to design checking experiments it is necessary to know the "initial state" of the network, which is determined by a "distinguishing" or a "homing sequence".

An input sequence is said to be a *homing sequence* for a machine if the machine's response to the sequence is always sufficient to determine uniquely its final state. For an example, consider the machine of Fig. 3.18. It has a homing sequence 101, for, as indicated in Fig. 3.19, each of the output

Present state	Input $x = 0$	$x = 1$
A	C,1	D,0
B	D,0	B,1
C	B,0	C,1
D	C,0	A,0

Next state/output

Fig. 3.18   State table of Machine M.

Initial state	Output sequence			Final state
A	0	0	1	C
B	1	0	0	A
C	1	0	1	B
D	0	1	1	C

Fig. 3.19   Response of Machine M to homing sequence 101.

sequences that might result from the application of 101 is associated with just one final state. A homing sequence need not always leave a machine in the same final state; it is only necessary that the final state can be identified from the output sequence.

A *distinguishing sequence* is an input sequence which when applied to a machine will produce a different output sequence for each choice of initial state. For example, 101 is also a distinguishing sequence for Machine M of Fig. 3.18. As shown in Fig. 3.19 the output sequence that the machine produces in response to 101 uniquely specifies its initial state. Every distinguishing sequence is also a homing sequence because the knowledge of the initial state and the input sequence is always sufficient to determine uniquely the final state as well. On the other hand not every homing sequence is a distinguishing sequence. For example, the machine of Fig. 3.20(a) has a homing sequence 010. As shown in Fig. 3.20(b) the output sequence produced in response to 010 uniquely specifies the final state of machine N but cannot distinguish between the initial states C and D. Every reduced sequential machine possesses a homing sequence, while only a limited number of machines have distinguishing sequences.

At the start of an experiment a machine can be in any of its n states. In such a case the "initial uncertainty" regarding the state of the machine is the set which contains all the states of the machine. A collection of states of the machine which is known to contain the present state is referred to as the "uncertainty"; the *uncertainty* of a machine is thus any subset of the state of the machine. For example, Machine M of Fig. 3.18 can initially be in any of its four states; hence the initial uncertainty is (ABCD). If an input 1 is applied to the machine, the successor uncertainty will be (AD) or (BC) depending on whether the output is 0 or 1 respectively. The uncertainties (C)(DBC) are the 0-successors of (ABCD). A *successor tree*, which is defined for a specified machine and a given initial uncertainty, is a structure which displays graphically the x_i-successor uncertainties for every possible input sequence x_i.

A collection of uncertainties is referred to as an "uncertainty vector"; the individual uncertainties contained in the vector are called the *components* of the vector. An uncertainty vector whose components contain a single state each is said to be a "trivial uncertainty vector". An uncertainty vector whose components contain either single states or identical repeated states is said to be a

Present state	Input		Present state	Response to 010			Final state
	$x = 0$	$x = 1$					
A	B,0	D,0	A	0	0	0	A
B	A,0	B,0	B	0	0	1	D
C	D,1	A,0	C	1	0	1	D
D	D,1	C,0	D	1	0	1	D
(a)				(b)			

Fig. 3.20   (a) Machine N; (b) response of Machine N to 010.

"homogeneous uncertainty vector". For example, the vectors (AA)(B)(C) and (A)(B)(A)(C) are homogeneous and trivial, respectively.

A homing sequence is obtained from the homing tree; a homing tree is a successor tree in which a node becomes terminal if one of the following conditions occurs:

1. The node is associated with an uncertainty vector whose non-homogeneous components are associated with the same node at a preceding level.
2. The node is associated with a trivial or a homogeneous vector.

The path from the initial uncertainty to a node in which the vector is trivial or homogeneous defines a homing sequence.

A distinguishing tree is a successor tree in which a node becomes terminal if one of the following conditions occurs:

1. The node is associated with an uncertainty vector whose non-homogeneous components are associated with the same node at a preceding level.
2. The node is associated with an uncertainty vector containing a homogeneous non-trivial component.
3. The node is associated with a trivial uncertainty vector.

The path from the initial uncertainty to a node associated with a trivial uncertainty defines a distinguishing sequence. As an example, the homing sequence 010 is obtained as shown in Fig. 3.21 by applying the terminal rules to Machine N of Fig. 3.20. The derivation of the distinguishing sequence 101 for Machine M of Fig. 3.18 is shown in Fig. 3.22.

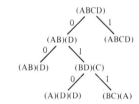

Fig. 3.21   Homing tree for Machine N.

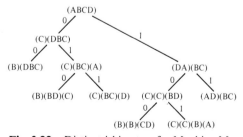

Fig. 3.22   Distinguishing tree for Machine M.

During the design of checking experiments it is often necessary to take the machine into a predetermined state, after the homing sequence has been applied. This is done with the help of a *transfer sequence*, which is the shortest input sequence that takes a machine from state S_i to state S_j. The procedure is an "adaptive" one, since the transfer sequence is determined by the response of the homing sequence. As an example, let us derive the transfer sequence that will take Machine M of Fig. 3.18 from state B to state C. To accomplish this we assume that the machine is in state B. We form the transfer tree as shown in Fig. 3.23; it can be seen from the successor tree that the shortest transfer sequence that will take the machine from state B to state C is 00.

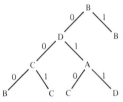

Fig. 3.23   Transfer tree.

Instead of a homing sequence, a *synchronizing sequence* may be used at the beginning of the checking experiment; it takes a machine to a specified final state regardless of the output or the initial state of the machine. Some machines possess synchronizing sequences—others do not. For a machine one can construct a synchronizing tree by associating with each node the uncertainty regarding the final states (regardless of the output) which results from the application of the input symbols. For example, if the initial uncertainty of Machine P of Fig. 3.24(a) is (ABCD), the 0-successor uncertainty is (ABC); it

Present state	Input	
	x = 0	x = 1
A	B,1	C,0
B	A,0	D,1
C	B,0	A,0
D	C,1	A,1
	Next-state/Output	

(a)

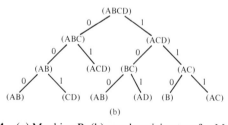

(b)

Fig. 3.24   (a) Machine P; (b) synchronizing tree for Machine P.

is not necessary to write down the repeated entries (BABC). A node becomes terminal whenever either of the following conditions occurs:

1. The node is associated with an uncertainty that is also associated with the same node at a preceding level.
2. A node in the nth level is associated with an uncertainty containing just a single element.

The synchronizing tree for Machine P of Fig. 3.24(a) is shown in Fig. 3.24(b). A synchronizing sequence is described by a path in the tree leading from the initial uncertainty to a singleton uncertainty. For Machine P, 110 is the synchronizing sequence which, when applied to the machine, synchronizes it to state B.

Designing checking experiments   Basically the purpose of a checking experiment is to verify that the state table of a finite state machine accurately describes the behavior of the machine. If during the execution of the experiment the machine produces a response that is different from the correctly operating machine, the machine is definitely faulty. Such experiments can be used only to determine whether or not *something* is wrong with a machine; it is not possible to conclude from these experiments *what* is wrong with the machine.

We will now show how to design a checking experiment for any strongly connected, "diagnosable" sequential machine. A *diagnosable machine* has the property of having at least one distinguishing sequence. The checking experiment can be divided into three phases:

1. *Initialization phase.* During the initialization phase the machine under test is taken from an unknown initial state to a fixed state. A reduced, strongly connected machine can be manoeuvered into some fixed state s by the following method:

   (a) Apply a homing sequence to the machine and identify the current state of the machine.
   (b) If the current state is not s, apply a transfer sequence to move the machine from the current state to s.

   It is apparent that the initialization phase is adaptive; however, it can be preset if a machine has a synchronizing sequence.
2. *State identification phase.* During this phase, an input sequence is applied so as to cause the machine to visit each of its states and display its response to the distinguishing sequence.
3. *Transition verification phase.* During this phase the machine is made to go through every state transition; each state transition is checked by using the distinguishing sequence.

Although these three phases are distinct, in practice the subsequences for state identification and transition verification are mixed up whenever possible, in order to shorten the length of the experiment.

As an example, the design of the checking experiment for the machine of Fig. 3.25 (Machine Q) is described.

The successor tree of this machine is shown in Fig. 3.26. It can be seen from Fig. 3.26 that the machine has two homing sequences (00 and 01), and one distinguishing sequence (11). The machine has no synchronizing sequences. The response of the machine to the homing sequence 00 is shown in Table 3.6. If the second part of the experiment is designed so that state A is the initial state, it is necessary to transfer the machine to that state. If the machine produces 00 in response to the homing sequence 00, it must be in state B. In this case it can be manoeuvred into state A by applying the transfer sequence 1. If the machine produces 01 in response to 00, it must be in state A; if it produces 10, it must be in state C. In the latter case it can be moved to state A by applying the transfer sequence 0.

Initial state	Response to 00	Final state
A	01	A
B	00	B
C	10	C
D	00	B

Table 3.6   Response to homing sequence 00

The second part of the experiment begins with the assumption that, if the machine is operating correctly, it is currently in state A. In order to ascertain that the current state is indeed A, the distinguishing sequence 11 is applied; the responses of the Machine Q to the distinguishing sequence are shown in Table 3.7. If the machine is operating correctly, the application of 11 will yield the

	$x = 0$	$x = 1$
A	C,0	D,1
B	B,0	A,1
C	A,1	B,0
D	B,0	C,0

Fig. 3.25   State table of Machine Q.

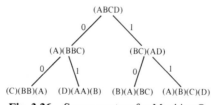

Fig. 3.26   Successor tree for Machine Q.

Initial state	Response to 11	Final state
A	10	C
B	11	D
C	01	A
D	00	B

Table 3.7   Response to distinguishing sequence 11

response 10 and leave the machine in state C. Applying 11 again will yield the response 01 and the machine will be back in state A. In order to display the response of state B to the distinguishing sequence, it is necessary to apply the transfer sequence 10, followed by 11. At this point the machine will be in state D. Applying 11 again will yield the response 00 and the machine will be in state B. To finish off this part of the experiment, the sequence 11 is applied, thereby getting the response of state B for the second time and leaving the machine in state D.

```
Time     1  2  3  4  5  6  7  8  9  10  11  12
Input    1  1  1  1  1  0  1  1  1  1   1   1
State  A     C     A     B     D     B       D
Output 1  0  0  1  1  0  1  1  0  0   1   1
```

It can be seen from the input–output sequence shown above that the machine produces four different responses to the distinguishing sequence 11. Hence the machine must have four states, each of which has been visited once. Consequently whenever the machine responds to the distinguishing sequence 11 in the same way at different points in the experiments, the state of the machine at each point is uniquely identifiable. Moreover, it can be established from the above input/output sequence that 111 takes the machine from state A to B, B to C and C to D.

To complete the experiment it is necessary to verify that the transitions of the actual machine match those of the given state table. The general procedure is to apply the input symbol which causes the desired transition and to identify it by applying the distinguishing sequence. Since the machine is currently in state D, the experiment is started by applying an input 0, followed by 11. If the machine is operating correctly, it will be back in state D as shown below. The arrow indicates the point at which the state transition occurred.

```
Time     1  2  3
Input    0  1  1
State  D → B     D
Output 0  1  1
```

If a 1 is applied now, the machine will move to state C, for it is known from the second part of the experiment that the sequence 111 takes the machine from state B to C. Since the 111-successor of state B is C and the 11-successor of B is D, the 1-successor of D must be C:

Time	1	2	3	4
Input	0	1	1	1
State			D → C	
Output	0	1	1	0

Since the sequence 111 takes the machine from C to D, the 1-successor of C must be B because it has already been established that D is the 11-successor of B:

Time	1	2	3	4	5	6	7
Input	0	1	1	1	1	1	1
State				C → B		D	
Output	0	1	1	0	0	1	1

If in response to the input sequence 011, the machine produces the output sequence 011, it can be concluded that the final state is again D and the 1-successor of B is A:

Time	1	2	3	4	5	6	7	8	9	10
Input	0	1	1	1	1	1	1	0	1	1
State							D	B → A	D	
Output	0	1	1	0	0	1	1	0	1	1

(Since from the earlier part of the experiment it is known that the 11-successor of B is D; hence the 1-successor of B must be A.)

The machine is presently in state D; the application of a 0 would take it to state B. The 0-transition out of state B is considered next:

Time	1	2	3	4	5	6	7	8	9	10	11	12	13	14	15
Input	0	1	1	1	1	1	1	0	1	1	0	0	1	1	1
State									D	B → B	A	D	C		
Output	0	1	1	0	0	1	1	0	1	1	0	0	1	1	0

This is done by applying 0 followed by 111, which takes the machine from state B to C. Since the 11-successor of B is D and the 1-successor of B is A, the 1-successor of A must be D. The 0-transition out of state C can then be checked by applying a 0 followed by 11. By inspecting the preceding sequence it can be verified that C is the 11-successor of A, hence the 0-successor of C must be A:

Time	1	2	3	4	5	6	7	8	9	10	11	12	13	14	15	16	17	18
Input	0	1	1	1	1	1	1	0	1	1	0	0	1	1	1	0	1	1
State															C → A			C
Output	0	1	1	0	0	1	1	0	1	1	0	0	1	1	0	1	1	0

Up to this point every state transition has been checked except the 0-transition out of state A. The application of an input sequence 00 followed by 11 verifies the transition from A to C under a 0 input. This verification is achieved by inspecting the earlier part of the experiment and observing that A is the 0-successor of C, and the 11-successor of C is A. Thus C is the 0-successor of A:

Time	1	2	3	4	5	6	7	8	9	10	11	12	13	14	15	16	17	18	19	20	21	22
Input	0	1	1	1	1	1	1	0	1	1	0	0	1	1	1	0	1	1	0	0	1	1
State																C	A → C		A			
Output	0	1	1	0	0	1	1	0	1	1	0	0	1	1	0	1	1	0	1	0	0	1

The state table verification technique can be considered as a form of functional testing. The major limitation of this technique is that it requires the generation of the state table of a given network, which is not practicable except for very small circuits. In addition, this technique results in excessively long test sequences for highly sequential circuits, i.e. for circuits in which memory elements constitute a significant portion of the circuitry. Thus the state-table verification technique although theoretically complete is not computationally feasible.

An alternative approach to testing sequential circuits, known as the "state diagram approach", uses an input sequence which forces a circuit under test to go through all the state and output transitions; this approach has been found to detect a large percentage of circuit faults |3.25|. It is independent of hardware fault modes and has the advantage in that a temporary fault can be detected as an incorrect state transition. A variation of this technique has been proposed by Yamada *et al.* |3.26| for testing highly sequential circuits. It involves decomposing a sequential circuit into several subcircuits, each subcircuit being represented by a finite state machine; the overall circuit is an interconnection of these subcircuits. Then an input sequence capable of completing a cycle of transitions for each subcircuit is derived by tracing through the state diagrams of the subcircuits. Experimental results show that test sequences obtained by this technique can detect more than 90% of single stuck-at-type faults.

3.5 RANDOM TESTING

Test generation for digital circuits can be classified as either *deterministic* or *probabilistic*. Examples of the former are one-dimensional path sensitization, Boolean difference and the *D*-algorithm, whereas the random test generation method falls under the latter category.

Deterministic test generation methods are often unable to cope with complex circuits of LSI and VLSI chips. The computation time, required by these methods to generate a test set that detects all single and some multiple stuck-at faults, becomes prohibitively expensive for large circuits. Random testing methods can reduce the computation cost and hence can be used very effectively for fault detection in today's digital devices.

There are two types of random testing procedures. In the first, known as the random test generation method, input patterns are randomly generated and applied to the primary inputs of circuits under test |3.27|. The input patterns can be generated by a linear feedback shift register (LFSR); such registers generate long, repetitive pseudo-noise sequences, short segments of which have properties similar to random patterns |3.28|. The outputs of the faulty and the fault-free networks for each random input pattern are compared by using a simulator. If the output values are different, the random input pattern is retained as a test. The ability of each new input pattern to detect faults in a fault list is determined. Successful tests are stored while the faults they detect are deleted from the fault list. In general this technique produces very large test sets. However, it is possible to optimize the tests by assigning different "weights" to the input leads of the circuit under test |3.29|.

The second type of random testing procedure does not require prior test generation and consists of comparing the output of the circuit under test with the output of a known good unit (also called "gold unit"), while both units are fed by the same sequence of random inputs (see Fig. 3.27) |3.30, 3.31|. Any difference in the output responses indicates the existence of faults. The procedure has certain weaknesses in that the reliability of the "known good circuit" is not guaranteed and the synchronization of the two circuits may cause problems, especially for sequential circuits, which would have different initial states.

For both types of random testing procedures, one needs to know the number of tests that should be applied to a given circuit to determine with a given

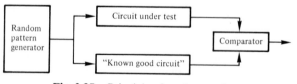

Fig. 3.27   Principle of random testing.

degree of confidence, that it is fault-free. The required number of tests could be determined only by analyzing the given circuit extensively. For very large circuits the analysis process may be of the same order as the formal test generation procedures being replaced. However, the decision whether a combinational circuit should be tested by random inputs can be made from certain easily observable characteristics of the circuit, such as the primary inputs, the number of levels and the average fan-in |3.32|.

3.6   TRANSITION COUNT TESTING

The *transition count* is defined as the total number of transitions from $1 \rightarrow 0$ and $0 \rightarrow 1$ in a response sequence for a given input sequence. For example, if a response sequence $Z = 10011010$, then the transition count $c(Z) = 5$. In transition count testing, as in conventional testing, a predetermined test sequence is applied to the circuit under test. The response of the circuit is monitored at some selected test point(s); however, this is done in a way different from that of conventional testing. Instead of recording the entire response sequence, only the transition count is recorded. This transition count is then compared with that expected at the test point(s). If the two transition counts differ, the circuit is declared faulty, otherwise it is fault-free |3.33|.

Figure 3.28(a) shows the response sequences, and the corresponding transition counts, at various nodes of a network resulting from the application of a test sequence of length 5. Let us suppose there is a fault α s-a-0 in the circuit (Fig. 3.28(b)). The presence of the fault changes the transition counts at certain nodes in the circuit (shown by arrow). As can be seen in the diagram, the

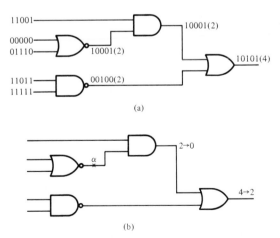

(a)

(b)

Fig. 3.28   (a) Response to test sequence of length 5; (b) changes in transition counts.

transition count at the output node changes from 4 to 2 resulting in the detection of the fault α s-a-0.

The transition count generator circuit consists of a counter and a transition detector that advances the counter when a change of state occurs in its input sequence. The main advantage of transition count testing is that it is not necessary to store either the correct response sequence or the actual response sequence at any test point; only the transition counts are needed. Clearly, this results in the reduction of data storage requirements. However, this data compression may give rise to fault-masking errors. This is because most transition counts correspond to more than one sequence; for example, the transition count 2 is generated by each of the following 5-bit sequences: 01110, 01100, 01000, 00110, 01000 and 00010. Hence, there is a possibility that a fault sequence will produce the same transition count as the good sequence, and therefore go undetected. However, as the sequence length increases the hazard of fault-masking diminishes.

Fault isolation by transition count testing can be carried out by monitoring the activity at each test point on a circuit and noting where the test results do not match those for a known-good board or those cited on the circuit diagram. Any circuit node stuck-at 0 or 1 produces sequences of all 0s and all 1s respectively; hence the transition counting gives very good coverage of stuck-at faults at circuit nodes. The main drawback of transition count testing is that the fault coverage achieved by a test pattern depends on the order of applying the patterns. Although this may not be a major problem in testing combinational circuits where test patterns can be applied in any order, this is not so in the case of sequential circuits. Besides, with multiple output circuits a particular test pattern may give different fault coverage at different outputs; the optimal test patterns can only be determined by using simulation techniques.

3.7 SIGNATURE ANALYSIS

Signature analysis is a technique pioneered by Hewlett-Packard Ltd, that detects errors in data streams caused by hardware faults |3.34|. It uses a unique data compression technique which reduces long data streams into four-digit hexadecimal signatures. By supplying known input sequences to a digital system, unique signatures can be obtained at various nodes in the system. These correct signatures can be recorded and later compared with the signatures obtained at the same nodes of a malfunctioning system. Any difference in signature at a node indicates that the node is not operating as expected. The cause of an incorrect signature may be discovered by tracing back through the circuit and observing the signatures at appropriate nodes; the fault giving rise to the error can eventually be located through the process of elimination. Thus the signature analysis technique is a digital equivalent of the voltage and waveform checking of analogue circuits, and is used in the same way. Unlike transition count testing the degree of fault coverage provided by signature analysis technique does not depend upon the order of test patterns.

Signatures can be created from data streams by feeding the data into an n-bit linear feedback shift register. The feedback mechanism consists of EX-ORing selected taps of the shift register with the input serial data as shown in Fig. 3.29. After the data stream has been clocked through, a residue of the serial data is left in the shift register. This residue is unique to the data stream and represents its "signature". Another data stream may differ by only one bit from the previous data stream, and yet its signature is radically different from the previous one. To form the signature of a data stream, the shift register is first initialized to a known state and then shifted using the data stream; normally, the all-0s state is chosen as the initial state.

The START signal in Fig. 3.29 resets all the bits in the shift register to logic 0 and initiates the "measurement window". During this time window the incoming data to the signature analyzer are entered into the shift register using the CLOCK signal. The STOP signal terminates the measurement window. All three control signals, START, CLOCK and STOP, are edge-triggered signals and may be selected to trigger on either the positive—or the negative—going edge.

Figure 3.30(a) shows a simplified 4-bit signature generator. Since the generator circuit is similar to that for generating pseudo-random binary sequences (PRBS), the circuit is also known as the PRBS generator. If a 1 is applied to the circuit, the EX-OR gate will have a 1 output. The next clock pulse will shift the gate output into the first stage of the register and 0s from the preceding stages into the second, third and fourth stages, which leaves the register containing 1000, i.e. in state 8. From the state diagram of Fig. 3.30(b), the register contents or signatures can be identified for any data stream.

Let us consider the circuit of Fig. 3.31 to show the application of the signature analysis technique for fault detection. Table 3.8 shows the six-bit input sequence, applied at inputs $X_1 - X_3$, the correct circuit responses, and the responses of the circuit in presence of the faults stuck-at-0 and B stuck-at-1.

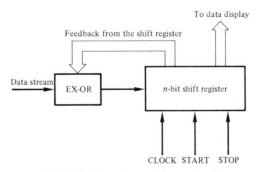

Fig. 3.29   Signature analyzer circuit.

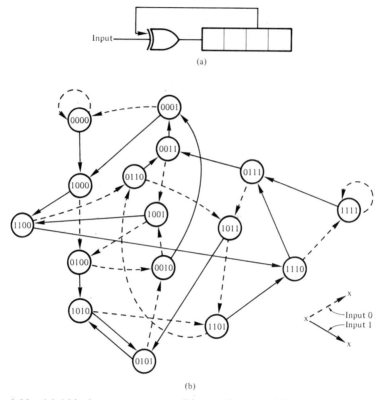

(a)

(b)

Fig. 3.30   (a) 4-bit signature generator; (b) state diagram of the signature generator.

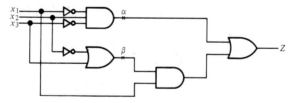

Fig. 3.31   Circuit under test.

When the sequences are shifted into the PRBS circuit, the register, after six shifts, will assume the status shown in the table. The hexadecimal equivalent of this status is stored as signatures. (Hewlett-Packard uses a non-standard hexadecimal character set, 0-9ACFHPU, to represent signatures; this character set was chosen for easy readability and compatibility with 7-segment displays.) It can be seen from the table that the signatures produced at the output node for the faulty circuits are different from that of the fault-free circuit.

	Input values			Fault-free output	Faulty output		
	X_1	X_2	X_3	Z	Z (α s-a-0)	Z (β s-a-1)	Z (α s-a-0 and β s-a-1)
Data streams	0	0	0	0	0	0	0
at the input	0	0	1	0	0	0	0
and output	0	1	0	1	0	1	0
nodes	0	1	1	0	0	0	0
	1	1	0	0	0	1	1
	1	1	1	1	1	1	1
Register	1	0	1	0	1	0	1
status after	1	1	1	0	0	1	1
six shifts	0	1	1	0	0	0	0
	0	1	0	1	0	1	0
Signature	F	7	P	1	8	5	F

Table 3.8   Generation of signatures for the circuit of Fig. 3.31

An n-bit PRBS can generate 2^n signatures. However, many input sequences can map into one signature. In general, if the length of an input sequence is m and n is the length of the PRBS generator, then $2^{(m-n)}$ input sequences map into each signature [3.35]. This mapping gives rise to fault-masking errors, because a signature generated from an input sequence carrying fault information may map into the same signature as the good sequence. The probability P that an input sequence has deteriorated into another which has the same signature as itself is

$$P = \frac{2^{(m-n)} - 1}{2^m - 1} \tag{3.1}$$

P is calculated on the assumption that any of the possible input sequences of a given length may be good or faulty. Expression (3.1) reduces to

$$P = \frac{1}{2^n} \quad \text{for } m \gg n$$

Hence the probability of fault-masking errors will be low if a PRBS generator has many stages, and thus capable of generating a large number of signatures. In Hewlett-Packard implementation of signature analysis a 16-bit PRBS generator (Fig. 3.32) is used; hence 65536 $(= 2^{16})$ signatures can be formed. The error-detection properties of the signature analysis technique are given below:

1. The probability that two identical data streams will produce the same signature during testing is 1.

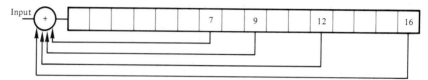

Fig. 3.32   A 16-bit signature generator.

2. The probability that two data streams will produce the same signature if they differ by precisely one bit is 0. For example, let us consider two long data streams, one differing from the other by only one bit. As the error bit gets shifted into the 16-bit register of Fig. 3.32, it has four chances to change the register's input before it overflows the register (after 16 clock cycles) and disappears. The effect of the erroneous bit continues to propagate around the feedback network changing the signature. For a single-bit error, therefore, no other error bit comes along to cancel the feedback's effect, and so signature analysis is bound to catch the single-bit error. Single-bit errors, incidentally, are typical of "soft failures" that occur in LSI devices.

3. The probability that two data streams shifted into the circuit of Fig. 3.32 will produce the same signature if one stream has multi-bit errors is 0.002% ($= 2^{-16}$). In other words there is a 99.998% probability of multi-bit errors being detected for the 16-bit **PRBS** generator.

The signature analysis technique identifies faults by tracing the signal flow in a circuit from input to output. If the signature at a circuit node does not match the empirically determined correct signature, one of the components connected to the node is faulty. In an alternative fault isolation approach, known as "half-splitting", a test point is selected where a fault is equally likely to exist ahead of or behind the point. A correct signature at that point means that the circuit fault exists further ahead. An incorrect signature indicates the reverse. Once the bad half is pin-pointed, it is split in half again and the process is repeated until the fault is located. Feedback loops produce particular difficulties, since faults within them propagate in circles, and can be located only by breaking a loop. Tracing from input to output generally proves useful for field-testing, whereas the half-splitting works well for automatic board testers |3.36|.

Signature analysis has been accepted as a valuable technique in locating hardware faults in bus-structured and processor-oriented digital systems. It offers unique alternatives to other test methods and can provide high test confidence at reasonable cost for both production and field testing |3.37|.

3.8   REFERENCES

3.1 Levendel, Y. H. and P. R. Menon, "Fault simulation methods—extension and comparison", *Bell Syst. Tech. Jour.*, 2235–2258 (November 1981).

3.2 Goel, P., "Test generation cost analysis and projections", *Proc. 17th Design Automation Conf.*, 77–84 (1980).

3.3 Armstrong, D. B., "On finding a nearly minimal set of fault detection tests for combinational logic nets", *IEEE Trans. Electron. Comput.*, 66–73 (February 1966).

3.4 Schneider, R. R., "On the necessity to examine D-chains in diagnostic test generation", *IBM Jour. of Res. and Develop.*, 114 (January 1967).

3.5 Sellers, F. F., M. Y. Hsiao and C. L. Bearnson, "Analyzing errors with the Boolean difference", *IEEE Trans. Comput.*, 676–683 (July 1968).

3.6 Chiang, A. C., I. S. Reed and A. V. Banes, "Path sensitization, partial Boolean difference and automated fault diagnosis", *ibid.*, 189–195 (February 1972).

3.7 Roth, J. P., "Diagnosis of automata failures: a calculus and a method", *ibid.*, 278–291 (July 1966).

3.8 Putzolu, G. R. and J. P. Roth, "A heuristic algorithm for the testing of asynchronous circuits", *IEEE Trans. Comput.*, 639–647 (June 1971).

3.9 Breuer, M. A., A. D. Friedman and A. Iosupovicz, "A survey of the art of design automation", *IEEE Computer*, 58–75 (October 1981).

3.10 Thomas, J. J., "Automated diagnostic test programs for digital networks", *Computer Design*, 63–67 (August 1971).

3.11 Goel, P., "An implicit enumeration algorithm to generate tests for combinational logic circuits", *IEEE Trans. Comput.*, 215–222 (March 1981).

3.12 Goel, P. and B. C. Rosales, "PODEM-X: An automatic test generation system for VLSI logic structures", *Proc. 18th Design Automation Conf.*, 260–268 (1981).

3.13 Goldstein, L. H., "A probabilistic analysis of multiple faults in LSI circuits", *IEEE Computer Society Repository*, R77–304 (1977).

3.14 Hayes, J. P., "A NAND model for fault diagnosis in combinatorial logic circuits", *IEEE Trans. Comput.*, 1496–1506 (December 1971).

3.15 McCluskey, E. J. and F. W. Clegg, "Fault equivalence in combinational logic networks", *ibid.*, 1286–1293 (November 1971).

3.16 Schertz, D. R. and G. A. Metze, "A new representation for faults in combinational digital circuits", *ibid.*, 858–866 (August 1972).

3.17 Klin To, "Fault-folding for irredundant and redundant combinational networks", *ibid.*, 1008–1015 (November 1973).

3.18 Cha, C. W., "Multiple fault diagnosis in combinational networks", *Proc. 16th Design Automation. Conf.*, 149–155 (1979).

3.19 Dias, F. J. O., "Fault masking in combinational logic circuits", *IEEE Trans. Comput.*, 476–482 (May 1975).

3.20 Schertz, D. R. and G. Metze, "On the design of multiple fault diagnosable networks", *ibid.*, 1361–1364 (November 1971).

3.21 Bossen, D. C. and S. J. Hong, "Cause-effect analysis for multiple fault detection in combinational networks", *ibid.*, 1252–1257 (November 1971).

3.22 Agarwal, V. K. and A. S. Fung, "Multiple fault testing of logic circuits by single fault test sets", *ibid.*, 854–855 (November 1981).

3.23 Kohavi, Z., *Switching and Finite Automata Theory*, Chap. 13, McGraw-Hill (1970).

3.24 Hennie, F. C., *Finite State Models for Logical Machines*, Chap. 3, John Wiley (1968).

3.25 Kovijanic, P. G., "A new look at test generation and verification", *Proc. 14th Design Automation Conf.*, 58–63 (1978).

3.26 Yamada, T., M. Saisho and Y. Kasuya, "Test generation method for highly sequential circuits", *Proc. COMPCON*, 104–107 (1979).

3.27 Agarwal, P. and V. Agarwal, "Probabilistic analysis of random test generation method for irredundant combinational logic circuits", *IEEE Trans. Comput.*, 691–695 (July 1975).

3.28 Golomb, S. W., *Shift Register Sequences*, Holden-Day (1967).

3.29 Schnurmann, H. D., E. Lindbloom and R. G. Carpenter, "The weighted random test-pattern generator", *IEEE Trans. Comput.*, 695–700 (July 1975).

3.30 David, R. and G. Blanchet, "About random fault detection of combinational networks", *ibid.*, 659–664 (June 1976).

3.31 David, R. and P. Thevenod-Fosse, "Random testing of integrated circuits", *IEEE Trans. Inst. & Measurement*, 20–25 (March 1981).

3.32 Agarwal, V. D., "When to use random testing", *IEEE Trans. Comput.*, 1054–1055 (November 1978).

3.33 Hayes, J. P., "Transition count testing of combinational logic networks", *ibid.*, 613–620 (June 1976).

3.34 Hewlett-Packard Ltd, "A designer's guide to signature analysis", Application Note 222 (1977).

3.35 Skilling, J. K., "Signatures take a circuit's pulse by transition counting or PRBS", *Electronic Design*, 65–68 (February 1980).

3.36 Wiseman, D., "Microprocessor trouble shooting techniques", *Electronics Test*, 42–48 (February 1980).

3.37 Humphrey, J. R. and K. Firooz, "Signature analysis for board testing", *The Radio & Electronic Engineer*, 37–50 (January 1981).

4 FAULT TOLERANT DESIGN OF DIGITAL SYSTEMS

4.1 THE IMPORTANCE OF FAULT TOLERANCE

There are two fundamentally different approaches that can be taken to increase the reliability of computing systems. The first approach is called *fault prevention* (also known as *fault intolerance*) and the second *fault tolerance*. In the traditional fault prevention approach the objective is to increase the reliability by *a priori* elimination of all faults (see Chap. 3). Since this is almost impossible to achieve in practice, the goal of fault prevention is to reduce the probability of system failure to an acceptably low value. In the fault tolerance approach, faults are expected to occur during computation, but their effects are automatically counteracted by incorporating redundancy, i.e. additional facilities, into a system, so that valid computation can continue even in the presence of faults. These facilities consist of more hardware, more software or more time, or a combination of all these; they are redundant in the sense that they could be omitted from a fault-free system without affecting its operation.

Fault tolerance is not a replacement but rather a supplement to the most important principles of reliable system design: (a) use the most reliable components (however, cost constraints often preclude their use); and (b) keep the system as simple as possible, consistent with achieving the design objectives.

The effectiveness of fault tolerance for enhancing computing system reliability is much more pronounced in a system composed of basically reliable components than in a system of unreliable components. In other words, while fault tolerance can be used to increase significantly the reliability of an already reliable system, it is of little use—and can even have a detrimental effect—if the original system is unreliable in the first place.

Most of the early work in fault-tolerant computer system design was

69

motivated by space applications, and in particular by the requirement for computers to be able to operate unattended for long periods of time. While this application is still an important one, fault tolerance is now regarded as a desirable, and in some cases an essential, feature of a wide range of computing systems especially in applications where reliability, availability and safety are of vital importance. For commercial systems, non-redundant, i.e. fault prevention techniques have been preferred mainly because a redundant design results in extra costs. The reliability is improved by using reliable components, refined interconnections, etc. However, this approach will be less and less viable in the future because it has limited effectiveness to counteract faults in hardware and reduce the number of system disruptions. There is an increasing number of applications where system failures once per day or even once per week are not acceptable. Besides it requires highly skilled system analysts and service engineers to maintain computer systems, which often makes the cost of repair and maintenance extremely high. A fault tolerant design can provide dramatic improvements in system availability and lead to a substantial reduction in maintenance costs as a consequence of fewer system failures |4.1|.

4.2 BASIC CONCEPTS OF FAULT TOLERANCE

The most widely accepted definition of a fault tolerant computing system is that "it is a system which has the built-in capability (without external assistance) to preserve the continued correct execution of its programs and input/output functions in the presence of a certain set of operational faults" |4.2|. An *operational fault* is an unspecified deviation of the correct value of a logic variable in the system hardware or a design fault in the software. "Correct execution" means that the programs, the data and the results do not contain errors and that the execution time does not exceed a specified limit. The types of fault that are encountered during system operation fall into two categories: (a) anticipated faults and (b) unanticipated faults |4.3|. *Anticipated faults* are those whose occurrence in an operational system can be foreseen. For example, hardware components in a system inevitably deteriorate and give rise to faults. In the past such faults have been modelled with relative success by the single, unidirectional multiple and bridging fault models based on stuck-at-fault effect (see Chap. 2). *Unanticipated faults* on the other hand cannot be foreseen but affect the operation of a system. For example, a VLSI chip can fail in so many modes that it is almost impossible to anticipate the consequences. Another example of faults in this category are design faults, which cannot be predicted except for the general assumption that a complex system is very likely to have such faults. Hence, tolerance of both anticipated and unanticipated faults must be considered in high-reliability applications.

4.3   STATIC REDUNDANCY

Static redundancy, also known as "masking redundancy", uses extra components such that the effect of a faulty component is masked instantaneously. Two major techniques employed to obtain fault masking are the triple modular redundancy and the use of error correcting codes.

4.3.1   Triple Modular Redundancy

The most general hardware masking technique is "triple modular redundancy" (TMR). The concept of TMR was originally suggested by von Neumann |4.4|. The concept is illustrated in Fig. 4.1, where the boxes labelled M are identical "modules" that feed a *voting element* V (called a "majority organ" by von Neumann). A module may be a microprocessor or it may be a less complex unit, e.g. an adder or a gate. The voting element accepts the outputs from the three sources and delivers the majority vote as its output.

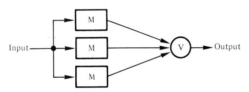

Fig. 4.1   Triple modular redundancy.

The concept of TMR could be expanded to include any number of redundant modules to produce an NMR (*N*-modular redundancy) system. An NMR system can tolerate up to n module failures, where $n = (N - 1)/2$. In general, in an NMR system N is considered to be an odd number, but it can also be even, e.g. the space shuttle has $N = 4$ in its main computer complex (see Sec. 4.13.1). The reliability equation for an NMR system is

$$R_{\text{NMR}} = \sum_{i=0}^{n} \binom{N}{i} \cdot (1 - R_M)^i \cdot R_M^{(N-i)}$$

For the TMR case $N = 3$ and $n = 1$.

The reliability of the TMR scheme can be determined as a function of the reliability R_M of one module, assuming the voting circuit does not fail. The redundant system will function properly as long as any two modules are operational. It is assumed that failures of the three modules are independent of each other. Hence, the reliability R_{TMR} of the TMR scheme is given by:

R_{TMR} = Probability of all three modules functioning

+ probability of any two modules functioning

$$= R_M^3 + 3R_M^2(1 - R_M)$$

$$= 3R_M^2 - 2R_M^3 \tag{4.1}$$

The reliability of the TMR system is usually better than that suggested by equation (4.1), since the system may continue to function correctly even if two modules fail. For example, if one module in Fig. 4.1 has a stuck-at-1 fault on its output while another module has a stuck-at-0 fault on its output, the system still produces the correct output. Such multiple module failures which do not lead to system failures are termed "compensating module failures" |4.5|. An interesting observation can be made on equation (4.1). If $R_M = 0.5$, $R_{TMR} = 0.5$, i.e. there has not been any improvement in the overall reliability of the system. This is an example of the general truth that reliability cannot be enhanced if redundancy is applied at a level where the non-redundant reliability is very low.

If it is assumed that each module has in a TMR system passed through an extensive burn-in period, then R_M is an exponential function of time with a constant failure rate λ, i.e. $R_M = e^{-\lambda t}$. Substituting the value of R_M in equation (4.1), we have

$$R_{TMR} = 3 e^{-2\lambda t} - 2 e^{-3\lambda t} \tag{4.2}$$

The MTBF* of the TMR system is

$$\int_0^\infty R_{TMR} \, dt = \frac{5}{6\lambda}$$

which is less than the MTBF of the individual modules.

Although the MTBF is a useful parameter which is frequently used in establishing the level of reliability in a system, it does not provide much insight into the improvement in reliability given by a fault-tolerant system |4.6|. The basic reason for this is that the MTBF computation evaluates the reliability function for $0 \leqslant t \leqslant \infty$. When redundancy is introduced to improve the reliability of a system, the only region of concern is $0 \leqslant t \leqslant T$, where T is some specified mission time for which the highest reliability is desired: what happens to the system after $t > T$ is not important.

Figure 4.2 shows the plot of reliability functions for $R_{TMR}(t)$ and $R_M(t)$. Although the MTBF $(5/6\lambda)$ of the TMR system is less than that $(1/\lambda)$ of the

---

* See Sec. 1.3.

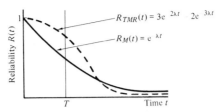

Fig. 4.2   Graph of functions $R_{TMR}(t)$ and $R_M(t)$.

simplex system, the reliability of the TMR system is much higher for the indicated mission time T.

A parameter that has been found more useful than MTBF for evaluating reliable systems is the *reliability improvement factor* (RIF). It is defined as the ratio of the probability of failure of the non-redundant system to that of the redundant system. If R_N and R_R are the reliabilities of the non-redundant and the redundant system respectively, for a fixed mission time T, then

$$\text{RIF} = \frac{1 - R_N}{1 - R_R}$$

In case a fixed mission time is not specified, the *mission time improvement factor* (MTIF) serves as a convenient comparison measure. It is defined by

$$\text{MTIF} = \frac{T_R}{T_N} \quad \text{at } R_f$$

where R_f is some predetermined reliability (e.g. 0.99 or 0.90), while T_R and T_N are times at which the system reliabilities $R_R(t)$ and $R_N(t)$, respectively, fall to the value R_f.

The reliability of the voting element ("voter") was not considered in the reliability expression for TMR. If the voter has the reliability $e^{\lambda_1 t}$, equation (4.2) becomes

$$R_{TMR} = e^{-\lambda_1 t}(3 e^{-2\lambda t} - 2 e^{-3\lambda t})$$

This means that the system will fail if the voter fails regardless of whether or not other modules fail. If $\lambda_1 \gg \lambda$, the reliability of the system is less than that of the original system for all values of t. The reliability of a voter in the basic TMR system can be improved by using three identical copies as shown in Fig. 4.3. This scheme is termed "triplicated TMR". Two out of the three system outputs are correct if and only if two out of the three replicated voter/module pairs function properly. Hence, the system reliability R_{sys} is given by

$$R_{sys} = (R_M R_1)^3 + 3(R_M R_1)^2(1 - R_M R_1) \tag{4.3}$$

where R_1 is the reliability of the voter.

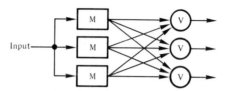

Fig. 4.3   Triplicated TMR system.

If $R_1 = 1$, equations (4.1) and (4.3) become equal but the basic TMR is preferable in this case because it uses fewer components. When $R_1 < 1$, the reliability of the triplicated TMR system $|= R_M^2 R_1^2 (3 - 2R_M R_1)|$ will be greater than the reliability of the basic TMR system $|= R_M^2 R_1 (3 - 2R_M)|$, if the inequality

$$2R_M R_1 \geqslant 3 - 2R_M$$

is satisfied |4.7|.

If a module fails in a TMR system, both the remaining modules must continue to operate correctly. Once a module has failed, therefore, the reliability of the TMR system is lower than that of an individual module. For example, if module 1 fails, the reliability of the system becomes

$$\{(\text{Reliability of module 2}) \times (\text{Reliability of module 3})\} = R_M^2$$

where the reliability of a module is R_M. It is possible, however, to improve reliability by switching out one of the remaining good modules together with the faulty module and thereby operating the system in a "simplex" (non-redundant) mode. Such a system is known as the "TMR/simplex" system |4.8|. The reliability expression for a TMR/simplex system may be derived as follows.

Let T denote the "mission time", i.e. the required duration of the reliable operation of the system. The probability that all the modules will survive the mission time is R_M^3 where $R_M = e^{-\lambda T}$. If a module fails at some time t $(0 \leqslant t \leqslant T)$ the module is removed together with one of the remaining good modules, reducing the system to a simplex system for the unelapsed time $(T - t)$. The probability of this event is

$$3 \int_0^T \left[\left\{ \frac{d}{dt} (1 - e^{-\lambda t}) \right\} e^{-2\lambda t} e^{-(T-t)} \right] dt = \tfrac{3}{2} |e^{-\lambda T} - e^{-3\lambda T}| = \tfrac{3}{2} |R_M - R_M^3|$$

Hence the probability that the system functions correctly for the mission time, $R_{\text{sim}}(T)$, is given by

$$R_{\text{sim}}(T) = R_M^3 + \tfrac{3}{2} |R_M - R_M^3| = 1.5 R_M - 0.5 R_M^3$$

One of the major implementation problems associated with an NMR scheme is the synchronization between the multiple modules. The most popular approach to the solution of the problem is to use a common clock. However, the clock must be fault tolerant otherwise there is a possibility that the system may fail due to a fault in the clock. The design of a fully synchronized TMR clock has been described by Davies et al. |4.9|. It uses three modules, each containing a crystal oscillator with feedback through a voter; inputs to the voter are the clock output themselves. Lewis |4.10| has described the design of a fault tolerant clock which uses the concept of stand-by spares (see Sec. 4.4). Two oscillators, one designated as the primary and the other as the secondary (spare), are used. Initially the primary oscillator is selected; the secondary is switched in if there is a fault in the primary.

Fault detection in a TMR system can be performed by using a set of disagreement detectors, one for each module. A disagreement detector is activated if the output of the module it is attached to is different from that of the voter. Both FTMP (fault tolerant multiprocessor) and C.vmp (computer voted multiprocessor), discussed in Secs 4.13.3 and 4.13.5, respectively, use disagreement detectors to diagnose module failures. The major advantages of the TMR scheme are:

1. The fault-masking action occurs immediately; both temporary and permanent faults are masked.
2. No separate fault detection is necessary before masking.
3. The conversion from a non-redundant system to a TMR system is straightforward.

Triple modular redundancy has been used in Saturn IB and Saturn V on-board computers to increase reliability |4.11|. In the fault tolerant space computer (FTSC), discussed in Sec. 4.13.6, three configuration control units (CCU) are used in TMR mode for reconfiguring the CPU modules. Both C.vmp and FTMP have TMR organizations. In a C.vmp three CPUs are connected to triplicated sets of memories and floppy-disk drives by three bi-directional buses attached to a voter. The processors and memories in a FTMP are configured in groups of three to form processor triads and memory triads respectively; a voter is used to mask the effect of a faulty module in a triad. It has been suggested that the TMR scheme could also be a practical technique for designing fault tolerant VLSI chips |4.12|.

4.3.2   Use of Error-correcting Codes

Error-correcting codes can also be used to provide automatic fault detection, location and masking. One form of such codes, Hamming single-error-correcting code (SEC), is extensively used to increase the reliability of the information stored in semiconductor memories (see Sec. 4.9). Error-correcting codes with different characteristics are also available |4.13, 4.14|.

Armstrong |4.15| has shown how reliable circuits can be constructed using error-correcting codes. The technique is in fact a generalization of a triple modular redundancy scheme, and is applicable to both combinational and sequential circuits. Design techniques for implementing single-fault tolerant sequential circuits using error-correcting codes have also been proposed by Russo [4.16] and Meyer [4.17]. A circuit is single-fault tolerant if it produces correct outputs even in the presence of a single fault. Single-fault tolerance in synchronous sequential circuits is achieved by state assignments with minimum Hamming distance of three; the minimum Hamming distance of three is required in order to detect and correct a single-bit error (see Sec. 4.9.1). The state assignment for a single-fault tolerant design of the machine of Fig. 4.4(a) is shown in Fig. 4.4(b). The state table is then modified so that each state and all its adjacent states are assigned the same next state entry. The modified state table is shown in Fig. 4.5.

The machine continues to operate properly even if a state variable assumes a false value; this is because of the single error-correcting properties of the state assignment. For example, when the input $x = 0$, the next state entry for 01111 (C), 11111, 00111, 01011, 01101 and 01110 is 11100, the binary assignment for state B. Thus the recovery from an erroneous state is possible provided the distance between the correct and the erroneous state is 1. The next state equations for the machine, Y_i ($i = 1, 5$) are derived from the modified state table and realized with D flip-flops by making $D_i = Y_i$. The sharing of logic among the flip-flops is not permitted in order to ensure that a single fault does not affect more than one state variable.

Osman and Weiss [4.18] have shown that a fault tolerant sequential machine can be implemented by using three copies of excitation equations and three copies of output expressions to obtain a TMR-like realization. Two copies of the excitation equations and the output expressions employ "shared logic-basis realization" of functions and are implemented using a set of modules. The third copy of each equation (excitation and output) can be realized by any technique. Such a sequential machine can tolerate any single module fault in the shared logic and any fault in the third copy.

Larsen and Reed [4.19] presented a technique for designing fault-tolerant sequential circuits using majority-logic decodable codes. They showed that for a specified ability to tolerate faults NMR redundancy is more reliable than coding redundancy. However, they indicated that for a fixed complexity,

Present state	Input x = 0	x = 1
A	C,0	B,0
B	A,1	D,0
C	B,1	A,1
D	D,1	C,0

Next state, output

(a)

	y_1	y_2	y_3	y_4	y_5
A	0	0	0	0	0
B	1	1	1	0	0
C	0	1	1	1	1
D	1	0	0	1	1

(b)

Fig. 4.4   (a) State table of a sequential machine; (b) state assignment.

Present state	Input $x = 0$	$x = 1$
0 0 0 0 0		
1 0 0 0 0		
0 1 0 0 0		
0 0 1 0 0	0 1 1 1 1	1 1 1 0 0
0 0 0 1 0		
0 0 0 0 1		
1 1 1 0 0		
0 1 1 0 0		
1 0 1 0 0		
1 1 0 0 0	0 0 0 0 0	1 0 0 1 1
1 1 1 1 0		
1 1 1 0 1		
0 1 1 1 1		
1 1 1 1 1		
0 0 1 1 1		
0 1 0 1 1	1 1 1 0 0	0 0 0 0 0
0 1 1 0 1		
0 1 1 1 0		
1 0 0 1 1		
1 1 0 1 1		
1 0 1 1 1		
1 0 0 0 1	1 0 0 1 1	0 1 1 1 1
1 0 0 1 0		
0 0 0 1 1		

Fig. 4.5   Fault-tolerant state table.

orthogonal (majority-logic decodable) codes provide a greater improvement in reliability.

4.4   DYNAMIC REDUNDANCY

A system with dynamic redundancy consists of several modules but with only one operating at a time. If a fault is detected in the operating module it is switched out and replaced by a spare. Thus dynamic redundancy requires consecutive actions of fault detection and fault recovery. Figure 4.6 illustrates the concept of dynamic redundancy.

A dynamic redundant system with S spares has a reliability

$$R = 1 - (1 - R_m)^{(S+1)}$$

where R_m is the reliability of each module, active or spare, in the system. This

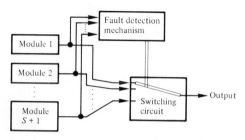

Fig. 4.6   Dynamic redundancy scheme with S spares (*courtesy of IEEE, © 1975*).

reliability function is obtained assuming that the fault detection and the switch-over mechanism are perfect. The reliability R is an increasing function of the number of spare modules (Fig. 4.7). However, the use of too many spares may have a detrimental effect on the system reliability. Losq |4.20| has shown that for every dynamic redundant system there exists a finite best number of spares for a given mission time. For extremely short mission times, one spare is best. The best number of spares is five or fewer, when the mission time is less than one-tenth of the simplex mean-life.

The detection of a fault in the individual modules of a dynamic system can be achieved by using one of the following techniques:

1.   Periodic tests.
2.   Self-checking circuits.
3.   Watchdog timers.

In periodic tests the normal operation of the functional module is temporarily suspended and a test routine is run to determine if faults are present in the module. A disadvantage of this technique is that it cannot detect temporary faults unless they occur while the module is tested.

Self-checking circuits provide a very cost effective method of fault detection

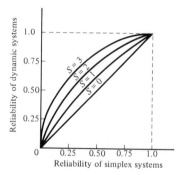

Fig. 4.7   Dynamic system reliability as a function of simplex system reliability (*courtesy of IEEE, © 1975*).

(see Chap. 5). They are designed so that for normal circuit inputs they provide correct output or indicate the presence of a fault in a module.

Watchdog timers are an effective and popular method of fault detection. Their principle of operation is relatively simple. Timers are set to certain values at pre-established points, called *checkpoints*, in the program executed by a module. A timer at a particular checkpoint counts down while the module performs its function, and is normally reset before the next checkpoint is reached. However, a software bug or a hardware fault will prevent the program from resetting the timer. The timer then issues an interrupt command which causes automatic switchover to a spare module. The Pluribus system |4.21| makes substantial use of watchdog timers. The console processor of VAX–11/780 also uses a watchdog timer. The fault recovery process in a dynamic redundant system starts after a fault has been detected in the operating module. It involves switching the faulty module out of service and selecting the system output to come from one of the alternative modules; this process is known as *reconfiguration*.

Before switching out a module from the system one should determine whether the fault in the module is temporary or permanent; otherwise a good module will be removed because of a temporary fault, which is not economical. A technique which is commonly used for this purpose is called *retry*. To retry a module the operation which resulted in the fault is repeated; this requires the knowledge of the module state immediately before the operation was attempted. If the fault is permanent the retry will be unsuccessful and the defective module must be replaced by a spare which performs the same logic function. In the classical dynamic redundant system, this replacement is invisible to the user and the system continues its operation uninterrupted; this is known as *self-repair*. The JPL–STAR computer |4.22| is the only known computer with full self-repair facilities.

In general dynamic redundant systems can be divided into two categories:

(a) Cold-standby system.
(b) Hot-standby system.

In a cold-standby system one module is powered up and operational, the rest are not powered, i.e. they are "cold" spares. Replacement of a faulty module by a spare is effected by turning off its power and powering a spare. In a hot-standby system all the modules are powered up and operating simultaneously. If the outputs of all modules are the same, the output of any arbitrarily selected module can be taken as the system output. When a fault is detected in a module the system is reconfigured so that the system output comes from one of the remaining modules.

The most common arrangement for a hot-standby system is to operate two modules in parallel with either module acting as a standby. This is known as a *duplex* system. A matching circuit continuously compares the outputs from both modules and interprets any mismatch as a fault in either of the modules or in the matching circuit itself. After the detection of a mismatch, diagnostic programs are run to locate the fault. If the fault is in a module, it is taken off-line and the normal operation is started as a simplex system. When found faulty, the matching circuit gets switched off-line and the reconfigured system returns to operation. The reliability R of a duplex system is:

$$R = [R_m^2 + 2CR_m(1 - R_m)]R_s R_c$$

where R_m is the module reliability, R_c the comparator reliability and R_s the reliability of the module selector circuit. C is the *coverage factor*, which is defined as the conditional probability of successful fault detection and reconfiguration given that a fault exists [4.23]. The reliability of a duplex system is increased if a faulty module is repaired and returned to operation (repairable duplex system). Such a system can be evaluated by Markov modelling. Examples of duplex configurations are the Bell ESS [4.24], the UDET 7116 telephone switching system [4.25] and the COMTRAC railway traffic controller [4.26].

4.5 HYBRID REDUNDANCY

Hybrid redundancy combines the static and the dynamic redundancy approaches. It consists of a TMR system (or in general an NMR system) with a set of spare modules. When one of the TMR modules fails, it is replaced by a spare and the basic TMR operation can continue. The "Test and Repair Processor" (TARP) in the JPL–STAR computer [4.22] is protected by a hybrid TMR redundancy scheme. The physical realization of a hybrid $(3, S)$ system is shown in Fig. 4.8. When a "core" of N active modules is used it is

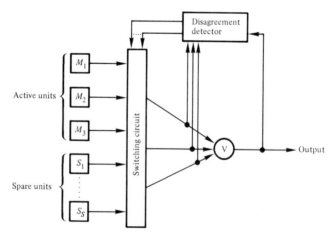

Fig. 4.8 Hybrid $(3, S)$ system.

called the hybrid (N, S) system. The "disagreement detector" detects if the output of any of the three active modules is different from the voter output. If a module output disagrees with the voter, the switching circuit replaces the failed module by a spare. The voter output will be correct as long as at least two modules have correct outputs. If a spare module were to fail in the dormant mode and was switched in on demand from the disagreement detector, this disagreement would still exist and the switching circuit would have to replace it by another module. If all the spares are used up, the system reduces to a hybrid $(3, 0)$ or just a standard TMR.

A hybrid (N, S) system cannot tolerate more than $n \mid = (N - 1)/2 \mid$ failed modules at a time in the core. For example, if there are two failed modules in the core of a hybrid $(3, S)$ system the voter will incorrectly switch out the fault-free module and switch a spare in. Since the majority of the modules are malfunctioning, the system will reject all the good spares until all of them are used up and the system will crash.

The reliability of a hybrid system with a TMR core and S spares is:

$$R(3, S) = 1 - \{\text{Probability of all } (S + 3) \text{ modules failing}$$

$$+ \text{ Probability of all but one modules failing}\}$$

$$= 1 - \{(1 - R_m)^{(S+3)} + (S + 3) \cdot R_m \cdot (1 - R_m)^{(S+2)}\}$$

$$= 1 - (1 - R_m)^{(S+2)}\{1 - R_m + S \cdot R_m + 3R_m\}$$

$$= 1 - (1 - R_m)^{(S+2)} \cdot \{1 + R_m(S + 2)\}$$

For systems with standby spares, even though the reliabilities of the spares are higher than those of core modules, it has been assumed in the above reliability expression that they are of equal value, R_m. The voter switch and the disagreement detector (VSD) are assumed to be perfect, for simplicity.

The reliability for a hybrid (N, S) system, where $N = 2n + 1$, can be derived in a similar manner and is equal to

$$R(N, S) = \sum_{i=0}^{i=n+S} \binom{N + S}{i} \cdot (1 - R_m)^i \cdot R_m^{(N+S-i)}$$

assuming no more than n modules fail simultaneously.

The VSD reliability is an important factor in determining the overall system reliability. A reliable switch design for a hybrid $(3, 2)$ system has been described by Siewiorek [4.27]; this is shown in Fig. 4.9. The five condition flip-flops (C–FF), referred to in Fig. 4.9, record whether a module has disagreed with the voter output. The disagreement detection is accomplished by the EXCLUSIVE-OR of the module and the voter outputs.

The same clock pulse that admits new data to the module flip-flops is used to record disagreement in the C–FFs. The clock pulse activating the C–FFs must be delayed to prevent a flip-flop being set by a transient signal. An iterative cell

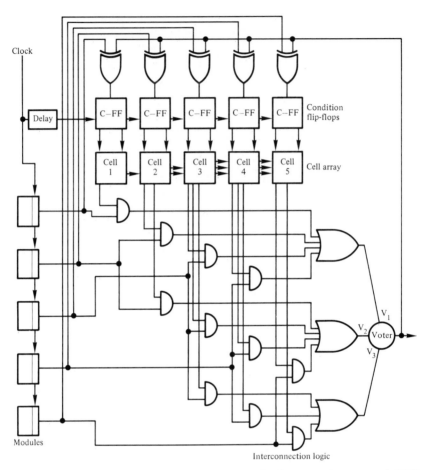

Fig. 4.9   An interactive cell switch for an hybrid (3, 2) system (*courtesy of IEEE,* © *1973*).

array determines the first three non-failed modules (as recorded by the C–FFs) and assigns them, via the interconnection logic, to be voted on. An iterative cell array is a cascade of identical combinational circuits, called "cells" (Fig. 4.10). The terminal behavior of a cell is described by means of a "cell table" which is analogous to the state table of sequential circuits (Table 4.1). Each cell receives as primary input the condition of the ith module (C_i), i.e. failed or functional, and the present state denotes the number of modules which have been found to be functional prior to the consideration of module i. The output function assigns the particular module to the appropriate voter position. For example, if the present state indicates one good module found so far and if C_i indicates a functional module, then a state of two is passed to the carry outputs. The output has a 1 on line V_2^i that instructs the interconnection logic to assign

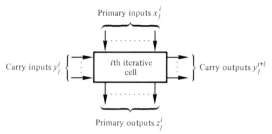

Primary inputs x_j^i

Carry inputs y_j^i { ith iterative cell } Carry outputs y_j^{i+1}

Primary outputs z_j^i

Fig. 4.10   An iterative cell (*courtesy of IEEE, © 1973*).

Present state: S (number of previous cells which are functional)	Next state: S⁺		Outputs: $V_1^i V_2^i V_3^i$*	
	$C_i = 0$ Failed	$C_i = 1$ Functional	$C_i = 0$ Failed	$C_i = 1$ Functional
A (zero)	A	B	0 0 0	1 0 0
B (one)	B	C	0 0 0	0 1 0
C (two)	C	D	0 0 0	0 0 1
D (three +)	D	D	0 0 0	0 0 0

* V_j^i: connect module i to voter input j.

Table 4.1   State and output table for an iterative cell (*courtesy of IEEE, © 1973*)

module i to the voter position 2. Voter position 1 is already occupied by the other functional module found so far.

For example, let us assume that module 2 has failed, i.e. $C_2 = 0$. Then the voter position 1 would be occupied by module 1, 2 by module 3, and 3 by module 4. If module 3 fails now then $C_3 = 0$ and voter positions 1, 2 and 3 would be occupied by modules 1, 4 and 5, respectively. Thus the iterative cell switch implements the rotary switching strategy which requires the least number of switch states. One of the problems associated with the iterative cell switch is that faults can propagate from one cell in the array to the next. Ogus [4.28] has described some techniques to improve the fault tolerance of the VSD using "fail-safe logic" (Chap. 5).

Mathur et al. [4.29] concluded that the reliability of a hybrid (N, 1) system can be improved by keeping $N = 3$ and adding more spares. Cochi [4.30] has shown that the reliability is not always improved by adding spares, because the complexity of the VSD logic increases as more modules are added. He proposed a method for finding an optimum value of spares for which the system reliability is the maximum. It depends upon the reliability of both the VSD and the individual modules. As in dynamic redundant systems a retry operation can also be used in hybrid systems to recover from temporary faults in modules.

4.6   SELF-PURGING REDUNDANCY

A basic self-purging system, shown in Fig. 4.11, consists of:

1. A set of N modules, each module being a copy of the system to be upgraded by the use of redundancy.
2. A set of N "elementary switches", one for each module.
3. A voter, which is a threshold gate with a threshold M and a weight of one for each input.

All the modules are initially fault-free. When an error occurs at the output of a module, its switch detects the disagreement between the module output and the voter output, and forces the module output to a logic 0. This is logically equivalent to disconnecting a failed module from the voter. The voter output is 1, if and only if the weighted sum of its inputs is equal to or greater than its threshold. So a 0 on one of the voter inputs does not influence the voter output as long as M modules or more are correct; hence the system operates correctly. For example, consider a self-purging system with five modules. If the threshold of the voter is 3, the output Z is

$$Z = m_1 \lfloor m_2(m_3 + m_4 + m_5) + m_3(m_4 + m_5) + m_4 m_5 \rfloor$$
$$+ m_2 \lfloor m_3(m_4 + m_5) + m_4 m_5 \rfloor + m_3 m_4 m_5$$

where $m_1 \ldots m_5$ are the outputs of the modules.

The main advantage of the self-purging system over the standard hybrid approach is the simplicity of the switching mechanisms. In a hybrid redundant system the switching circuit has to turn off a faulty module, locate an unused spare and then turn the spare on. The self-purging switching circuit only has to switch off a faulty module, by forcing its output to 0, if the module output is not the same as the voter output. Figure 4.12 shows the switching circuit for the self-purging systems.

A module is retried after its first disagreement with the voter, instead of removing it from the system. To retry a module, the control AND gate of the elementary switch (Fig. 4.12) is arranged so that the module output is recon-

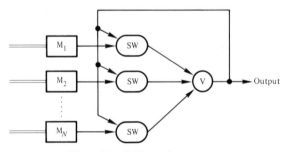

Fig. 4.11   Self-purging system.

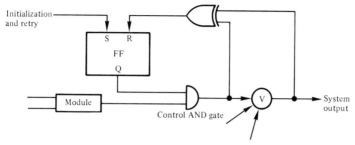

Fig. 4.12   Elementary switch for self-purging systems (*courtesy of IEEE,* © *1976*).

nected to the voter input; this can be done by using the S-input of the flip-flop. If the disagreement is due to a permanent fault in the module, the module is removed from the system. Self-purging systems are very advantageous when module repair facilities are available. Failed modules can be physically disconnected from the system, repaired and reconnected without system interruption. Self-purging systems with perfect voters, perfect switches and a voter threshold of M will perform correctly as long as they have M or more fault-free modules. Let R_m denote the reliability of each module at time t. The general reliability expression for self-purging systems having N modules and with perfect switches and voters is

$$R = \sum_{x=M}^{N} \binom{N}{x} \cdot |R_m|^x \cdot |1 - R_m|^{(N-x)}$$

where

$$\binom{N}{x} = \frac{N!}{x! \, (N-x)!}$$

This reliability expression indicates that the system survives provided M, $M + 1$, $M + 2, \ldots, N - 1$ or N modules survive. $|R_m|^x$ is the probability of exactly x modules surviving. $|1 - R_m|^{(N-x)}$ is the probability of exactly $(N - x)$ modules failing, and the number of ways it can happen is N-combinatorial-x.

The above reliability expression has two special cases:

Case 1 $M = 2$
The system survives provided at least 2 out of the N modules are operative. This is the condition for a hybrid redundant system having 3 modules in TMR and the remaining $(N - 3)$ modules as standby spares. The system reliability is given by

$$R = 1 - |1 - R_m|^{(N-1)} \cdot |1 + R_m \cdot (N - 1)|$$

However, self-purging systems have simpler switches than hybrid systems. The elementary switches for self-purging systems have one flip-flop and two gates whereas the iterative cell switch developed for hybrid systems (Fig. 4.9) has one flip-flop and seven gates for each module. Furthermore, the failure of one cell in the iterative array can affect the other cells. So, switches for hybrid systems are less reliable than switches for self-purging systems.

Case 2 $M = (N + 1)/2$

This is the N-modular redundant (NMR) system where N is any odd number of modules operating in a majority configuration, i.e. a $(N + 1)/2$-out-of-N configuration. The reliability expression is

$$R = \sum_{x=0}^{(N-1)/2} \binom{N}{x} |1 - R_m|^x \cdot |R_m|^{(N-x)}$$

The self-purging redundancy scheme is a very efficient way of increasing the reliability of digital systems. It is probably the best solution for applications, where the mission times range from one-tenth to a few tenths of the module mean life [4.31]. However, the major problem with the self-purging scheme is that the complexity of the threshold voter increases significantly if the number of modules is large. This is because large threshold gates are not currently available in integrated circuit (IC) packages. Therefore, they must be designed using logic gates or discrete components, which in turn increases the cost of the voter and decreases its reliability [4.32].

4.7   SIFT-OUT MODULAR REDUNDANCY (SMR)

In this scheme a system is organized into L identical "channels", where L is any integer [4.33]. The channels are synchronized with one another and perform simultaneous operations. A checking unit is placed at the output of the channels. It compares the output signals; if one of the channels disagrees with others, the corresponding channel is sifted out and its contribution to the system output stops. The system becomes an $(L - 1)$ redundancy scheme. If another channel fails, the process repeats itself. The system can tolerate up to $(L - 2)$ channel failures. When the number of channels reduces to two and one of them fails, the system loses the fault detection capability. SMR is sometimes called an "L-down-to-2" redundancy scheme. Figure 4.13 shows the main components of the checking unit, which include the comparator, detector and collector.

The comparator is a set of $\binom{L}{2}$ exclusive-OR gates that checks the L channels against each other. This is illustrated in Fig. 4.14 for $L = 3$. The detector shown in Fig. 4.15 is a sequential circuit with two levels of NOR gates; the first level contains $\binom{L}{2}$ NOR gates and the second level contains (L) NOR gates. A clocked flip-flop is added to each feedback loop to provide a reset/retry proce-

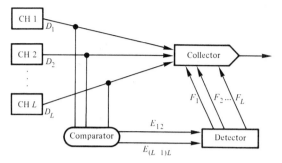

Fig. 4.13   Sift-out redundancy scheme.

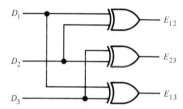

Fig. 4.14   Comparator for a three-channel SMR.

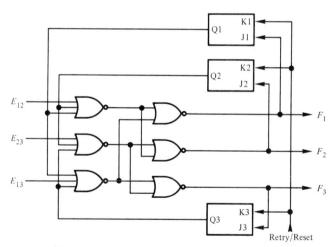

Fig. 4.15   Detector for a three-channel SMR.

dure. When a channel i is fault-free, the signal F_i is equal to 0. F_i is equal to 1 when channel i has failed. For example, if the channel 1 has failed, it will disagree with other channels, causing lines E_{12} and E_{13} to be at logic 1. Line F_i will then be set to 1 and the corresponding flip-flop will force it to stay that way. The retry procedure makes the structure tolerant to temporary faults. Initial checkout of the circuit is also simplified with the availability of the reset

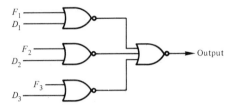

Fig. 4.16   Collector for three-channel SMR.

facility. The collector is a combinational circuit with $(L + 1)$ NOR gates; it is shown in Fig. 4.16. Each good channel feeds one input $(\bar{D}_i)$ to the last NOR gate. Each bad channel provides a logic 0 input to the last gate. The output of the gate is the correct output of the system provided that at least two channels are good.

A sift-out configuration with three channels has the same fault tolerance as a TMR system but it has the capability of automatic fault diagnosis. For example, if channel i fails, the output variable F_i in the detector circuit is set to 1. This is an important advantage over the TMR, because it eases maintenance operations and thereby improves system availability. A sift-out configuration with N channels can tolerate $(N - 2)$ channel failures whereas an NMR configuration can tolerate $(N - 1)/2$ module failures. The voter unit of the NMR is less complex than the sift-out checking unit for small N, but the situation reverses as N increases. Sift-out redundancy also compares favorably with hybrid and self-purging redundancy schemes.

4.8   5MR RECONFIGURATION SCHEME

This scheme begins with a basic 5MR (five-modular redundancy) system; it changes into a TMR when two modules fail simultaneously |4.34|. When only a single module fails, the system becomes a TMR with a spare. The spare module replaces the faulty module in the TMR. Whereas in 5MR systems a maximum number of two-module failures can be tolerated, the reconfiguration scheme can tolerate either three-module faults occurring sequentially or a single fault following a double fault.

Let us consider a five-module system with binary variables $x_1, x_2, \ldots, x_5$ as the outputs for the modules. If $x_1 - x_5$ feed into a majority gate, then the output of the majority gate is

$$Z = M(x_1, x_2, x_3, x_4, x_5)$$

$$= x_1x_2x_3 + x_1x_2x_4 + x_1x_2x_5 + x_1x_3x_4 + x_1x_3x_5 + x_1x_4x_3$$

$$+ x_2x_3x_4 + x_2x_3x_5 + x_2x_4x_5 + x_3x_4x_5 \tag{4.4}$$

Substituting $x_4 = 0$ and $x_5 = 1$ into the above expression, we obtain

$$Z = M(x_1, x_2, x_3, 0, 1)$$

$$= x_1 x_2 + x_1 x_3 + x_2 x_3$$

It can be seen from the above equation that a TMR can be obtained from a 5MR by replacing any variable by 0 and any other variable by 1. For example, if module 1 is faulty, by letting $x_1 = 0$ and $x_2 = 1$ a TMR scheme with inputs x_3, x_4 and x_5 is obtained from equation (4.4).

The block diagram for the automatic configuration scheme is shown in Fig. 4.17. Block A consists of five "equivalence detectors", each having two inputs x_i ($i = 1, 5$) and Z. The output $g_i = 1$ if x_i has a different value from the system output Z, i.e. when the ith module is faulty. Figure 4.18 shows the logic diagram of block A. Initially all RS flip-flops are reset. If module i is faulty, Z and x_i are different from each other and hence $S_i = 1$ sets flip-flop i when the clock pulse occurs. Therefore, $g_i = 1$. If all the modules are fault-free, $g_i = 0$ ($i = 1, 5$) and the network B causes a direct transmission from x_is to α_is, i.e. $\alpha_i = x_i$. Figure 4.19 shows the detailed diagram of block B. If the ith module is

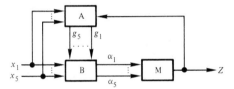

Fig. 4.17   Automatic reconfiguration scheme (*courtesy of IEEE, © 1980*).

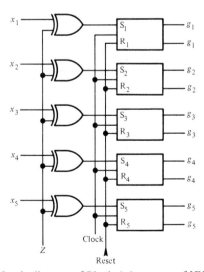

Fig. 4.18   Logic diagram of Block A (*courtesy of IEEE, © 1980*).

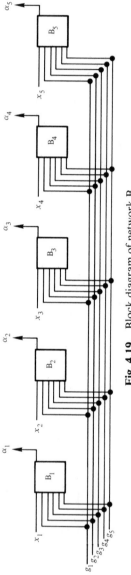

Fig. 4.19   Block diagram of network B.

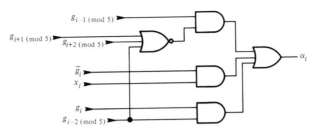

Fig. 4.20   Logic diagram of each B_j in Fig. 4.19 (*courtesy of IEEE,* © *1980*).

faulty α_i becomes stuck-at-0, and the module can no longer participate in the voting. The lead $\alpha_{i+1 (\text{mod } 5)}$ is forced to become temporarily stuck-at-1, thus a spare is obtained. The remaining α_is being unaffected by the flip-flop allow the x_i to transfer to α_i.

If there is a double fault among the modules, two cases have to be considered:

1.   Non-adjacent double fault. Two faulty modules are regarded as non-adjacent if they are separated by "distance" of 2, i.e. if the module i is faulty then the other faulty module is $(i - 2)$.
2.   Adjacent double fault. The ith and $(i - 1)$th modules are faulty.

The following equation for α_is, as a function of the x_is and g_is, assures the desired performance of the reconfiguration network.

$$\alpha_i = g_{i-1} \sum_{K \neq i-1, i} g_K + x_i \bar{g}_i + g_i g_{i-2} \tag{4.5}$$

The logic diagram for realizing α_i (each of the five blocks B_i in Fig. 4.19) is shown in Fig. 4.20. To verify that equation (4.5) is valid for both single and multiple faults, let us consider the following cases:

Case 1   Single fault
Let us assume that module m_2 is faulty. Hence $g_2 = 1$ and $g_1 = g_3 = g_4 = g_5 = 0$. Substituting these values in equation (4.5) gives

$$\alpha_2 = g_1 \overline{(g_3 + g_4 + g_5)} + x_2 \bar{g}_2 + g_2 \cdot g_5$$

$$= 0 + 0 + 0 = 0$$

Similarly, it can be shown that $\alpha_1 = x_1$, $\alpha_3 = 1$, $\alpha_4 = x_4$ and $\alpha_5 = x_5$. Thus the 5MR becomes a TMR with a module m_3 as the spare.

Case 2   Double fault
Let modules m_2 and m_5 be faulty. Substituting $g_2 = g_5 = 1$ and

$g_1 = g_3 = g_4 = 0$ in equation (4.5), we obtain

$$\alpha_2 = g_1\overline{(g_3 + g_4 + g_5)} + x_2\bar{g}_2 + g_2 g_5$$
$$= 0 + 0 + 1 = 1$$

and

$$\alpha_5 = g_4\overline{(g_1 + g_2 + g_3)} + x_5\bar{g}_5 + g_5 g_3$$
$$= 0 + 0 + 0 = 0$$

Similarly, $\alpha_1 = x_1$, $\alpha_3 = x_3$ and $\alpha_4 = x_4$. Therefore, the system changes correctly with the three fault-free modules 1, 3 and 4, becoming a TMR system.

Case 3   Treble fault

Suppose module 1 fails, after the system has become a TMR following the double fault considered in Case 2. Substituting $g_1 = g_2 = g_5 = 1$ and $g_3 = g_4 = 0$ in equation (4.5), we obtain $\alpha_1 = 0$, $\alpha_2 = 1$, $\alpha_3 = x_3$, $\alpha_4 = x_4$ and $\alpha_5 = 0$. Therefore, from equation (4.4) we get $Z = x_3 \cdot x_4$, i.e. the majority gate in the TMR is changed to an AND gate.

The reconfiguration scheme is superior to the 5MR and the hybrid redundancy systems since it can tolerate a double fault followed by a single fault, which can be tolerated neither by a 5MR nor by a hybrid redundancy system with a TMR core. The switching mechanism which performs the necessary reconfiguration function can be implemented with only five gates (or six NAND gates) and a flip-flop. The modular structure of the logic design for the scheme should make the testing of the system easier. However, the reliability of the NMR reconfiguration scheme decreases as N increases; this is because the complexity of block B grows with N.

4.9   FAULT TOLERANT DESIGN OF MEMORY SYSTEMS USING ERROR CORRECTING CODES

Error correcting codes are extensively used in mainframes and minicomputers to improve memory reliability. Among these are some models of DEC system 20, the UNIVAC 1100/60, several models of IBM 360/370, the VAX–11/780 and VAX–11/750, and the Data General ECLIPSE. The basic idea of coding is to add check bits to information bits in such a way that if errors occur in information bits they can be detected (error detection) or the original information bits can be reconstructed (error correction). The process of adding check bits to the information bits is called *encoding*. The error detecting and correcting capability of a code can be defined in terms of the *Hamming distance* of a code. This is the number of positions in which the bits of any two distinct codes differ. The relationship between the Hamming distance of a code and its error detecting and correcting capabilities can be defined as

$$d = C + D + 1 \qquad \text{with } D \geqslant C$$

where

$d =$ Hamming distance of a code.
$D =$ Number of bit errors which can be detected.
$C =$ Number of bit errors which can be corrected to obtain a correct code.

The relationship is shown below:

d	D	C
1	0	0
2	1	0
3	1	1
	2	0
4	3	0
	2	1
5	4	0
	3	1
	2	2

The simplest and the most common method for error control is the use of a single check bit called a *parity bit*. The parity bit is determined by the oddness or evenness of the number of 1s contained in the information bits. For "even" parity, if the number of 1s is even, the parity bit is 0; if the number of 1s is odd, the parity bit is 1 (see Fig. 4.21). Even though the odd and the even parity checks are mathematically equivalent, the odd parity is generally preferred since it ensures at least 1 in any code. The advantage of using a simple parity check is that the information bits in a code word can be processed without decoding. However, it can detect only single-bit errors and cannot correct errors. If a double-bit error occurs in information bits, the parity is unchanged leaving the error undetected.

Information bits	Odd parity	Even parity
0 1 0 0 1 1 0	0	1
1 0 0 1 0 1 1	1	0
0 0 0 0 0 0 0	1	0

Fig. 4.21   Parity check.

4.9.1   Error Detection and Correction using Hamming Codes

A technique which has gained wide acceptance as a means of increasing the reliability of semiconductor memory systems is the coding of data using Hamming codes [4.35]. Implementation of these codes for memory systems involves generating several check bits for the data word, by using multiple parity checks on certain subsets of the data bits. The check bits are then combined with the data bits to form the Hamming code.

A Hamming code can be described by its "parity check matrix" P of n columns each corresponding to one of the n bits of the encoded word; k rows each corresponding to one of the parity check bits. The elements of the matrix are 0s and 1s, the position of the 1s in the ith row indicate which bit positions are involved in the parity check. Similarly, the positions of 1s in the jth column indicate the parity pattern corresponding to the jth bit.

Single-error correcting Hamming codes have a distance of 3. The minimum number of parity check bits required for single-error correction is determined from the relationship (known as the Hamming relationship):

$$2^k \geqslant m + k + 1$$

where m = number of data bits; k = number of check bits.

The construction of a Hamming code with $m = 4$ will now be explained. It can be seen from the Hamming relationship that if $m = 4$, $k = 3$. Thus 3 check bits have to be appended to the 4 data bits in order for the Hamming code to be single-error correcting. The bit positions of the code are labelled, with numbers 1 through 7:

Bit positions	1	2	3	4	5	6	7
Bit names	C_1	C_2	b_1	C_3	b_2	b_3	b_4

The bit positions corresponding to powers of 2 are used as check bits C_1, C_2 and C_3 respectively. The other bit positions correspond to the data bits b_1 to b_4.

The parity check matrix for the Hamming code with $m = 4$, $k = 3$ is

$$
P = \begin{array}{c}
\begin{array}{ccccccc} C_1 & C_2 & b_1 & C_3 & b_2 & b_3 & b_4 \end{array} \\
\left(\begin{array}{ccccccc}
1 & 0 & 1 & 0 & 1 & 0 & 1 \\
0 & 1 & 1 & 0 & 0 & 1 & 1 \\
0 & 0 & 0 & 1 & 1 & 1 & 1
\end{array} \right)
\end{array}
$$

It can be seen from the parity check matrix that

$$C_1 = b_1 \oplus b_2 \oplus b_4$$

$$C_2 = b_1 \oplus b_3 \oplus b_4$$

$$C_3 = b_2 \oplus b_3 \oplus b_4$$

For example, if $b_1 b_2 b_3 b_4 = 1010$, then $C_1 = 1$, $C_2 = 0$ and $C_3 = 1$. Thus the corresponding Hamming code is

$$\begin{array}{c|ccccccc}
\text{Bit positions} & 1 & 2 & 3 & 4 & 5 & 6 & 7 \\
& 1 & 0 & 1 & 1 & 0 & 1 & 0
\end{array}$$

Suppose that the encoded word is stored in the memory and on a read operation bit 3 changes from 1 to 0. To determine whether the word is correct or not, the check bits for the word are regenerated and compared with the check bits generated before storing the word in the memory. The new check bits are

$$C'_1 = 0 \quad \text{(for even parity)} \qquad C'_2 = 1 \quad \text{(for even parity)}$$

and

$$C'_3 = 1 \quad \text{(for even parity)}$$

The "error address", i.e. the location of the bit in error, is generated from the following equations:

$$e_1 = C_1 \oplus C'_1, \quad e_2 = C_2 \oplus C'_2 \quad \text{and} \quad e_3 = C_3 \oplus C'_3$$

Hence

$$e_1 = 1 \oplus 0 = 1, \quad e_2 = 0 \oplus 1 = 1 \quad \text{and} \quad e_3 = 1 \oplus 1 = 0$$

Therefore the error address is 011 (i.e. 3_{10}) and bit position 3 must be inverted; the word is corrected to 0101101. If the error address is all 0s, then no bit error has occurred in the stored word.

Hamming codes with distance 3 can detect two-bit errors but can only be used to correct single-bit errors. For example, if bits 3 and 5 are erroneous in the previous example,

$$\begin{array}{c|ccccccc}
\text{Bit positions} & 1 & 2 & 3 & 4 & 5 & 6 & 7 \\
& 1 & 0 & \underline{0} & 1 & \underline{1} & 1 & 0
\end{array}$$

then $C'_1 = 1$, $C'_2 = 1$ and $C'_3 = 0$. Hence the error address is $e_3 = 1(1 \oplus 0)$, $e_2 = 1(0 \oplus 1)$ and $e_1 = 0(1 \oplus 1)$, which points to bit position 110 (6_{10}). But bit position 6 is not erroneous! Thus any attempt to execute double-bit error correction with distance-3 Hamming code will result in incorrect correction.

The single-error correcting Hamming code can be made into a distance-4 code with the addition of another parity check bit at bit position 8.

$$\begin{array}{c|cccccccc}
\text{Bit positions} & 1 & 2 & 3 & 4 & 5 & 6 & 7 & 8 \\
& C_1 & C_2 & b_1 & C_3 & b_2 & b_3 & b_4 & C_4
\end{array}$$

This bit checks for even parity over the entire eight-bit word. When the overall parity check of the encoded word is correct and the error address is zero, there is no bit error. If the overall parity is wrong and the error address has a non-zero value, there is a single, correctable bit error. If the overall parity of the

Data word length	Single-error correction/ double-error detection	
	Check bits	Increase, %
8	5	62.5
16	6	37.5
32	7	21.9
48	7	14.6
64	8	12.5

Table 4.2   Increase in word length with single-error correction and double-error detection

encoded word is correct, but the error address is not zero, there is a non-correctable double-bit error in the word.

Table 4.2 shows the increase in word length with Hamming single-error correcting/double-error detecting codes. It can be seen from the table that the percentage increase in word length decreases with the increase of data word length. In other words, the use of error correction becomes more efficient as the number of bits per word becomes large. For example, for an 8-bit data word, 5 check bits—62.5% of the data word—are required, but for a 64-bit word, 8 check bits—12.5% of the data word—are required. The check bits are treated in exactly the same way as data bits, in that a single-bit error in either category will be detected and corrected.

4.9.2   Error Checking and Correction in Semiconductor Memory Systems

Semiconductor memory systems are composed of a host of individual RAMs; each RAM is assigned to one bit of a word in memory. The probability of failure of such a system is directly related to the error rate of the individual RAMs and the number of RAMs in the system. RAM chips are subject to two types of error—"soft" and "hard".

Hard errors are permanent errors due to physical defects in chips. Three major defects can create hard errors in RAM chips: metallization and bonding failures, oxide defects and ion contamination [4.36]. Poor metallization can result in open-circuits between device inputs and outputs. Oxide defects may disable a whole chip or just cause a single-bit failure. Ion contamination can induce failure in the row or column decoders. Initial testing and burn-in significantly reduce hard errors in RAMs during system operation. *Soft errors*, sometimes referred to as "soft-fails" or "upsets", are apparently random non-recurring changes in memory logic states. For example, a logical 1 may change to a logical 0 or vice versa. Traditional sources of soft error have been power supply noise, board noise and marginal devices. It has recently been observed that α-particles produced by the radioactive decay of minute quantities of uranium and thorium in the packaging materials can cause bits to flip in dynamic RAMs [4.37]. These bit-flips are soft failures in that they have no permanent effect on a device; the cell which suffers a failure is completely recovered when a new bit is written into it and, thereafter, has no greater probability of failure than any other cell in the RAM.

Soft failures in semiconductor memories due to α-particles were not significant until the introduction of 16K and 64K dynamic RAMs (Table 4.3) [4.38]. As the dynamic RAM memory cell shrinks to fit more bits per chip, the capacitance of the cell decreases, and that makes the cell more vulnerable to soft errors due to α-particles. Memory manufacturers have taken various precautions to minimize the radiation that hits the chips, but they still get random hits; hence precautions must be taken to make sure these soft errors do not cause system failure.

Density (bits/chips)	Typical error rate (% per 1000 hours)	
	Soft	Hard
1K	0.001	0.0001
4K	0.02	0.002
16K	0.10	0.011
64K (predicted)	0.13	0.016

Table 4.3   Memory density v. error rate (*courtesy of IEEE, © 1979*)

The technique that is commonly used nowadays to accommodate soft errors is the use of error checking and correction (ECC). Error correction reduces the effect of RAM failures dramatically. Figure 4.22 shows the block diagram of a 16-bit word memory system with error correction. The code used is a subset of Hamming's single-error correcting and double-error detecting codes called "Maintenance (M)" code. An M-code has the property that the check bits for a

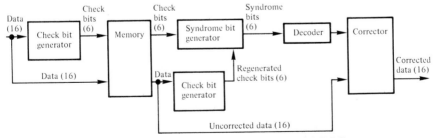

Fig. 4.22   A 16-bit word memory system with ECC.

1	2	3	4	5	6	7	8	9	10	11	12	13	14	15	16	C_1	C_2	C_3	C_4	C_5	C_6
1	1	1	1	1	1	1	1	1	0	0	0	0	0	0	0	1	0	0	0	0	0
0	0	0	0	0	1	1	1	1	1	1	1	1	1	0	0	0	1	0	0	0	0
1	0	1	0	1	1	0	0	1	0	1	0	0	0	1	1	0	0	1	0	0	0
1	0	0	1	0	0	1	0	1	0	0	1	1	1	0	1	0	0	0	1	0	0
0	1	0	1	1	0	0	1	0	1	0	1	0	1	1	0	0	0	0	0	1	0
0	1	1	0	0	0	0	0	0	1	1	0	1	1	1	1	0	0	0	0	0	1

Fig. 4.23   Parity check matrix for M(22, 16) code (*courtesy of IEEE*, © *1976*).

word W are the same for W and its bit-wise complement $\overline{W}$ [4.39]. This not only facilitates error correction but also allows identification of the locations of bits that have been corrected. M-codes can be constructed by choosing the parity check matrix so that all columns have an odd number of 1s (check bits have exactly 1), and so that the number of 1s in each row is odd. The maximum length of data handled by an M-code is even. M-codes exist to handle all data of even lengths beginning with 4. Figure 4.23 shows the parity check matrix which can be used to generate six M-code check bits for any 16-bit word of memory data.

The memory system of Fig. 4.22 receives each 16-bit word of incoming memory data and generates the check bits, which are stored with the 16 data bits to form a 22-bit memory word. When a memory word is read, the check bits are again generated from the data bits. Then these check bits are exclusive-ORed with the previously stored check bits to produce outputs called "syndrome" bits. These syndrome bits reveal whether no error occurred, a single-bit error occurred (identifying that bit) or a multiple-bit error occurred. If a single-bit error occurred, a signal is generated that corrects the bit in error before it is latched in the output register.

4.9.3   Improvement in Reliability with ECC

The degree of reliability improvement using ECC depends on the failure modes of the RAMs. The RAM devices are subject to various types of faults: these can affect a single bit, a row, a column or the whole chip [4.40]. In fact, if all RAM failures were single-bit failures, they could effectively be eliminated by using ECC. Failure mode distributions also change with time for a given device as the fabrication process matures. Nevertheless, there is good evidence that the dominant failure mode is either single-bit or partial-memory-array failure, not the entire chip as is frequently assumed. The distribution of failure modes experienced for 16K RAMs at Intersil Incorporated in the USA is shown in Table 4.4 [4.41]. The majority of the failures involved isolated single bits, 9.2% involved failure of entire rows or entire columns and 1.2% of the failures resulted from failure of the entire RAM.

ECC memory reliability is also strongly dependent on the reliability of control/support circuits. The reliability of a memory system which incor-

Failure type	Percent	(Resulting bits failed)/(100 RAMs)
Single-bit	89.6	90
128-bit	9.2	1177
Total RAM	1.2	19660

Table 4.4 16K RAM failure distribution (*courtesy of* Computer Design)

porates error correction is evaluated below for single-bit failure, whole-chip failure and row (column) failure modes [4.42]:

1. *Single-bit failure mode.* Single-bit failures are assumed to be independent events with each cell having a failure rate λ_b and reliability R_b:

$$R_b(t) = e^{-\lambda_b t}$$

Each m-bit word can tolerate a single-bit failure. Thus the reliability R_{sb} of a given word is

$$R_{sb}(t) = R_b^m + m(1 - R_b) \cdot R_b^{(m-1)}$$

If λ_E is the total failure rate of control/support circuits, then the reliability of the complete W word memory, $R(t)$, is

$$R(t) = e^{-\lambda_E t} \cdot \{R_{sb}(t)\}^W$$
$$= e^{-\lambda_E t} \cdot [e^{-m\lambda_b t} + m \cdot e^{-(m-1)\lambda_b t} - m\, e^{-m\lambda_b t}]^W$$
$$= e^{-\lambda_E t} \cdot [m\, e^{-(m-1)\lambda_b t} - (m - 1)\, e^{-m\lambda_b t}]^W \qquad (4.6)$$

2. *Whole chip failure mode.* A single-error correcting system cannot tolerate multiple-bit failures in a word. If a whole chip failure mode is dominant, the memory system must be designed in such a way so that no word has more than one bit on the same chip. Thus, for a memory with m bit words implemented with d bit chips, the parameter W (number of words in memory) in the single-bit-failure-model is transformed to $\gamma = W/d$. In effect the memory is organized into rows of m chips each, every row containing d words; γ is then the number of such rows.

Substituting $\lambda_b = \lambda_C = $ memory chip failure rate, and $W = \gamma$ in equation (4.6), the reliability $R(t)$ of the memory system becomes

$$R(t) = e^{-\lambda_E t} \cdot [m\, e^{-(m-1)\lambda_C t} - (m - 1)\, e^{-m\lambda_C t}]^\gamma$$

3. *Row (column) failure mode.* In this failure mode, a word can have more than one bit on the same chip as long as it does not have more than one bit on the same row (column) of the chip. For a memory of m bits words implemented with d bit memory chips having q bits per row (column), W of equation (4.6) is replaced by $p = Wq/d$, which is the number of one-word-wide sets of rows (columns) in the memory architecture.

Substituting $\lambda_b = \lambda_\gamma =$ row (column) failure rate, and $W = p$ in equation (4.6), the reliability of the system is given by

$$R(t) = e^{-\lambda_E t} [m\, e^{-(m-1)\lambda_\gamma t} - (m-1)\, e^{-m\lambda_\gamma t}]^p$$

Maximum gain from an error-correcting system can be obtained only if the system is checked periodically for faults that are being corrected. Otherwise the probability of multiple-bit failures in a word increases [4.43]. For example, if in a 22-bit-word (16 data bits and 6 check bits) memory system, a failure affects all of the memory words, then, after the first failure, the probability of system failure is higher than that of the system without error correction; there are 21 bits which can fail instead of 16. Therefore, to gain maximum benefit from a single-error correcting system, periodic checking should be made to repair hard faults before they become implicated in a double non-correctable error. The effectiveness of periodic maintenance is dependent on memory size, service intervals, failure distribution, etc.

4.9.4   Commercially Available Error Detection and Correction Chips

Several semiconductor manufacturers have recently introduced error detection and correction chips. Among these are the Advanced Micro Devices Am 2960 and Am Z8160, the Motorola MC68540, the Fujitsu MB1412A, the Intel 8206 and National Semiconductor DP8400. Most of these chips can detect both single- and double-bit errors and correct single-bit errors. Although all of them are oriented to 16-bit systems, they are also expandable to larger-word memory systems.

The architecture of Intel 8206 is different from the rest in that it uses separate input and output data buses, a feature that reduces the amount of control logic to be added to a system for single-bit error correction. The National Semiconductor DP8400 permits an easy implementation of a two-bit error-correction system through the use of a "rotational syndrome word generator matrix" [4.44]. This matrix is formed by adding a second DP8400 to the memory system with data bits shifted by one bit position. Both chips together produce a unique 12-bit syndrome word for any two bits in error. This syndrome word can be decoded to identify and correct the two bits in error.

4.9.5   Multiple Error Correction using Orthogonal Latin Squares Configuration

A memory system with built-in single-error correction/double-error detection (SEC/DED) capability can correct any single-bit error in a given word, but fails if any word contains two or more bit errors. Goldberg et al. [4.45] suggested a reconfiguration strategy for correcting multi-bit errors, by replacing faulty memory chips with spares. The number of additional chips required to implement such a strategy is equal to the number of bit errors the memory system should be able to tolerate. As an alternative to total chip replacement, Hsiao and Bossen [4.46] proposed a scheme which uses the concept of address skewing to dispense multi-bit errors in a word into several locations, so that the word in each of these locations contains at most a single-bit error. Thus the error correction capability of the SEC/DED can be utilized despite the presence of multi-bit errors in a word. The skewing is derived from the theory of "orthogonal Latin squares".

Let x be a set of n elements $\{x_1, x_2, \ldots, x_n\}$. A Latin square of order n is then an $n \times n$ array of elements of x such that each row and each column of the array contains each element of x exactly once. A pair of Latin squares of order n is said to be orthogonal if, when one square is superimposed on the other, each of the n^2 possible ordered pairs occurs exactly once in the array [4.46]. For example, with $n = 4$, there exist three possible orthogonal Latin squares L_1, L_2, L_3:

$$L_1 = \begin{vmatrix} 0 & 1 & 2 & 3 \\ 1 & 0 & 3 & 2 \\ 2 & 3 & 0 & 1 \\ 3 & 2 & 1 & 0 \end{vmatrix} \qquad L_2 = \begin{vmatrix} 0 & 2 & 3 & 1 \\ 1 & 3 & 2 & 0 \\ 2 & 0 & 1 & 3 \\ 3 & 1 & 0 & 2 \end{vmatrix} \qquad L_3 = \begin{vmatrix} 0 & 3 & 1 & 2 \\ 1 & 2 & 0 & 3 \\ 2 & 1 & 3 & 0 \\ 3 & 0 & 2 & 1 \end{vmatrix}$$

The result of the superimposition of the first two Latin squares is shown below:

$$\begin{vmatrix} 0,0 & 1,2 & 2,3 & 3,1 \\ 1,1 & 0,3 & 3,2 & 2,0 \\ 2,2 & 3,0 & 0,1 & 1,3 \\ 3,3 & 2,1 & 1,0 & 0,2 \end{vmatrix}$$

Let us now consider how the orthogonal Latin square structure can be built into a 4-word $\times$ 4-bit memory system consisting of 4 memory cards, each card having a 4-word $\times$ 1-bit memory. Figure 4.24 illustrates the concept. The L_0 square represents the original address distribution. This is exactly the same as the conventional memory without any reconfiguration capability. If a double error is detected by the SEC/DED logic, the memory system is reconfigured so that it uses the L_1 configuration; this separates a double-bit error in an addressed location into two single-bit errors at two different addresses. If an error occurs at a location in the L_1 configuration which already has a single error in it, the memory system changes itself into an orthogonal Latin square L_2. Although the probability that this new double error will create another double error at a different location is very low, it should be ruled out by conducting a diagnostic test. If a new double error is detected in the L_2 configuration, the address pattern of the memory system is changed to L_3.

For a memory of 2^r addresses there exist $(2^r - 1)$ copies of orthogonal Latin squares. The $(2^r - 1)$ copies of orthogonal Latin square can be achieved by an r-stage linear feedback shift register characterized by a primitive polynomial of

Address	Bit locations					
0	0	0	0	0	(a)	L_0 configuration
1	1	①	①	1		Two single-bit errors (circles)
2	2	2	2	2		cause a double error.
3	3	3	3	3		
0	0	①	☐2	3	(b)	L_1 configuration
1	1	0	3	2		The two single errors in L_0
2	2	3	0	1		configuration are tolerable; a third uncorrectable error occurs
3	3	2	①	0		(box).
0	0	2	3	1	(c)	L_2 configuration
1	1	3	②	0		The errors in L_1 configuration are tolerable; a fourth
2	2	0	①	☐3		uncorrectable error occurs (box).
3	3	①	0	2		
0	0	3	①	2	(d)	L_3 configuration
1	1	2	0	③		No double errors exist, but any other error is uncorrectable.
2	2	①	3	0		
3	3	0	②	1		

Fig. 4.24   Three possible Latin squares of order 4.

degree r. In general, if a memory has 2^r words each having n-bits ($2^r \geqslant n$), any k-bit error in a single word, where $1 \leqslant k \leqslant n$, can be dispersed into k single-bit errors occurring in k different words using orthogonal Latin squares of order 2^r. As an example, Fig. 4.25(a) shows a memory block in which all the bits of the word addressed by #2 are erroneous. In the skewed version (Fig. 4.25(b)), using an orthogonal Latin square the erroneous bits are dispersed so that each addressed word has a single-bit error.

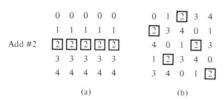

Fig. 4.25   Skewed memory-address configuration: (a) original address form; (b) Latin square address form.

4.9.6 Soft Error Correction using Horizontal and Vertical Parity Method

An alternative to Hamming codes is the horizontal and vertical parity method [4.47], and this can be economically used to detect and correct soft errors in memory systems. It uses a combination of firmware/software and hardware logic for error correction and is less expensive than Hamming codes for smaller

Bit number

	7	6	5	4	3	2	1	0	
0	1	1	1	1	1	0	1	1	0
1	0	0	1	0	1	1	0	1	1
2	1	0	0	1	1	0	0	0	0
3	0	0	0	0	0	0	0	0	1
4	1	1	1	1	1	1	1	1	1
5	0	0	0	①	0	1	1	1	1
6	1	1	1	0	0	1	0	1	0
7	0	0	1	0	0	0	1	1	0
	0	1	1	0	0	0	0	0	

Word number (rows 0–7)

Fig. 4.26 An eight-word memory block.

memory systems. The memory is partitioned into a number of blocks. A horizontal parity bit is added to each word of a block in order to detect an erroneous bit in the word. Once the failed word is identified, the CPU initiates a firmware routine that uses the vertical parity word of the block to locate the erroneous bit. The odd vertical parity word for a block is obtained by EX-ORing the words in the block; every memory write operation updates one vertical parity word. When the horizontal parity bit detects an error in a word on a read operation, the firmware recalculates the vertical parity word of that block by EX-ORing all words except the failed word. This newly calculated vertical parity word is EX-ORed with the original vertical parity word of the block; the result produces the correct data to be stored in the failed location.

Figure 4.26 shows a memory block of 8 words with 8 bits/word, although a block can have any number of words. If, for example, bit 4 of word 5 is in error, i.e. changed from 1 to 0, the firmware is started. It saves the current vertical parity word and calculates the EX-OR of all words except word 5. The result 01110111 is EX-ORed with 01100000 to produce 00010111 which is the original content of location 5. The correct word is then rewritten into location 5 and the original vertical parity word is restored. The method can correct all errors detectable by horizontal parity, including multiple errors in a single word. This is an advantage over Hamming codes which correct only single-bit errors in a memory word. However, unlike Hamming codes the method can correct only soft errors.

4.10   TIME REDUNDANCY

Time redundancy is commonly used in the detection and correction of errors caused by temporary faults. It involves the repetition or *rollback* of instructions [4.48], segments of programs [4.22] or entire programs [4.49], immediately after a fault is detected. The rollback operation requires that a program restarts processing from the last checkpoint, where all the information relevant to the successful execution of the program beyond the checkpoint is stored. If a fault is temporary, rolling back the program to a checkpoint should allow successful recovery. However, if the fault is permanent, the fault detection mechanism will be activated again and an alternative recovery method should be attempted. The JPL–STAR [4.22] and the Tandem computer (see Sec. 4.13.10) make extensive use of checkpoints.

The selection of the correct number of checkpoints is important. If too many checkpoints are used, the computation time increases since the normal flow of the program is stopped at each checkpoint in order to save state information. On the other hand if the checkpoints are too far apart, the recovery time will increase since the program will have to be re-executed from the last checkpoint. The choice of strategic checkpoints is itself a complex problem. Chandy [4.50] has studied several rollback and recovery models and has determined an optimum checkpoint interval which uses the hardware failure rate. O'Brien [4.51] has also studied the strategies for inserting checkpoints.

If a fault occurs during the creation of a checkpoint, it may result in incorrect resumption of a program. In the COPRA system (see Sec. 4.13.2) protection of the rollback mechanism is provided by saving the checkpoint information in two separate areas. When a fault occurs, the program restarts from the area indicated to be valid by a flag. Finally, care must also be taken not to repeat certain events, called "singular events", which should only be carried out once. The re-execution of such events because of rollback may have serious consequences on a computer-controlled system.

Time redundancy can also be effectively employed to detect faults in digital systems. The "alternating logic design" technique proposed by Reynolds et al. [4.52] achieves its fault detection capability by utilizing a redundancy in time instead of the conventional space redundancy. It is based on the successive execution of a required function and its self-dual. A function for which the normal output is the complement of the output, when complemented inputs are applied, is known as a self-dual function, e.g. a function $f(x)$, where $x = (x_1, x_2, \ldots, x_n)$, is a self-dual if for all x, $f(\bar{x}_1, \bar{x}_2, \ldots, \bar{x}_n) = \bar{f}(x_1, x_2, \ldots, x_n)$. Thus the principal characteristic of alternating logic is that it provides a true output in one time period and the complementary output in the next time period. The main disadvantage of the technique is that it requires twice as much time to obtain the verified output. Hence it should not be considered for designs for which time is a major factor. However, the increase in hardware it involves is generally modest in comparison to the space redundancy approach, e.g. the duplex system, where two identical functions have to be used for fault detection.

4.11   SOFTWARE REDUNDANCY

It is now widely recognized that even the most thoroughly debugged software still contains faults. In order to improve the reliability of software, provisions may be incorporated to tolerate such faults. Redundancy, used to achieve fault tolerance in hardware, has not found wide application in software. The main problem is that it is not possible to quantify the expected improvement in reliability that can be achieved by using additional software.

Chen and Avizienis [4.53] have suggested the idea of "N-version programming" for providing fault tolerance in software. In concept this approach is similar to the NMR scheme used to provide tolerance against hardware faults. The standard NMR scheme, however, does not provide protection against design faults, since each of the N copies is of identical design. In the N-version programming approach a number of independently written programs for a given function are run simultaneously; results are obtained by voting upon the outputs from the individual programs. In general the requirement that the individual programs should provide identical outputs is extremely stringent. Therefore, in practice "sufficiently similar" output from each program is regarded as equivalent; however, this increases the complexity of the voters [4.54]. In addition to its ability to tolerate design faults, N-version programming is also capable of masking certain categories of temporary hardware faults [4.55].

Basically, an N-version program incorporates redundancy in design. However, in practice it has been found that as many as 50% of the faults in software for control systems can be attributed to faults in the specification [4.80]. Hence N-versions of a design to the same specification are all likely to be faulty. Redundancy in the specification may be a solution to this problem [4.56]. Randell [4.57] proposed a technique, known as "the recovery block", for masking software design faults. The recovery block is a program composed of checkpoints, acceptance tests and alternative procedures for a given task. A typical structure of a recovery block is shown below:

$$
\begin{array}{ll}
\text{ensure} & \text{T} \\
\text{by} & \text{A} \\
\text{else by} & \text{B} \\
\text{else by} & \text{C} \\
\text{else} & \text{error}
\end{array}
$$

where T is an acceptance test which is evaluated after the execution of the "primary" procedure A, to check that no errors are present; a primary procedure is preceded by the keyword "by". If the acceptance test is passed, control passes to the next statement following the recovery block. If A fails the acceptance test, the "alternate" procedure B is entered; an "alternate" procedure is tried only after restoring the system state to what it had been before the primary procedure was executed. The acceptance test is repeated to check the successful execution of procedure B. If it fails, procedure C is executed. The "alternate" procedures are identified by the keywords "else by". When all "alternate" procedures are exhausted, the recovery block itself is considered to have failed; the final keywords "else error" emphasizes the fact. The organization of the FTMR^{2}M (fault-tolerant multiprocessor with a rollback recovery mechanism) system, which was designed to be tolerant of hardware faults with minimum time overhead, is based on the use of backward recovery and recovery blocks [4.58, 4.59].

The N-version programming and the recovery block techniques have been discussed in detail by Anderson and Lee in their text on fault tolerant systems [4.3].

4.12   FAIL-SOFT OPERATION

The redundancy techniques discussed so far enhance the fault tolerance characteristics of digital systems by using substantial amounts of additional resources. An alternative approach involves disconnecting a faulty module from the system and reconfiguring the rest of the system so that continued (through degraded) operation is possible. This ability of a faulty system to continue to operate at an acceptable but reduced level of performance is known as "graceful degradation" or "fail-soft operation".

Fail-soft systems have been finding increasing applications in time-sharing and real-time applications where a system must have the highest possible availability. In order to achieve the capability of fail-soft operation a system must have a distributed architecture, a comprehensive fault detection capability, the ability to achieve both logic and power isolation between functional modules, and the ability to reconfigure itself to operate as efficiently as possible without a faulty module [4.60].

An early example of a fail-soft computer system is PRIME [4.61], which was designed at the University of California, Berkeley, but was never actually implemented. The Pluribus system, used as a node in a packet switching network (the ARPANET), is a multiprocessor network which can operate in degraded mode (see Sec. 4.13.9). It contains an additional processor to increase throughput. If any processor is found to be faulty, the system loses this extra capability but still continues to perform as required. The Tandem system can also tolerate a processor failure and continue operation with lowered capacity until repairs are done (see Sec. 4.13.10).

4.13   PRACTICAL FAULT TOLERANT SYSTEMS

It is universally accepted now that computers cannot achieve the reliability needed in aerospace missions, aircraft traffic control, communication systems or crucial business transactions without employing redundancy. As discussed in the previous sections, several techniques have been developed to achieve fault tolerance using redundant hardware or software. A number of centralized and distributed computing systems which employ a combination of these techniques have been designed in recent years. Although no formal design methodology for implementing fault tolerant systems has evolved yet, these systems have certainly contributed to the knowledge required to achieve such an objective. The fault tolerance aspects of some of these systems are examined in this section.

4.13.1   Space Shuttle Computer Complex

The space shuttle is totally dependent on its computer complex for safe operation during a mission. Hence fault tolerance has been considered as vital in the design of the space shuttle computer. It uses five identical computers which can be assigned to redundant operation under program control [4.62]. During critical mission phases, such as boost, re-entry and loading, four of its five computers operate in an NMR configuration, receiving the same inputs and executing identical tasks. The fifth computer is used to perform non-critical tasks in the simplex mode. The reason for having four redundant computers is to keep the shuttle operational after any single computer failure. It should still be safe after the second failure, although the mission might have to be aborted. Each computer in the redundant set can compare the outputs of the other three with its own via special software. In addition, each computer also contains dedicated redundancy management circuitry. This circuitry incorporates a four-bit register, known as "failure vote register"; each bit position of the register corresponds to a computer in the system. The output bits of a failure vote register are connected to the voters of the computers corresponding to the dedicated register positions. If a computer fails, i.e. its output is different from the rest, then the bit position associated with the computer is set in all other vote registers. The failure is also reported to the crew. The shuttle can tolerate up to two computer failures. After the second failure it operates as a duplex system and uses comparison and self-test techniques to survive a third fault.

4.13.2   COPRA

COPRA is a reconfigurable multiprocessor system designed mainly for aerospace applications [4.63]. It consists of three kinds of replicated modules: processors, memory blocks and input/output (I/O) units. They are all interconnected through a matrix network. All modules remain powered, with the processors sharing the computing load. Processor allocation is carried out by a multi-tasking operating system. A processor can be connected at every memory request with one or several memory blocks. It is therefore possible to write simultaneously in two or more blocks and to replace a failing block by a spare one easily.

Failure detection in the COPRA system is done through hardware. As soon as a fault is detected, the system stops temporarily and an automatic roll-back occurs in the software organization, i.e. a specified sequence of the current program is repeated. This is done with a delay of a few milliseconds so that a possible temporary fault may vanish. Computation is then resumed and the number of unsuccessful attempts in going through that sequence of the program is counted. Two or three unsuccessful attempts are interpreted as a permanent fault and a reconfiguration occurs. The setting of the roll-back points is affected automatically by the assembler which splits the program into repeatable sequences [4.64]. Detection, retry and reconfiguration are performed automatically at various levels: hardware for detection, microprogramming for roll-back and software for reconfiguration.

The detection of a processor failure is determined by duplication and comparison. Each processor consists of two identical subprocessors; a subprocessor is built with four AMD 2901 ALU/reg. slices. The subprocessors are operated synchronously and their outputs are compared on a bit-by-bit basis at each computation. If a fault is detected and the retry is unsuccessful, the processor is "disabled" and an interrupt signal is sent to other processors. Reconfiguration and recovery then occur at the operating system level and the work load is divided among the remaining processors.

Errors in the memory blocks are detected by four bits of parity; such an economical method can be used because the blocks are arranged in four-bit slices. Any single failure occurring in one of the four-bit slices can be detected by a processor connected to the memory block at the moment (parity check is hard-wired). When such an error is detected, the processor initiates a retry. After attempting the number of retries allowed for in the roll-back mechanism, the processor reads from the second memory block which is a duplication of the first. If the reading is successful, the processor writes the correct information into the first memory block and checks, through a new reading, that the content has been properly restored.

An interconnection failure in the COPRA system cannot result in the loss of more than one processor and one memory block. The clock operates in TMR mode and has a failure probability of less than 10^{-12} per hour. Two separate power supplies are used and a network is provided to protect each supply against the failure of the other. Failure probability of the duplicated power supply is of the order of 10^{-9} per hour.

4.13.3 FTMP (Fault Tolerant Multiprocessor)

The FTMP computer is one of the two computers (the other is SIFT) which has been designed under NASA sponsorship to meet the safety-critical requirements for commercial transport aircraft [4.65]; as a practical guide for design this requirement means a probability of failure of less than 10^{-9} for a ten-hour flight. It consists of three types of hardware modules: processor modules with cache memory, memory modules and I/O access units. A simplified block diagram of the computer is shown in Fig. 4.27. It employs triple-redundant serial buses for memory and interface access. Actually there are five buses for both memory and interface accesses, of which three operate as a triad at any one time with the remaining two constituting spares. Each module in the system has an internal voter; it accepts the redundant information from all three active bus lines and forms the voted result. The processor-cache modules are organized into groups of three called *processor triads*. Each processor triad acts as one functional processor unit, of which several can work in parallel on different job steps. An error in one processor module is manifested as a disagreement that is visible to the other two processors in the triad. In such a case the two valid modules continue the current job step. However, before these two modules embark on another job step, the faulty module is replaced with a spare. If no spare is available, the triad is taken out of the system. Thus the multiprocessor is reduced by one processor unit, but the two valid processor modules are now available as spares should further module failures occur.

Memory modules are also organized into groups of three, called *memory triads*. The three members of a memory triad store identical data. If one of the memory modules of a triad is faulty, it can be replaced by a spare. However, unlike the processor modules, the memory modules are not anonymous. For example, a read-only memory is totally dedicated to its assigned function and cannot be used as a spare. Hence, if a read-only memory triad has a faulty module, a read–write memory must be used to replace it, unless an extra dedicated copy of the read-only memory is available. The spare read–write memory will be assigned to the same address space as the two modules it is joining. It must then be loaded to agree with the surviving triad members.

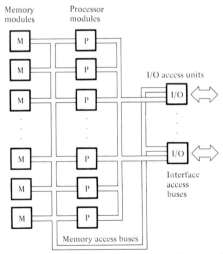

Fig. 4.27   The FTMP structure (*adapted from Ref. 4.69*).

In addition to the internal voting, each module also contains a pair of sub-units called "bus guardian units". The bus guardians control access to the buses; they are also used to reconfigure module assignments. The connections of bus guardians is shown in Fig. 4.28. Each guardian derives its power, its bus inputs and its timing reference independently of all other guardians. A guardian unit also contains a voter to mask erroneous bus data. The output of each module in an FTMP system is connected to one of the buses via a "bus isolation gate", as shown in Fig. 4.28. A module can be assigned to any bus; however, the module itself is not empowered to enable the bus isolation gates. Bus guardian units receive control commands from processor triads via the active bus triad, and accordingly enable selected bus isolation gates and control power to their associated modules. Isolation gates are non-redundant. The failure of any isolation gate into a mode, which allows unwanted data to enter the bus, can render the bus line useless. As can be seen in Fig. 4.28, both the bus guardian units inside a module would have to fail in order to cause a bus isolation gate to be improperly enabled. The failure of a single bus guardian unit does not affect the buses; it can at worst cause the loss of one processor or memory module.

The FTMP uses a common system clock to achieve synchronization between the members of each triad. The clock is quadruply redundant. The power supply to the FTMP is also quadruply redundant. All four units supply power under normal circumstances. But a single unit is capable of running the whole system. Therefore, up to three main power supply unit failures can be tolerated.

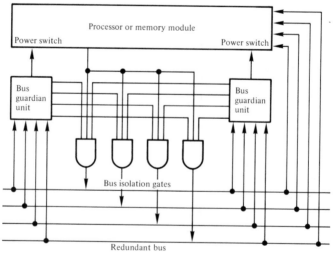

Fig. 4.28   Bus guardian connections (*courtesy of IEEE, © 1978*).

4.13.4   SIFT (Software Implemented Fault Tolerance)

The SIFT system is designed to the same specification as the FTMP, and is intended to execute a given flight-control program in the presence of internal hardware faults. It uses software techniques for fault detection, diagnosis and reconfiguration [4.49]. Figure 4.29 shows the SIFT system configuration. It consists of a number of modules, each composed of a processing unit and some memory. A processing unit within a module is connected to its memory by a high-bandwidth bus. The I/O processing modules are structurally similar to the main processing modules, but have much smaller computational and memory capacity. The processing modules are interconnected by a system of independent buses.

The basic principle of the SIFT system is to break down any computation into a number of "tasks", each of which consists of a sequence of "iterations". According to a task's criticality a number of modules is assigned to it. Non-critical tasks are performed concurrently in different modules, while critical

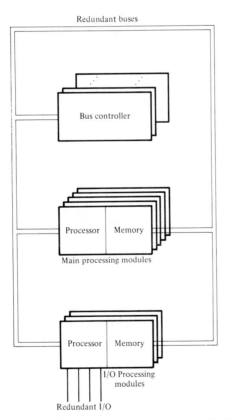

Fig. 4.29   The SIFT structure (*adapted from Ref. 4.49*).

tasks are performed in a TMR fashion. The output of each iteration of a task, executed by a processor, is placed in the memory associated with the processor. After an iteration has been executed by all the assigned modules, the results are compared by software. Any disagreement among the results indicate the occurrence of errors. The errors are recorded in the processor's memory; the records are used to locate the faulty units. An iteration of a task can be executed at slightly different times by different processors. This reduces the probability of correlated failures in the replicated version of a task, in the event of simultaneous temporary failures of several processors.

The processing modules in the SIFT system are interconnected so that a processor can read from, but not write into, the memory of any other processing module other than its own. Thus a faulty processor can corrupt data only in its own memory and not in that of any other processing modules. All faults within a module are assumed to produce bad data in that module's memory. Moreover the system does not distinguish between a faulty memory and a faulty processor that puts bad data into a non-faulty memory.

A non-faulty processor can obtain bad data either from a faulty processing module or over a faulty bus. In order to prevent these bad data from generating incorrect results, each processor receives multiple copies of the data. Each copy of the data is obtained from a different memory over a different bus, and the processor uses two-out-of-three voting to obtain the correct version of the data. If any of the copies of the data are found not to agree, the system identifies the unit providing the bad data and prevents it from taking part in any further computation. If the faulty unit is a processing module, its assignments are taken over by other modules. If it is a bus which is faulty, the processors receive their data over other buses. After reconfiguration the system can tolerate a new failure, provided that there are enough non-faulty units available.

4.13.5   C.vmp (Computer Voted Multiprocessor)

C.vmp is a multiprocessor system capable of operating correctly in the presence of both permanent and temporary hardware faults |4.66|. It provides real-time computation with software transparency to the fault tolerant aspects of the system. The basic design is modular, and it includes separate power distribution networks so that parts of the system can be deactivated while the rest of the system is in operation. The ability to deactivate parts of the system helps in the on-line maintenance, thus making the system highly available.

A block diagram of the C.vmp system is shown in Fig. 4.30. The processors P are DEC LSI–11s. Each processor has a memory M and a disk associated with it; the user terminals are interfaced via the serial line unit (SLU). The multiplexed data/address buses connecting the processors and the memories pass through a bidirectional voter V; the buses are standard DEC Q. The voter puts its output on bus A and multiplexes it to the other buses. A processor can have

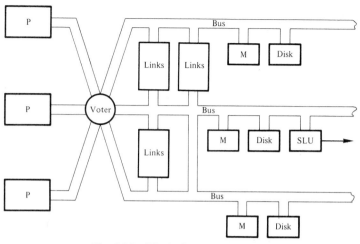

Fig. 4.30   Block diagram of C.vmp.

a certain bit failure in one bus, but if that bit is correct in the two other buses, the voter will produce the correct information for that bit. Thus any disagreement among the processors will not be propagated to the memories and vice versa. The voter also includes disagreement detectors, one for each bus; they can be used to monitor the failures in each of the three parts of the system.

In addition to the voting mode as discussed above the voter can also operate, under program control, in two other modes: broadcast mode and independent mode. In the broadcast mode the requests of one processor bus are broadcast onto all three buses. This mode is used for system initialization as well as for selective triplication of I/O devices. In the independent mode the voter is inoperative, with each processor working separately and interprocessor communication taking place via the parallel interfaces (Links). Clearly, the C.vmp can trade off reliability for higher performance by operating in the independent mode as a loosely coupled three-processor non-fault tolerant system. The reliability of C.vmp has been measured and reported in terms of a failure record and a failure recovery data [4.66]. Currently it is being used to gather statistics on transient faults in order to determine what provisions are needed to tolerate such faults [4.32].

4.13.6   FTSC (Fault Tolerant Spaceborne Computer)

The FTSC is a 32-bit general-purpose aerospace computer with self-repair capabilities [4.51, 4.67]. It is designed to have a 95% probability of remaining fully operational for a full five-year period. The main hardware modules in the FTSC are four central processing units (CPUs), up to 24 4K-word memory modules, three configuration control units (CCUs) and a bus network. One CPU is active and a second, known as a "monitor", performs the same sequence of operations as the active CPU and compares its output with those of its own. The remaining two CPUs are unpowered. The FTSC can have as many as 15 memory modules powered at any time. The CCUs operate in TMR mode and initiate reconfiguration activities if a fault is detected. The bus network consists of a data bus, address bus, control bus, status bus and interrupt bus; all inter-module communication takes place over this bus network.

The FTSC uses a shortened cyclic code for error protection in data transfers and in storage. This code protection is retained during all manipulations except those taking place within the CPU. Both the active and the monitor CPU receive only coded information and check the validity of the code before processing. The active CPU re-encodes all information before it is sent over either the address bus or the data bus. The advantage of this code protection is that only simultaneously occurring multiple faults can cause an undetected error. The probability of a multiple fault is minimized by partitioning the hardware in such a way so that failures are restricted to a single eight-bit byte. The cyclic code structure assures that any errors within a single byte will be detected.

Control signal errors are monitored by the monitor CPU, if the signals are generated by the active CPU, or by internal monitors in other modules. Software diagnostics are periodically run during normal system operation to ensure that the hardware is operating correctly. In addition, watchdog timers in the powered CPUs indicate error condition, if too much time is spent by a module to complete data transfer once it gains access to the bus network. The control lines interconnecting various modules are triplicated and the signals voted on at each module to mask the effect of a fault on a line.

The detection of a fault is signalled to the CCUs, which initiate the execution of the recovery program. The recovery program identifies the faulty module, eliminates it by power switching, selects a spare module and finally conditions the spare into the operational system. This program resides in a ROM within each of the CPU modules so that when the CCU automatically cycles the CPU modules the availability of this program is guaranteed.

4.13.7   FTBBC (Fault Tolerant Building Block Computer)

The fault-tolerant building block computer has been designed at the Jet Propulsion Laboratory to meet the requirements for military and long-life space applications [4.68, 4.69]. It consists of several self-checking computer modules (SCCM) with interfaces to a redundant busing system. This redundant busing allows the modules to combine off-the-shelf microprocessors and memory chips to form a fault tolerant system. The self-checking computer modules are designed using several buidling block circuits, each of which can be implemented as a single VLSI chip.

Figure 4.31 shows the block diagram of the FTBBC's self-checking com-

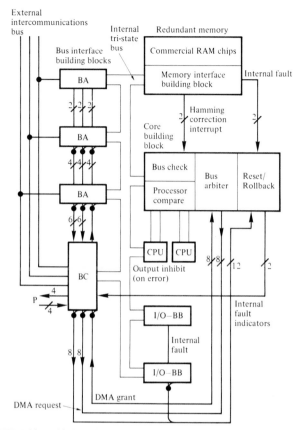

Fig. 4.31 FTBBC's self-checking computer module (*courtesy of IEEE,* © *1980*). BA. Bus adaptor. BC. Bus controller. P. Bus assignment priority signals.

puter module. It contains four types of building block circuits which interface processors, memories, I/O functions and external buses to the SCCM's internal bus. The internal bus employs error correcting codes to verify transmission of addresses and data between the building blocks. Each building block can detect faults both within itself and in its associated circuitry. The SCCM disables its output and raises a flag, when an internal fault is detected. An external SCCM can sense the fault by recognizing the absence of activity from the faulty module or interrogating the module through the redundant busing system. The four types of building blocks used in an SCCM are:

1. Memory interface building block (MIBB).
2. Bus interface building block (BIBB).
3. Core interface building block (core-BB).
4. I/O building block (IOBB).

1. The memory interface building block   The MIBB interfaces a memory array (consisting of RAM chips) to the SCCM internal bus. It provides single-error correction or double-error detection to damaged memory data. The circuits used for error correction and detection are self-testing. The bit plane replacement logic inside a MIBB can replace any two specified bits in a word with the two spare bit planes. The bits to be replaced are specified by an external command.

2. The bus interface building blocks   The BIBBs are used in each SCCM to provide communications with other computer modules through a redundant bus system. Each BIBB can be microprogrammed either to be a bus controller (BC) or a bus adapter (BA). When a SCCM wants to initiate data transfers between the memories of the SCCM modules on its bus, it alerts the BIBB which has been microprogrammed to be a BC. The BC reads the information necessary for the transfer from the host SCCM's memory. It specifies one BA as the data source and one or more BAs as data acceptors. The source BA extracts the specified information from its host SCCM's memory and places them on the bus. Simultaneously, the acceptor BA(s) transfers this information from the bus into its host SCCM's memory. An SCCM can obtain several BAs to provide an interface to a number of redundant intercommunication buses. Communications can occur simultaneously over three buses with an SCCM without any bus conflict. The BIBBs employ parity coding to protect memory information and duplication with "morphic" comparison for most of the logic circuitry.

3. The core building block   The core BB is responsible for two CPUs which carry out identical computations. It continuously compares their outputs and signals a fault if there is a disagreement. The core BB also serves as a bus arbiter and collects fault indications from itself and other building blocks. If a fault is detected, the core BB attempts recovery either by rolling back or by reloading memory and restarting. If the fault is permanent, it disables its host SCCM. The core BB uses internal duplication and self-checking logic so that most faults in the checking logic will isolate the SCCM from the rest of the system. When an SCCM fails, other SCCMs can access its internal building blocks via one of its BAs to read out its status, correct its memory and command internal reconfiguration.

4. The I/O building block   The implementation of a multi-function I/O building block as a single VLSI chip is currently under consideration.

The cost of a building block self-checking computer is approximately 23% more than that of an equivalent non-redundant module. If a spare bit-plane is included in the memory to provide single-fault recovery, the cost increase is 29%. However, if full single-error correcting/double-error detecting capability is employed in a memory with two spare bit-planes the cost increase rises to 60%.

4.13.8   Sperry Univac 1100/60

The Sperry Univac 1100/60 is a medium-scale general-purpose computer designed to achieve a high degree of fault tolerance |4.70|. Figure 4.32 shows a block diagram of the 1100/60 system. Each system support processor (SSP) incorporates a maintenance processor and a console. The instruction processors (IP) are microprogrammed and use four-bit slices (Motorola 10800). An optional 8K-word cache buffer is supplied with each IP. Each I/O unit can support—as a maximum—12 word channels and three-block multiplexor channels, and it has a direct interface main storage. The IP and cache hardware are ECL, the I/O units are TTL and the main store uses 16K MOS RAM chips.

The 1100/60 instruction processor consists of two 36-bit subprocessors. Each of these two subprocessors is constructed from nine four-bit slices and associated control circuitry; both subprocessors are also duplicated. During any microcycle only one of the subprocessors is allowed to drive the data bus; its duplicate drives the duplicate data bus. The results are compared at the end of the microcycle; any disagreement will cause interruption of operations. The main storage unit of the 1100/60 employs an error-correcting code to correct single-bit error and detect double-bit error during every read cycle. The control store also uses error correction; however, the approach is different than that used in the main storage. If the parity code of a micro-instruction indicates a single fault, a macro-instruction retry is attempted. If the retry fails, the SSP

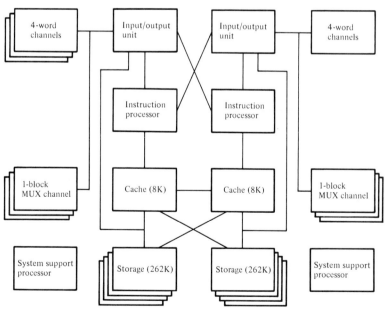

Fig. 4.32   System block diagram (two processor, two I/O configuration) (*courtesy of IEEE, © 1980*).

support processor initiates a procedure to rewrite the failed position of the control store. After each attempt at rewriting, the SSP checks to verify whether the proper correction has been made. It signals the IP to start action again if the correction is satisfactory.

Two different fault isolation techniques are used in the 1100/60. One relies on the on-line fault detection capabilities in the processor, the other uses a diagnostic program to determine the status of major test points in a failing unit. The second technique is necessary only if a fault is not sufficiently isolated by the fault detection logic in the system. The combination of fault detection logic and the diagnostic program can isolate any fault in the data logic to one or two PCBs. Since there is no manual diagnosis involved, the repair time is considerably reduced, resulting in the reduction of field support cost and increase of the system availability.

The 1100/60 has an efficient error recovery procedure to deal with both permanent and temporary faults. The procedure uses a combination of hardware and firmware. When a fault is detected, the system is halted until a special timer expires. If the fault is temporary, it will die out without further interference, because the system is not operating. The timer is variable for periods up to five seconds, allowing for adjustments to different program environments. At the end of the period, a fault recovery microroutine is executed which assembles a fault status word to be presented to the software. The next step is to determine whether the failing micro-instruction can be retried; an error-interrupt signals the operating system to log the fault in case the retry is not possible. If the fault is retriable the micro-instruction is re-fetched and re-executed. If the retry is unsuccessful, an interrupt is issued to the operating system for logging the fault. Should either the retry or the fault recovery microroutine fail, the IP is halted and the SSP is interrupted. If the fault is in the control store the system maintenance processor attempts to correct the fault by rewriting the control store with its original values. In case this is unsuccessful the maintenance processor writes the complement of the control store contents into the control store, and sets a designator to indicate that the control words must be reinverted before use. This allows both hard and soft errors in the control store to be corrected. The IP is restarted if the correction is successful and a second retry is attempted. The program execution can continue if the retry is successful. If the retry is unsuccessful or if the fault was not in the control store, the SSP selects another IP in the configuration (assuming multiprocessor reconfiguration) in which the failing instruction sequence can be restarted; this is known as "program transplant". The SSP initializes again the internal registers of the failing IP, irrespective of whether "program transplant" is possible or not, and then starts a microdiagnostic program. If this is executed successfully, the rejected IP can be introduced into the system. Should the microdiagnostic program fail, the operator is notified, and the fault is isolated and repaired by using the information provided by the automatic error log, macrodiagnostic tests, and scan-compare tests (see Sec. 6.5).

4.13.9 Pluribus

The Pluribus system serves as an interface message processor (IMP) in the ARPA network [4.21]. Its goal is high availability. The system consists of a set of modules which fall into three types: processor modules, memory modules and I/O modules (Fig. 4.33).

A processor module contains one or more processors and their associated local memory (8–12K), a bus arbiter and one bus coupler per logical path. A memory module contains an arbiter, bus couplers and 32K to 80K words of memory, depending on the application. Collections of memory modules serve as the shared memory. An I/O module contains an arbiter, bus couplers and various I/O interfaces. The system contains extra modules of each type so that a failure of any one resource or the module containing that resource will not result in system failure.

Each processor module is connected to each memory module via a bus coupler; hence all processors can access the shared memory. Bus couplers connect each I/O module to each memory module. They are also used to connect each processor module to each I/O module. A processor can access another processor module via its processor-to-I/O bus coupler.

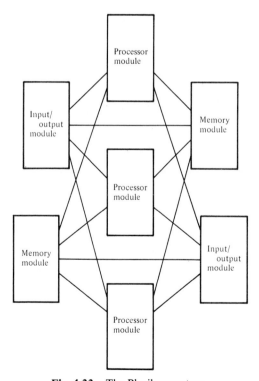

Fig. 4.33 The Pluribus system.

Processors can be incorporated into or withdrawn from the system by enabling or disabling the program-settable switches in the coupler paths that connect memory and I/O modules to processor modules. A processor cannot enable or disable its own access paths, but can remove a malfunctioning processor from the system by "amputating" the processor module containing the offending processor. Newly acquired or repaired processor modules can be incorporated into the system in a similar manner. Faults in bus couplers and defects in memory are detected by checking parity across all bus coupler paths; the parity computation is based on both data and address.

Pluribus uses software to provide most of its fault tolerance. When hardware faults are detected, the system software forms a new logical system by replacing the failing resources with redundant counterparts available in the system. Pluribus also checks the validity of its software structure. Data structures are redundantly constructed so that they can be checked for correctness. Time-out counters are employed for hardware/software fault detection. A number of Pluribus systems are currently in operation. The availability of these systems has been above 99.7%; the downtime was mainly due to software bugs.

4.13.10   Tandem Nonstop System

The Tandem nonstop system is a reconfigurable multiple processor system designed for on-line transaction processing [4.71, 4.72]. The fundamental design concept behind the Tandem system is to duplicate everything, so that no single hardware fault could cause a system failure. Maintenance and replacement of failed components are done on-line without bringing down the system. The architecture of the system comprises multiple processor modules, all interconnected by a dual interprocessor bus system known as the DYNABUS. The buses are completely independent, separately powered and controlled; each operates at 13 megabytes per second. Power supply is derived from more than one source, so that single failure can never affect more than one processor. Figure 4.34 shows a typical system configuration.

The Tandem system can contain up to 16 processor modules. Each processor module is a totally autonomous computer system consisting of an instruction processor unit (IPU), memory, a DYNABUS control unit, an I/O channel and a diagnostic data transreceiver (DDT). The IPU is a pipe-lined microprogrammed processor with a cycle time of 100 ns. The basic set of 242 machine instructions provides stack operations, 16-, 32- and 64-bit integer arithmetic, and byte-oriented functions such as scanning and comparing strings. A processor module may have up to 2 megabytes of storage. Each memory word is 22 bits wide; six bits of a word are used to correct any single-bit error and detect any double-bit error in the word.

The DYNABUS control provides high-speed interprocessor communication with a minimum of processor interruption. Messages are sent in 16-byte packets and can be up to 32K bytes in length. Each packet is protected by a

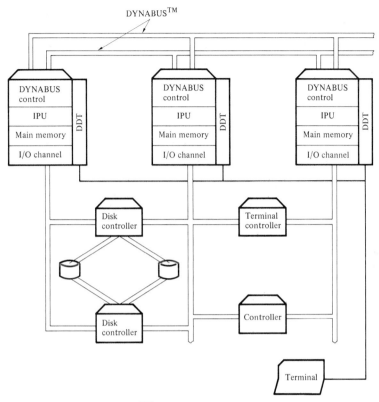

Fig. 4.34   A Tandem nonstop^{TM} system (*courtesy of Tandem Computers Inc.*).

check sum with automatic transmission if an error is detected. The I/O channel of each processor module has its own processor, which handles transfers between I/O devices and the memory. Because the I/O processor operates independently from the IPU, I/O transfers are extremely efficient and require only a minimum of IPU intervention.

The DDT monitors the status of the IPU, DYNABUS interface, memory and the I/O channel processor, and reports any error to the operations and service processor (OSP). The OSP is located in the console of the Non-Stop II system; this enables the diagnosis of the software and hardware problems through the operator's console. I/O devices are interfaced to the processor modules by dual-port device controllers; each port of a controller is connected to a separate processor. At any one time, one of the ports is used, the other one plays a back-up role. The processor connected to the active port is said to "own" the processor. In case of a failure, the system software transfers the ownership of the I/O device to another processor. Thus the system can complete an I/O operation without any loss of data even if a failure occurs while an I/O operation is in progress.

Tandem system provides automatic "mirroring" of the data base to ensure that it is available even if a disk fails. A pair of physically independent disk drives is treated as a mirrored disk volume. Each disk drive is dual-ported and is connected to a dual-ported disk controller as shown in Fig. 4.35; a pair of controllers can support up to 8 drives (4 mirrored pairs). During write operation the system writes data to the mirrored pair and during read operation the system can access data from either drive. When a failed member of a mirrored pair is restored to operation, the system automatically brings the disk up to

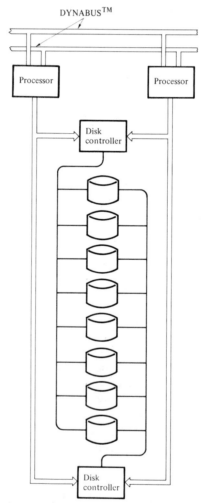

Fig. 4.35   Mirrored disk configuration (*courtesy of Tandem Computers Incorporated*).

date while at the same time it continues operation using the other member of the pair. Each processor module of the Tandem system contains a copy of the operating system GUARDIAN. When two processor modules operate in fault tolerant mode, one processor runs the primary program and the other runs a back-up program. The primary program is the active application program, whereas the back-up program is a passive copy of the primary program. At critical points, like before altering a disk file, the primary program passes the data and processor status information to the back-up. If the primary program fails, the GUARDIAN automatically activates the back-up program.

4.13.11   Stratus/32 System

The Stratus/32 supermini system, like the Tandem system, addresses the transaction-processing market [4.73]. However, unlike the Tandem system, the Stratus system uses hardware redundancy to achieve fault tolerance. A Stratus system can have up to 32 processing modules. Each module contains duplicated processors, memory, disks, magnetic tape terminals and printers. All the modules are interconnected via a high speed "Strata LINK" to form a single computing system. The fault tolerance in a Stratus system is achieved by using a pair of Motorola 68000 processors on two independently powered processor boards. The outputs of the processors on each board are con-tinuously compared; checking logic is incorporated in each board to detect a mismatch. If there is a mismatch on a board, a red light indicates a failure on the board; meanwhile the duplicated board continues to function normally, and so the system remains operational. The nature of the fault which caused the mismatch on the failed board is determined by the maintenance software. If the mismatch is due to a temporary fault, the failed board is restarted, otherwise it is replaced. Replacement of a board, as well as other units, can be carried out on-line without causing system interruption.

4.13.12   ESS (Electronic Switching System)

The Bell-ESS (Electronic Switching System) is an interesting example of a fault tolerant computing system [4.24]. The first generation of ESS processors, ESS–1 and ESS–2, went into operation in 1965 and 1969 respectively. The ESS–1 is designed to serve large telephone offices while the ESS–2 is used in medium-sized offices. Because of the small size of the ESS–2, cost was one of the particularly important considerations in its design. However, the reliability objective for both the configurations is the same—maximum two hours down-time in 40 years.

   In order to achieve this high reliability all critical parts in both processors are duplicated, including the central processing unit (CPU), the program store and the store's buses. Both CPUs operate in a step-by-step match mode; however, only one of these CPUs actually controls the telephone switching network, the other runs in a stand-by mode. If a mismatch occurs, a fault recognition program is used to identify the faulty CPU. The faulty CPU is automatically disconnected from the system by fault identification logic. The ESS–2 uses a watchdog timer to check whether the active CPU gets stuck while executing the fault recognition program. If it does, the timer will time out and transfer control to the stand-by processor.

Both ESS–1 and ESS–2 can run in simplex mode until the faulty CPU is repaired; a self-checking high-resolution diagnostic aids the maintenance personnel in repairing. Thus a system failure can result only if both the CPUs fail simultaneously. The possibility is included in the two-hour down-time estimate. The ESS–1A and ESS–3A are the second generation of ESS systems. The ESS–1A processor design is an improvement of the ESS–1 processor. It uses faster logic and faster memory and incorporates considerably more hardware for rapid fault detection. Besides, more extensive matching of internal nodes is used in order to increase the fault isolation capability.

The ESS–3A processor is different from the other processors—it operates in the non-matched mode of duplex operation. During normal operation it uses self-checking logic (see Chap. 5) for detecting faults, thus eliminating the need for synchronous-match mode of operation. Another new feature of the ESS–3 processor is that its control section is microprogrammed.

4.13.13   COMTRAC (Computer Aided Traffic Control System)

COMTRAC is a fault tolerant computer system, designed to control the Japanese railways' "bullet train" (Shinkansen). It consists of three symmetrically interconnected computers (Hitachi H–700). Two computers are synchronized at the program task level, the third computer acts as a stand-by spare. Figure 4.36 shows the hardware system concept. Each computer can be

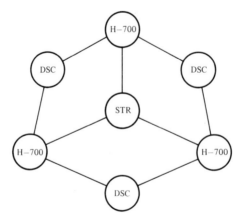

Fig. 4.36   Three-computer system.

in one of the following states: on-line control, stand-by and off-line. The DSC (dual system controller) compares the processing results of two computers. If the results do not match it starts a special test program. The output of a program is constant if the computer under test is fault-free. The DSC compares the results from the two computers with a stored constant as shown in Fig. 4.37. Based on the result of the test program, the DSC reconfigures the system, i.e. it replaces the faulty computer with one which is on stand-by. Figure 4.38 illustrates the procedure. The DSC also activates the timing control when the system returns to dual-computer operation.

A 16-bit register (STR) is used for the configuration control hardware. Bits 1–7 of the STR are used for entering an interrupt command for a specified computer. This is employed when fault diagnosis in a dual system is required or when the stand-by computer is to replace one of the computers under dual operation. The status bits 8–15 indicate the operating state of the system and are valid only when two computers are under dual operation. Bit 0 of the STR is called the "valid" bit; it is 1 when the data in the other 15 bits are valid, and is 0 during reloading or when there is a failure in the STR. If the "valid" bit is 0, it is re-read a fixed number of times and, if it is still 0, an STR failure is assumed. In general, the system goes down in the event of an STR failure in order to avoid mistaken configuration control.

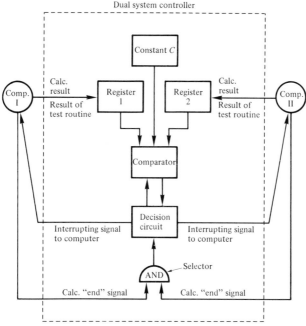

Fig. 4.37   Organization of the dual system controller with respect to configuration control (*courtesy of IEEE,* © *1978*).

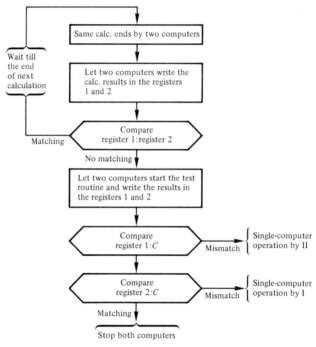

Fig. 4.38   Algorithm for fault detection by comparison, synchronization, and reconfiguration (*courtesy of IEEE, © 1978*).

The COMTRAC software, like the hardware, has a symmetric configuration (Fig. 4.39). The COS (configuration system) contains the configuration control program and the DMS (dual monitor system) contains the state control program. When one of the computers under dual operation has a fault, the state control program switches the system to single operation and reports the completion of the system switching to the configuration control program. The

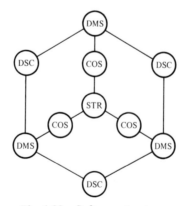

Fig. 4.39   Software structure.

configuration control program commands the state control program to switch over to dual operation with the stand-by computer. The state control program executes the system switch-over and transfers control to the configuration control program, which judges the correctness of the report it received from the state control program and indicates its own state to the other computers. The actual running record of the COMTRAC shows that it went down only seven times during a three-year period—once because of a hardware failure, five times because of software failures and once for unknown reasons.

4.13.14 AXE

AXE is a telephone exchange system and was first put into operation in 1977 [4.74]. It was designed to achieve high availability, with built-in facilities to ease system maintenance. AXE has two processors. Each processor is structured into a number of separate functional units, which communicate via an internal bus, as shown in Fig. 4.40. At one time one processor is executive

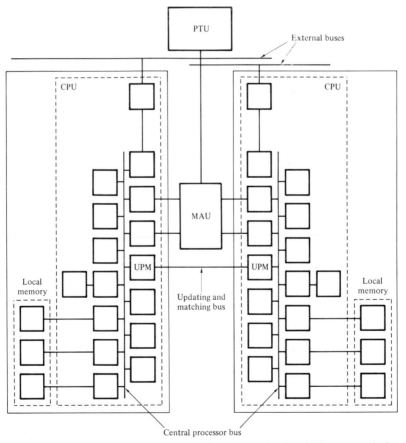

Fig. 4.40   The organization of the control processor in the AXE system (*adapted from Ref. 4.74*).

and the other is stand-by. The stand-by processor can be in one of the following states: parallel working, updating, separated and halted. The system includes a processor test unit (PTU), which is mainly used for initial load and start of the system but can also be used to fetch diagnostic information. The system contains a maintenance unit (MAU) for automatic and manual maintenance of the control part of the system. If a fault is detected in a processor, MAU controls the recovery procedure until one fault-free processor returns to normal program execution. The task of the manual maintenance part of MAU is to transfer signals between the PTU and the stand-by processor.

Each processor contains an update and match unit (UPM). Data on the internal bus of the executive processor are transferred to a buffer in the UPM of the stand-by processor for comparison with the data on the stand-by processor's bus. The loading of the buffer is controlled by the data input pulse from the executive processor and the reading is controlled by data input pulse from the stand-by processor. Synchronization of the two processors is performed by the UPMs, which keep a count of the data input pulses. The UPM on the faster side keeps its processor in synchronization by simulating a busy signal and thus delaying the next data input pulse.

If a mismatch is detected between the output of the buffer and the corresponding data on the internal bus, a malfunction interrupt signal stops both the processors. The processors then execute self-tests independently of each other. As soon as MAU has indication of which processor is faulty, it commands the fault-free processor to skip the remaining tests and resume processing as executive; the other processor becomes the halted stand-by. In the updating mode the stand-by processor is allowed to synchronize with the executive. Information is transferred from the executive to the stand-by until all registers and memory elements get loaded with the same information as the executive. Parallel operation in the stand-by is then resumed.

4.14   A SCHEME FOR FAULT TOLERANT DESIGN FOR VLSI CHIPS

The current state of very large scale integrated (VLSI) technology yields 16K-bit memory chips and 5K-gate random logic microprocessor chips. In the near future 64K-bit memory chips and 10K-gate random logic chips will be in production, while 50-to-100K-gates/chip will be possible within the next decade [4.75, 4.76, 4.77]. The effort required for VLSI testing would require an enormous amount of both human and computer resources and may become practically impossible [4.78]. However, as circuit density increases and cost per gate decreases, the idea of incorporating self-testing capability (see Chap. 6) and/or fault tolerant features inside chips becomes attractive.

A technique for incorporating redundancy in the design of digital systems on single chips has been proposed by Lala [4.79]. The redundancy scheme is illustrated in Fig. 4.41. The simplex (non-redundant) circuit is replaced by two

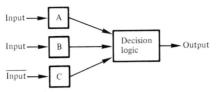

Fig. 4.41   Redundancy scheme (*courtesy of* Computer Design).

identical copies A and B; the third copy C is the logical complement of the functional circuits A and B. Data inputs and control signals from the external pins are received by all three copies. The signals going into the copy C are of opposite polarities to those of copies A and B [4.12]. For simplicity, it is assumed that each copy has only one output. If there is no fault, the output polarities of A and B will be the same, and opposite to that of C, for the same input pattern; faults are assumed to be of stuck-at type.

When the output of copy A or copy B is of the same polarity as that of copy C, the presence of a fault is indicated in the copy (A or B) whose output polarity is identical to that of C (see Table 4.5). Once the faulty copy is identified it can be replaced by the copy which is functioning correctly. Thus this scheme can tolerate output faults in either A or B by reconfiguring the system so that the fault-free copy takes over from the faulty copy. If the output of copy C is equal to that of copies A and B, i.e. when the outputs of copies A, B and C are 000 or 111, then the output of copy A or copy B is selected as the correct output of the system. Thus the proposed scheme produces correct outputs as long as not more than one copy has faulty output value. If two copies fail simultaneously the scheme takes wrong corrective action. For example, if due to faults in copies A and C, the correct output values 110 are transformed into 011, then the output of copy A is interpreted as being correct,

Output state			
A	B	C	Inference
0	0	1	No fault
1	1	0	No fault
0	1	0	A faulty
1	0	1	A faulty
0	0	0	C faulty
1	0	0	B faulty
1	1	1	C faulty
0	1	1	B faulty

Table 4.5   Fault diagnosis from the output states (*courtesy of Computer Design*).

instead of that of copy B. The probability of having output faults which result in wrong corrective action is

$$q_1 = P_B P_C(1 - P_A) + P_A P_C(1 - P_B) + P_A P_B(1 - P_C)$$

where P_A, P_B and P_C are the probabilities of A, B and C, respectively, being faulty. If all three copies produce faulty outputs simultaneously, the scheme does not detect the faults. For example, if the correct output values 001 change to 110 due to faults in all three copies, no failures are detected; this is because 001 and 110 are the expected output values during the normal operation. The probability of having faulty outputs in all three copies is

$$q_2 = P_A \cdot P_B \cdot P_C$$

Therefore the reliability of the proposed scheme is

$$R = 1 - (q_1 + q_2)$$
$$= 1 - [P_B P_C(1 - P_A) + P_A P_C(1 - P_B) + P_A P_B(1 - P_C) + P_A P_B P_C]$$

Let $P_A = P_B = P_C = P$; then

$$R = 1 - [3P^2(1 - P) + P^3]$$
$$= 1 - 3P^2 + 2P^3$$

If the reliability of the decision logic, R_D, is also taken into account, the overall reliability of the scheme, R_{ov}, is

$$R_{ov} = R_D[1 - 3P^2 + 2P^3]$$

It can be seen from the above expression that the overall system reliability is critically dependent on the decision logic. Figure 4.42 shows the block diagram of the decision logic. The 2-out-of-4 code* is used to represent the output states

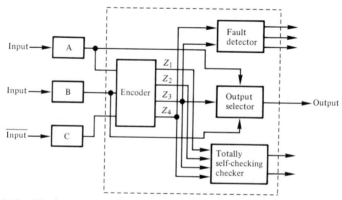

Fig. 4.42   Block diagram of the decision logic (*courtesy of Computer Design*).

---

* See Sec. 5.2.2 for explanation of an *m*-out-of-*n* code.

Output state			Assigned code			
A	B	C	Z_1	Z_2	Z_3	Z_4
0	0	1	0	1	0	1
1	1	0	1	0	0	1
0	1	0	0	0	1	1
1	0	1	0	0	1	1
0	0	0	0	1	1	0
1	0	0	1	1	0	0
1	1	1	1	0	0	0
0	1	1	1	1	0	0

Table 4.6   Code assignments for the output states (*courtesy of Computer Design*).

of copies A, B and C as shown in Table 4.6. The code assignments have been made in such a way so that the resulting encoder circuit can be realized economically using AND–OR logic. Figure 4.43(a) shows the encoder circuit.

The output of the encoder is monitored by a checker which is totally self-checking (see Chap. 5). The checker circuit, shown in Fig. 4.43(b) has outputs (0, 1), (1, 0) when its inputs are within the assigned codes. Since only the assigned codes should appear at the checker input during normal operation, the appearance of a non-code word can only be due to fault(s) in the encoder circuit. The checker outputs (0, 0) or (1, 1) indicate the presence of non-valid codes at the checker input or of fault(s) in the checker circuit.

The circuit of Fig. 4.43(c) interprets the information on code words and indicates whether or not a copy has an incorrect output value. The outputs of the circuit, $(W_1 W_2 W_3)$, take the value (000) when all three copies have correct outputs; it has outputs (001), (010) and (100) when copy A, B and C, respectively, has the faulty output value. Any other output combinations can result only from the sequential failures of two copies or due to circuit faults. The output selector circuit shown in Fig. 4.43(d) is used to select the output of the copy which is functioning correctly. The output of copy A or copy B is selected depending on whether $Z_3 = 0$ or 1 respectively.

In order to simplify the testing of the decision circuit, extra logic in the form of the circuit of Fig. 4.44 is built into the system. The outputs of copies A, B and C feed the decision logic via the test circuit as shown in Fig. 4.45. When $S = 0$, the circuit operates in its normal mode, i.e. the outputs of copies A, B and C are directly transferred to the inputs of the decision circuit. If S is set to 1, the flip-flops in the circuit are connected together in a chain to behave as a shift register (see Sec. 6.5). When the circuit is in the shift register mode, the first flip-flop can be directly set from the T input. This means that the circuit can be set to any state by clocking in the input value set at T. Thus the off-line testing of the decision logic can be carried out by switching the built-in test

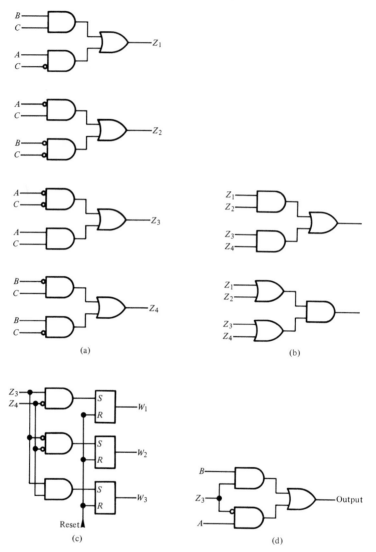

Fig. 4.43   (a) Encoder; (b) self-checking checker; (c) fault-detection circuit; (d) output-selection circuit (*courtesy of Computer Design*).

circuit to the shift-register mode and by setting the eight possible input combinations to the decision logic via the input T.

The redundancy scheme proposed here has the same reliability as the TMR scheme and also has the additional capability of automatic fault detection and isolation; this is an important advantage when redundancy is incorporated for easing test problems and improving reliability. Unlike the voter in the TMR,

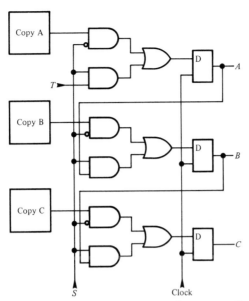

Fig. 4.44   Extra test logic (*courtesy of Computer Design*).

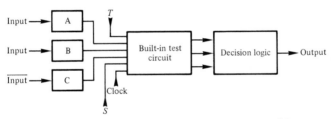

Fig. 4.45   Testable design of the fault-tolerant scheme (*courtesy of Computer Design*).

the decision logic used in this scheme is self-checking. If one of the circuit copies is faulty, externally observable signals (W_1, W_2, W_3, in Fig. 4.43(c)) indicate which copy has a fault in it. For example, if $W_1 W_2 W_3 = 100$, then copy C is faulty. Subsequently if another copy, say B, fails, then $W_1 W_2 W_3$ are set to 101 indicating that two copies have failed sequentially. There are also certain disadvantages associated with the scheme. If more than two copies fail simultaneously the scheme takes wrong corrective action as in the TMR. This scheme requires more than three times as many gates and connections to realize as would a conventional logic scheme. Since with VLSI the rate of increase in cost as a function of added gates is comparatively low, more logic in the proposed design would not lead to a significant rise in manufacturing cost.

4.15   REFERENCES

4.1 Champine, G. A., "What makes a system reliable?", *Datamation*, 195–206 (September 1978).

4.2 Avizienis, A., "Fault-tolerant systems", *IEEE Trans. Computers*, 1304–1311 (December 1976).

4.3 Anderson, A. and P. Lee, *Fault-tolerance: Principles and Practice*, Prentice-Hall International (1980).

4.4 von Neumann, J., "Probabilistic logics and synthesis of reliable organisms from unreliable components", Automata Studies, in *Annals of Mathematical Studies*, No. 34, 43–98 (Ed.: C. E. Shannon and J. McCarthy), Princeton University Press (1956).

4.5 Siewiorek, D., "Reliability modelling of compensating module failures in majority voted redundancy", *Proc. Int. Symp. Fault-tolerant Computing*, 214–219 (1974).

4.6 Avizienis, A., "Fault-tolerance: the survival attribute of digital systems", *Proc. IEEE*, 1109–1125 (October 1978).

4.7 Carter, W. C., "Hardware fault-tolerance", in *Computing System Reliability*, Camb. Univ. Press (1979).

4.8 Ball, M. and H. Hardie, "Majority voter design considerations for TMR computers", *Computer Design*, 100–104 (April 1969).

4.9 Davies, D. and J. F. Wakerly, "Synchronization and matching in redundant systems", *IEEE Trans. Comput.*, 531–539 (June 1978).

4.10 Lewis, D. W., "A fault-tolerant clock using stand-by sparing", *Proc. Int. Symp. Fault-tolerant Computing*, 33–40 (1979).

4.11 Dickinson, M. M., *et al.*, "Saturn V launch vehicle digital computer and data adapter", *Proc. Fall Joint Computer Conf.*, **26**, 501–516 (1964).

4.12 Sedmak. R. M. and H. L. Libergot, "Fault-tolerance of a general purpose computer implemented by very large scale integration", *Proc. Int. Symp. Fault-tolerant Computing*, 137–143 (1978).

4.13 Paterson, W. W. and E. J. Weldon, *Error-correcting codes*, MIT Press (1972).

4.14 Lin, S., *An Introduction to Error Correcting Codes*, Prentice-Hall (1970).

4.15 Armstrong, D. B., "A general method of applying error-correction to synchronous digital systems", *Bell Syst. Tech. Jour.*, 577–593 (March 1961).

4.16 Russo, R. L., "Synthesis of error-tolerant counters using minimum distance three state assignments", *IEEE Trans. Computers*, 359–366 (June 1965).

4.17 Meyer, J. F., "Fault-tolerant sequential machines", *ibid.*, 1167–1177 (October 1971).

4.18 Osman, M. Y. and C. D. Weiss, "Shared logic realizations of dynamically self-checked and fault-tolerant logic", *ibid.*, 298–306 (March 1973).

4.19 Larsen, R. W. and I. S. Reid, "Redundancy by coding versus redundancy by replication of failure-tolerant sequential circuits", *ibid.*, 130–137 (February 1972).

4.20 Losq, J., "Influence of fault detection and switching mechanisms on the reliability of stand-by systems", *Proc. Int. Symp. Fault-tolerant Computing*, 81–86 (1975).

4.21 Katsuki, D., *et al.*, "Pluribus—an operational fault-tolerant multiprocessor", *Proc. IEEE*, 1146–1157 (October 1978).

4.22 Avizienis, A., *et al.*, "The STAR (Self-testing and repairing) computer: an investigation of the theory and practice of fault-tolerant computer design", *IEEE Trans. Comput.*, 1394–1403 (November 1971).

4.23 Arnold, T. F., "The concept of coverage and its effect on the reliability model of a repairable system", *ibid.*, 251–254 (March 1973).

4.24 Toy, W. N., "Fault-tolerant design of local ESS processors", *Proc. IEEE*, 1126–1145 (October 1978).

4.25 Morganti, M. G., *et al.*, "UDET 7116—Common control for PCM telephone exchange: diagnostic software design and availability evaluation", *Proc. Int. Symp. Fault-tolerant Computing*, 16–23 (1978).

4.26 Ihara, H., *et al.*, "Fault-tolerant computer system with three symmetric computers", *Proc. IEEE*, 1160–1177 (October 1978).

4.27 Siewiorek, D. P. and E. J. McCluskey, "An iterative cell switch design for hybrid redundancy", *IEEE Trans. Comput.*, 290–297 (1973).

4.28 Ogus, R. C., "Fault-tolerance of the iterative cell array switch for a hybrid redundancy", *ibid.*, 667–681 (July 1974).

4.29 Mathur, F. P., "On reliability modelling and analysis of ultra-reliable fault-tolerant digital systems", *ibid.*, 1376–1382 (November 1971).

4.30 Cochi, B., "Reliability modelling and analysis of hybrid redundancy", *Proc. Int. Symp. Fault-tolerant Computing*, 75–80 (1975).

4.31 Losq, J., "A highly efficient redundancy scheme: self-purging redundancy", *IEEE Trans. Comput.*, 569–577 (June 1976).

4.32 Elkind, S. A., "Reliability and availability techniques", Chap. 3 of *Reliable System Design: Theory and Practice* (Ed.: D. Siewiorek and S. Swarz), Digital Press (1982).

4.33 DeSousa, P. T. and F. P. Mathur, "Sift-out modular redundancy", *IEEE Trans. Comput.*, 624–627 (July 1978).

4.34 Su, S. Y. H. and E. DuCasse, "A hardware redundancy reconfiguration scheme for tolerating multiple module failures", *ibid.*, 254–257 (March 1980).

4.35 Hamming, R. W., "Error detecting and correcting codes", *Bell Syst. Tech. Jour.*, 147–160 (April 1950).

4.36 Zachan, M. P., "Hard, soft and transient errors in dynamic RAMs", *Electronics Test*, 42–54 (March 1982).

4.37 Geilhufe, M., "Soft errors in semiconductor memories", *Proc. COMPCON*, 210–216 (1979).

4.38 Westerfield, E. C., "Memory system strategies for soft errors and hard errors", *Proc. WESCON*, 9/1, 1–5 (September 1979).

4.39 Carter, W. C. and C. E. McCarthy, "Implementation of an experimental fault-tolerant memory system", *IEEE Trans. Comput.*, 557–568 (June 1976).

4.40 Wang, S. Q. and K. Lovelace, "Improvement of memory reliability by single-bit error correction", *Proc. COMPCON*, 175–178 (1977).

4.41 Koppel, R., "RAM reliability in large memory systems—improving MTBF with ECC", *Computer Design*, 196–200 (March 1979).

4.42 Elkind, S. A. and D. P. Siewiorek, "Reliability and performance of error-correcting memory and register arrays", *IEEE Trans. Comput.*, 920–926 (October 1980).

4.43 Rickard, B., "Automatic error correction in memory systems", *Computer Design*, 179–182 (May 1976).

4.44 Nelson, B., "Simplification of 2-bit error correction", *Computer Design*, 127–136 (January 1982).

4.45 Goldberg, J., K. N. Levitt and J. H. Wensley, "An organization for a highly survivable memory", *IEEE Trans. Comput.*, 693–705 (July 1974).

4.46 Hsiao, M. Y. and D. C. Bossen, "Orthogonal Latin square configuration for LSI yield and reliability enhancement", *ibid.*, 512–516 (May 1975).

4.47 Edwards, L., "Low cost alternative to Hamming codes corrects memory errors", *Computer Design*, 143–148 (July 1981).

4.48 Hopkins, A. L., "A fault-tolerant information processing concept for space vehicles", *IEEE Trans. Comput.*, 1394–1403 (November 1971).

4.49 Wensley, J. H., *et al.*, "SIFT: Design and analysis of a fault-tolerant computer for aircraft control", *Proc. IEEE*, 1240–1255 (October 1978).

4.50 Chandy, K. M., "A survey of analytic models of rollback and recovery strategies", *IEEE Computer*, 40–47 (May 1975).

4.51 O'Brien, F., "Rollback point insertion strategies", *Proc. Int. Symp. Fault-tolerant Computing*, 138–142 (1976).

4.52 Reynolds, D. and G. Metze, "Fault detection capabilities of alternating logic", *IEEE Trans. Comput.*, 1093–1098 (December 1978).

4.53 Chen, L. and A. Avizienis, "*N*-version programming: a fault-tolerant approach to reliability of software operation", *Proc. Int. Symp. Fault-tolerant Computing*, 3–9 (1978).

4.54 Randell, B., "Fault-tolerant computing system", 6th School of Computing— European organization for nuclear research, 362–389 (September 1980).

4.55 Hecht, H., "Fault-tolerant software", *IEEE Trans. Reliability*, 227–232 (August 1979).

4.56 Pyle, I. C., Private communication.

4.57 Randell, B., "System structure for software fault-tolerance", *IEEE Trans. Software Eng.*, 220–232 (June 1975).

4.58 Feridun, A. M. and K. G. Shin, "A fault-tolerant multiprocessor system with rollback recovery capabilities", *Proc. 2nd Int. Conf. Distributed Computing System*, 283–298 (April 1981).

4.59 Lee, Y. H. and K. G. Shin, "Rollback propagation, detection and performance evaluation of FTMR^{2}M—a fault-tolerant multiprocessor", *Proc. Computer Architecture*, 171–180 (1982).

4.60 Borgerson, B., "A fail-softly system for time-sharing use", *Proc. Int. Symp. Fault-tolerant Computing*, 89–93 (1972).

4.61 Baskin, H. B., B. R. Borgerson and R. Roberts, "PRIME—a modular architecture for terminal oriented system", *Proc. Spring Joint Comput. Conf.*, 431–437 (1972).

4.62 Sklaroff, J. R., "Redundancy management technique for space shuttle computers", *IBM Jour. Res. Develop.*, 20–27 (January 1976).

4.63 Meraud, C. and P. Lloret, "COPRA: a modular family of reconfigurable computers", *Proc. IEEE Nat. Aerospace and Electronics Conf.*, 822–827 (May 1978).

4.64 Meraud, C. and F. Browaeys, "Automatic rollback techniques of the COPRA computer", *Proc. Int. Symp. Fault-tolerant Computing*, 23–29 (1976).

4.65 Hopkins, A. L., T. B. Smith and J. H. Lala, "FTMP—a highly reliable fault-tolerant multiprocessor for aircraft", *Proc. IEEE*, 1221–1239 (October 1978).

4.66 Siewiorek, D. P., *et al.*, "A case study of C.mmp, Cm and C.Vmp: Part 1—Experiences with fault-tolerance in multiprocessor systems", *ibid.*, 1178–1199 (October 1978).

4.67 Stiffler, J. J., "Architectural design for near–100% fault coverage", *Proc. Int. Symp. Fault-tolerant Computing*, 134–137 (1976).

4.68 Rennels, D. A., "Architectures for fault-tolerant spacecraft computers", *Proc. IEEE*, 1255–1268 (October 1978).

4.69 Rennels, D. A., "Distributed fault-tolerant computer systems", *IEEE Computer*, 55–64 (October 1980).

4.70 Boone, L. A., H. L. Liebergot and R. M. Sedmak, "Availability, reliability and maintainability aspects of the Sperry Univac 1100/60", *Proc. Int. Symp. Fault-tolerant Computing*, 3–8 (1980).

4.71 Tandem Computers Ltd, "Continuous operation in the Tandem fashion", *Which Computer* (March 1980).

4.72 Katzman, J. A., "A fault-tolerant computing system", *Proc. 11th Int. Conf. on Syst. Sciences, Hawaii*, 85–102 (January 1978).

4.73 Herbert, E., "Computers: minis and mainframes", *IEEE Spectrum*, 28–33 (January 1983).

4.74 Ossfeldt, B. E. and I. Jonsson, "Recovery and diagnostics in the central control of the AXE switching system" *IEEE Trans. Comput.*, 482–491 (June 1980).

4.75 Bloch, E. and D. Galage, "Component progress: its effect on high speed computer architecture and machine organization", *IEEE Computer*, 64–75 (April 1978).

4.76 Faggin, F., "How VLSI impacts computer architecture", *IEEE Spectrum*, 28–31 (May 1978).

4.77 Vancleemput, W. M., "A structured design automation environment for digital systems", *Proc. COMPCON*, 139–142 (1978).

4.78 Ando, H., "Testing VLSI with random access scan", *Proc. COMPCON*, 50–52 (1980).

4.79 Lala, P. K., "An onchip, fault-tolerant design scheme", *Computer Design*, 143–148 (August 1982).

4.80 European Workshop of Industrial Computer System TC.7, *Hardware of Safe Computer Systems* (1982).

5 SELF-CHECKING AND FAIL-SAFE LOGIC

5.1 INTRODUCTION

As digital systems get more and more complex it is becoming highly desirable for maintenance and repair to have systems that have the capability of self-checking. *Self-checking* can be defined as the ability to verify automatically, whether there is any fault in logic (chips, boards or assembled systems) without the need for externally applied test stimuli.

One way to achieve self-checking design is through the use of error-detecting codes. The principle of such designs can be better understood in terms of input/output mappings of the network. Let a network have m primary input lines and n primary output lines. Then the 2^m binary vectors of length m form the "input space" X of the network; the "output space" Z is similarly defined to be the set of 2^n binary vectors of length n. During normal, i.e. fault-free, operation, the network receives only a subset of X called the "input code space" A and produces a subset of Z called the "output code space" B. Members of a "code space" are called "code words".

A non-code word at the output indicates the presence of a fault in the network. However, a fault may also result in an incorrect code word at the output, rather than a non-code word, in which case the fault is not detectable.

The following two definitions describe the manner in which self-checking circuits deal with faults [5.1]:

Definition 1 A circuit is *fault-secure* for a given set of faults, if for any fault in the set the circuit never produces an incorrect code word at the output for the input code space.

Definition 2 A circuit is *self-testing*, if for every fault from a given set of faults, the circuit produces a non-code word at the output for at least one input code word.

These two properties of self-checking circuits can be described in the following manner. Let F represent a set of faults for which a circuit is self-checking. Let I and Y_1 be the input and output code spaces respectively for the circuit. If Z is the output space and Y_2 is the set of non-code words then $Z = Y_1 \cup Y_2$. Let $i \in I$ (i.e. i is an element of set I), and the correct output of the network be $y_1 \in Y_1$; and for the same input i, the output of the network is $y_1' \in Y_1$ in the presence of a fault $f \in F$.

Fault secureness implies that if $y_1' \in Y_1$, then $y_1' = y_1$. In other words, the output of a faulty network cannot be a code word and at the same time be different from the correct code-word output y_1. Thus, as long as the output is a code word, it must be assumed to be correct. The self-testing property, on the other hand, ensures that for every fault $f \in F$, there is at least one input, $i_2 \in I$, for which the resulting output is a non-code word $y_2 \in Y_2$, i.e. the presence of the fault is detected by input i_2. In other words, the occurrence of any fault from the prescribed set will be detected by at least one member of the input set.

A circuit is "totally self-checking" if it is both fault-secure and self-testing. Totally self-checking circuits are very desirable for highly reliable digital system design, since during normal operation all faults from a given set would cause a detectable, erroneous output. Such circuits have many significant advantages [5.10], such as:

1. Temporary faults as well as permanent faults are detected.
2. Faults are immediately detected upon occurrence. This prevents corruption of data.
3. Software diagnostic programs are eliminated or greatly simplified.

The model of a totally self-checking circuit is shown in Fig. 5.1. It consists of a functional circuit and a checker (check circuit) both of which are totally self-checking.

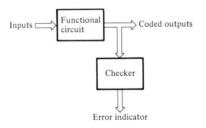

Fig. 5.1 Totally self-checking circuit.

The function of the checker is to check the validity of the output code words. It maps code word inputs into code word outputs, and non-code words into non-code word outputs; such a circuit is said to be *code disjoint* [5.1]. Thus by observing the output of the checker it is possible to detect any fault in the functional circuit or the checker itself. However, it is not possible to locate the fault (i.e. whether it is in the functional circuit or in the checker itself) from the information provided by the checker output.

5.2 DESIGN OF TOTALLY SELF-CHECKING CHECKERS

As yet there is no systematic technique available for the design of totally self-checking circuits, but considerable work has been done in recent years on the design of totally self-checking checkers for various types of error-detecting codes. A totally self-checking checker must have two outputs and, hence, four output combinations (Fig. 5.2). Two of these output combinations are considered as valid, namely (01, 10). The reason that no output takes a constant value, say 1, for code inputs is that the output would then not be tested for the s-a-1 fault during normal operation. A non-valid checker output, 00 or 11, indicates either a non-code word at the input of the checker or a fault in the checker itself.

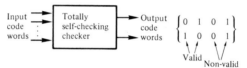

Fig. 5.2 Totally self-checking checker.

5.2.1 The Two-rail Checker

The two-rail checker has two groups of inputs $(x_1, x_2, \ldots, x_n)$ and $(y_1, y_2, \ldots, y_n)$, and two outputs f and g. The signals observed on the outputs should always be complementary, i.e. a 1-out-of-2 code if and only if every pair x_j, y_j is also complementary for all j $(1 \leqslant j \leqslant n)$. This technique can be understood by looking at the circuit of Fig. 5.3, where $y_i = \bar{x}_i$. In a non-error situation when $x_0 x_1 = 11$, $y_0 y_1 = 00$; the result of this is $f = 0$, $g = 1$. Now consider a situation where due to a fault $y_0 y_1 = 10$. The circuit of Fig. 5.3 will

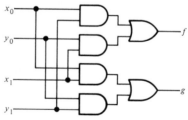

Fig. 5.3 Totally self-checking two-rail checker.

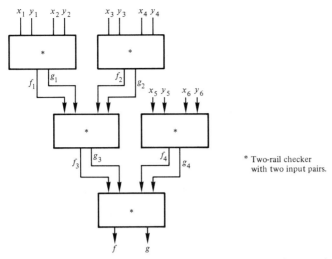

Fig. 5.4   Totally self-checking two-rail checker with six input pairs.

then produce $f = g = 1$, a non-code output thus giving an error indication. In fact the circuit is totally self-checking for all single and unidirectional multiple faults.

Although a two-rail checker for an arbitrary number of input pairs may be designed using two-level AND-OR logic, it is more efficiently realized as a tree by interconnecting the checker modules with two input pairs [5.1]. In general a multi-level tree realization for a checker with m input pairs, formed by interconnecting checker modules with x input pairs, requires $\lceil (m - 1)/(x - 1) \rceil$ modules, and $\lceil \log_2 m \rceil$ module levels. For example, Fig. 5.4 shows a two-rail checker with $m = 6$, formed by interconnecting checker modules with $x = 2$ input pairs (Fig. 5.3). Anderson [5.1] has shown that such a tree can be tested with 2^x input combinations, i.e. all possible input code words to a module. Thus the test set for the circuit of Fig. 5.4 is the normal input set {0101, 1010, 0110, 1001} of the circuit of Fig. 5.3. The cost of a two-rail checking scheme is 50–80% greater than that of an unchecked circuit [5.2]. Results show that two-rail checking could be effectively utilized in the design of self-checking LSI chips [5.3, 5.4].

5.2.2   Totally Self-checking Checker for *m*-out-of-*n* Codes

An m-out-of-n code is one in which all valid code words have exactly m 1's and $(n - m)$ 0's. Such codes are "non-separable" codes, because the information is embedded in the code word with the redundancy. If the information is required in another form elsewhere in the system, a code translator is needed to convert the coded information into the desired format: m-out-of-n codes are useful because of their ability to detect single and unidirectional multiple faults.

The m-out-of-n checker consists of two independent subcircuits, each subcircuit having a single output. For normal m-out-of-n code inputs, the checker output is (01) or (10). If the number of 1's at the checker input are greater or less than m (i.e. invalid code inputs), then the output is (11) or (00), respectively. In order for the m-out-of-n checker to be self-testing, the code words must contain the same number of 1's and 0's, i.e. $n = 2m$. Codes of this type are known as k-out-of-$2k$ codes [5.1].

The k-out-of-$2k$ checker is fault-secure for single faults, because it has two subcircuits; a single fault can affect the output of only one of the subcircuits. Hence, the checker is totally self-checking for all single faults. If the checker is realized with AND-OR logic, it is also totally self-checking for unidirectional multiple faults because it contains no inverters. Thus, a unidirectional multiple fault in the checker can cause only a faulty 1 or faulty 0 at the output, but not a faulty 1 and 0 at the same time. The number of tests required to diagnose all single and unidirectional multiple faults in the checker is 2^k.

To design the k-out-of-$2k$ checker, the $2k$ bits are partitioned into two disjoint subsets $A(x_1, x_2, \ldots, x_k)$ and $B(x_{k+1}, x_{k+2}, \ldots, x_{2k})$. If the two outputs of the checker are designated as Z_1 and Z_2, then

$$Z_1 = \sum_{i=0}^{k} T(k_A \geqslant i) \cdot T(k_B \geqslant k - i) \quad (i = 1, 3, 5, \ldots \text{ an odd number})$$

$$Z_2 = \sum_{i=0}^{k} T(k_A \geqslant i) \cdot T(k_B \geqslant k - i) \quad (i = 0, 2, 4, \ldots \text{ an even number})$$

where k_A and k_B are the number of 1's occurring in subsets A and B respectively. $T(k_A \geqslant i)$ represents the function which has the value 1 if and only if the number of 1's in subset A is greater than or equal to the value i; similarly $T(k_B \geqslant k - i)$ has the value 1 if and only if the number of 1's in subset S_2 is greater than or equal to the value $(k - i)$.

As an example of this checker, the design of a totally self-checking 2-out-of-4 checker is described. In this example $k = 2$ and $A = (x_1, x_2)$ and $B = (x_3, x_4)$. The two output functions become:

$$Z_1 = T(k_A \geqslant 1) \cdot T(k_B \geqslant 1)$$
$$= (x_1 + x_2) \cdot (x_3 + x_4)$$
$$Z_2 = T(k_A \geqslant 0) \cdot T(k_B \geqslant 2) + T(k_A \geqslant 2) \cdot T(k_B \geqslant 0)$$
$$= 1 \cdot T(k_B \geqslant 2) + T(k_A \geqslant 2) \cdot 1$$
$$= x_3 x_4 + x_1 x_2$$

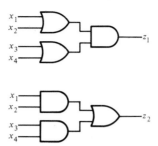

Fig. 5.5   Logic circuit for the 2-out-of-4 checker.

The circuit diagram for the 2-out-of-4 checker is shown in Fig. 5.5.

A general m-out-of-n checker, where $n \neq 2k$, can be realized by translating the given code to a 1-out-of-$\binom{n}{m}$ code, which is converted to a k-out-of-$2k$ code

$$\left[2^k \leqslant \binom{n}{m} \leqslant \binom{2k}{k} \right]$$

via a totally self-checking translator. As an example, we describe the design of a 2-out-of-5 code checker. The design consists of changing the 2-out-of-5 code into a 1-out-of-10 code, which is then translated into a 3-out-of-6-code. Figure 5.6 shows the circuit for decoding the 2-out-of-5 code into the 1-out-of-10 code. The decoder is totally self-checking and consists of ten two-input AND gates; each AND gate recognizes only one code word input. Table 5.1 shows the decoded output.

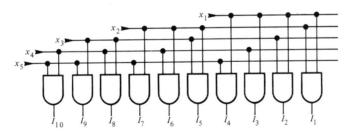

Fig. 5.6   A 2-out-of-5 to 1-out-of-10 decoder.

The 1-out-of-10 code is translated into a 3-out-of-6 code (Table 5.2) via a single level of OR gate as shown in Fig. 5.7.

A systematic procedure for designing two-level totally self-checking checkers for m-out-of-$(2m + 1)$, $m > 1$, codes has been presented by Reddy [5.5]. Such checkers are basically composed of two sub-checkers, an m-out-of-$(2m + 1)$ to 1-out-of-$^{(2m+1)}C_m$ code translator, and a 1-out-of-$^{(2m+1)}C_m$ to 1-out-of-2 code translator. The first translator is realized by using $^{(2m+1)}C_m$

2-out-of-5 code					1-out-of-10 code									
x_1	x_2	x_3	x_4	x_5	I_1	I_2	I_3	I_4	I_5	I_6	I_7	I_8	I_9	I_{10}
1	1	0	0	0	1	0	0	0	0	0	0	0	0	0
1	0	1	0	0	0	1	0	0	0	0	0	0	0	0
1	0	0	1	0	0	0	1	0	0	0	0	0	0	0
1	0	0	0	1	0	0	0	1	0	0	0	0	0	0
0	1	1	0	0	0	0	0	0	1	0	0	0	0	0
0	1	0	1	0	0	0	0	0	0	1	0	0	0	0
0	1	0	0	1	0	0	0	0	0	0	1	0	0	0
0	0	1	1	0	0	0	0	0	0	0	0	1	0	0
0	0	1	0	1	0	0	0	0	0	0	0	0	1	0
0	0	0	1	1	0	0	0	0	0	0	0	0	0	1

Table 5.1

1-out-of-10 code										3-out-of-6 code					
I_1	I_2	I_3	I_4	I_5	I_6	I_7	I_8	I_9	I_{10}	Z_1	Z_2	Z_3	Z_4	Z_5	Z_6
1	0	0	0	0	0	0	0	0	0	1	1	1	0	0	0
0	1	0	0	0	0	0	0	0	0	1	1	0	0	0	1
0	0	1	0	0	0	0	0	0	0	1	0	1	0	1	0
0	0	0	1	0	0	0	0	0	0	1	0	0	0	1	1
0	0	0	0	1	0	0	0	0	0	0	1	1	1	0	0
0	0	0	0	0	1	0	0	0	0	0	1	0	1	0	1
0	0	0	0	0	0	1	0	0	0	0	0	1	1	1	0
0	0	0	0	0	0	0	1	0	0	0	0	0	1	1	1
0	0	0	0	0	0	0	0	1	0	0	1	0	0	1	1
0	0	0	0	0	0	0	0	0	1	1	0	1	1	0	0

Table 5.2

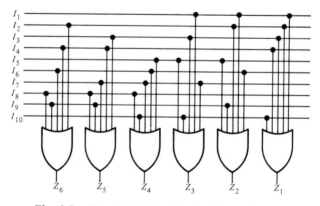

Fig. 5.7   A 1-out-of-10 to 3-out-of-6 translator.

Group I

$$A_i = \{i\,|\,0\,|\,(m-i),\ i\ \text{even and}\ 2 \leqslant i \leqslant m\}$$

$$A\dagger = \{i\,(m+i_1)\,(m+i_2)\ldots(m+i_{m-1}),\ 1 \leqslant i \leqslant m,\ 2 \leqslant i_j \leqslant (m+1),\ \text{and}\ i_j - 1 \neq i\}$$

and

$$B_i = \{i\,|\,1\,|\,(m-i-1),\ i\ \text{even and}\ 0 \leqslant i \leqslant m-1\}$$

Group II

$$A_i = \{i\,|\,0\,|\,(m-i),\ i\ \text{odd and}\ 3 \leqslant i \leqslant m\}$$

$$A^* = \{\text{all elements of}\ (1\,|\,0\,|\,(m-1)\ \text{not included in}\ A\dagger\}$$

$$A_0 = (0\,|\,0\,|\,m)$$

and

$$B_j = \{j\,|\,1\,|\,(m-1-j),\ j\ \text{odd and}\ 1 \leqslant j \leqslant m-1\}$$

Fig. 5.8   Partitioning of a set of AND gates (*courtesy of IEEE, © 1974*).

number of m-input AND gates. The second translator consists of only two OR gates, with a total of $^{(2m+1)}C_m$ inputs. The output of each AND gate is connected to an input of a single OR gate. Hence the set of AND gates has to be partitioned into two disjoint subsets.

The partitioning of the set of AND gates into two sub-groups Group I and Group II is shown in Fig. 5.8. A code word in a partitioned set is represented in two different ways. In the first representation, indications of the positions of 1's in a code word are given. For example, 00111 is represented by 345 and 1100001 is represented by 127. In the second representation a code word is assumed to be divided into three regions A, B, C with both A and C containing m-bits and C containing only 1-bit. A code word is then represented by the 3-tuple $(a\,|\,b\,|\,c)$, where a, b and c are the number of 1's in the A, B and C regions, respectively. For example, 00111 is represented by $(0\,|\,1\,|\,2)$ and 1100001 is represented by $(2\,|\,0\,|\,1)$. The second type of representation is used in Fig. 5.8 except for $A\dagger$, for which the first type of representation is used.

As an example, we consider the design of a totally self-checking 2-out-of-5 code checker circuit. Table 5.3 shows the truth table for the first translator circuit. This can be designed using the two-input AND gates.

The set of AND gates is partitioned into two groups:

Group I	*Group II*
$A_2 = \{11000\}$	$A^* = \{01001, 10010\}$
$A\dagger = \{15, 24\} = \{10001, 01010\}$	$A_0 = \{00011\}$
$B_0 = \{00101, 00110\}$	$B_1 = \{10100, 01100\}$

Each group represents the subset of AND gates which feed an OR gate. The complete circuit for the 2-out-of-5 checker is shown in Fig. 5.9.

x_1	x_2	x_3	x_4	x_5	I_1	I_2	I_3	I_4	I_5	I_6	I_7	I_8	I_9	I_{10}
1	1	0	0	0	1	0	0	0	0	0	0	0	0	0
1	0	1	0	0	0	1	0	0	0	0	0	0	0	0
1	0	0	1	0	0	0	1	0	0	0	0	0	0	0
1	0	0	0	1	0	0	0	1	0	0	0	0	0	0
0	1	1	0	0	0	0	0	0	1	0	0	0	0	0
0	1	0	1	0	0	0	0	0	0	1	0	0	0	0
0	1	0	0	1	0	0	0	0	0	0	1	0	0	0
0	0	1	1	0	0	0	0	0	0	0	0	1	0	0
0	0	1	0	1	0	0	0	0	0	0	0	0	1	0
0	0	0	1	1	0	0	0	0	0	0	0	0	0	1

Table 5.3   Truth table for 2-out-of-5 to 1-out-of-10 code

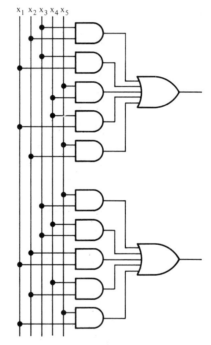

Fig. 5.9   Totally self-checking checker for 2-out-of-5 code (*courtesy of IEEE*, ©
1974).

Reddy [5.5] has also developed a procedure for cellular realization of totally
self-checking checkers for k-out-of-$2k$ codes. This method uses the same
technique as Anderson's method in deriving the logical expressions for the two
outputs. For example, when $k = 4$, the expressions for the outputs are

$$Z_1 = \sum_{i=0}^{4} T(k_A \geqslant i) \cdot T(k_b \geqslant 4 - i) \qquad (i = 1, 3)$$

$$Z_2 = \sum_{i=0}^{4} T(k_A \geqslant i) \cdot T(k_b \geqslant 4 - i) \qquad (i = 0, 2, 4)$$

Reddy and Wilson [5.6] have shown that functions $T(k_A \geqslant i)$ and $T(k_B \geqslant j)$ can be realized using two-dimensional cellular logic networks. An n-variable cellular array, T^n, can realize all the nT_p^n functions of the n variables (a T_p^n function takes the value 1 if and only if p or more of the n variables are 1). The T^n array requires $(n \cdot (n + 1)/2 - 1)$ cells containing $(n \cdot (n - 1)/2)$ AND gates and $(n \cdot (n + 1)/2)$ OR gates; each gate has a fan-in of two and a maximum fan-out of two. For example, a T^4 array can realize the functions T_1^4, T_2^4, T_3^4 and T_4^4 as shown in Fig. 5.10.

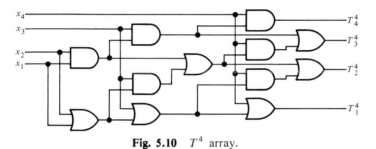

Fig. 5.10 T^4 array.

The output expressions Z_1 and Z_2 for a k-out-of-$2k$ checker can be expressed in the following form:

$$Z_1 = T_{1A}^4 \cdot T_{3B}^4 + T_{3A}^4 \cdot T_{1B}^4$$

$$Z_2 = T_{4B}^4 + T_{2A}^4 \cdot T_{2B}^4 + T_{4A}^4$$

Thus Z_1 and Z_2 can be realized using two T^4 arrays, three AND gates and two OR gates, as shown in Fig. 5.11.

It is shown in reference [5.6] that a checker designed with cellular array requires only $2k$ tests to detect all stuck-at faults. The test set is given below.

Test set for
k-out-of-$2k$ =
checkers

1	1	1	.	.	.	.	.	.	1		0	0	.	.	.	.	.	.	.	.	0
0	1	1	.	.	.	.	.	.	1		1	0	.	.	.	.	.	.	.	.	0
0	0	1	.	.	.	.	.	.	1		1	0	.	.	.	.	.	.	.	.	0
0	0	0	.	.	.	.	.	1			1	1	1	.	.	.	.	.	.	0	
1	1	.	.	.	.	.	1	0			0	0	.	.	.	.	.	0	1		
1	1	.	.	.	1	1	0				0	0	.	.	.	0	1	1			
1	0	.	.	.	.	.	.	0			0	1	.	.	.	.	.	1	1		
0	0	.	.	.	.	.	.	0			1	1	.	.	.	.	.	.	1			

$$\longleftarrow k \longrightarrow \qquad \longleftarrow k \longrightarrow$$

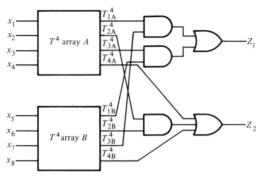

Fig. 5.11   Cellular realization of a 4-out-of-8 checker.

Therefore, the test set for the 4-out-of-8 checker is

1111	0000
0111	1000
0011	1100
0001	1110
1110	0001
1100	0011
1000	0111
0000	1111

Smith [5.7] has presented a general design procedure for the construction of totally self-checking circuits for a large number of "unordered" codes, including m-out-of-n codes, which satisfy Ramsey's theorem [5.8]. The procedure consists of the following steps:

1.   Partition the code words into two blocks B_1 and B_2 so that:
     (a)   block B_1 contains the minimal number of code words;
     (b)   there is some non-code word, $(m + 1)$-out-of-n, which is covering a member of B_1 and a member of B_2. For example, 111100 covers 110100; and
     (c)   there is some non-code word, $(m - 1)$-out-of-n which is covered by a member of B_1 and by a member of B_2. For example, 100100 is covered by 101100.

However, a procedure for generating a partition with "minimal" number of code words in B_1 has not been found. Actually the "minimal" numbers are generally unknown except for 2-out-of-4, 3-out-of-6 and 4-out-of-8 code words for which they have been derived to be 2, 6 and 14 respectively [5.7].

2. Form an AND gate for each code word in B_1, with inputs corresponding to the 1 positions in code words.

    Connect the outputs of the AND gates to the inputs of an OR gate to form the first output bit of the checker circuit.

3. Form an OR gate for each code word in A_1, with the inputs corresponding to the 0 positions in code words.

    Connect the outputs of the OR gates to the inputs of an AND gate to form the second output bit of the checker circuit.

As an example, let us design a totally self-checking checker for 3-out-of-6 code. The application of the above procedure results in

$$B_1 = \{111000, 110100, 001110, 001101, 100011, 010011\}$$

$$B_2 = \{\text{all code words not in } B_1\}$$

Figure 5.12 shows a minimal two-level 3-out-of-6 totally self-checking checker.

Smith also proposed a method for cellular realization of two-output k-out-of-$2k$ totally self-checking checkers [5.7]. Fig. 5.13 illustrates the construction

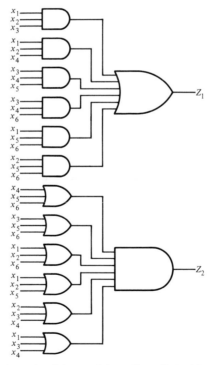

Fig. 5.12 A minimal two-level 3-out-of-6 totally self-checking checker (*courtesy of the Journal of Digital Systems*).

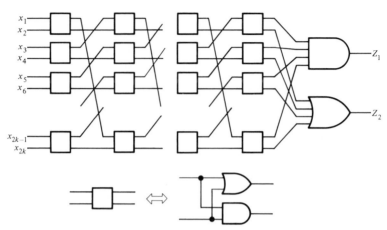

Fig. 5.13 A totally self-checking checker for k-out-of-$2k$ codes (*courtesy of the Journal of Digital Systems*).

of k-out-of-$2k$ checkers; such checkers can be tested by $2k$ code words resulting from the circular shift of k 1's followed by k 0's.

As an example, the cellular realization of 4-out-of-8 codes is shown in Fig. 5.14(a); the test words for the checker are given in Fig. 5.14(b). In general, k-out-of-$2k$ checkers designed by Smith's approach will be faster, and require fewer gates than that of Reddy's [5.5]. For example, the 4-out-of-8 checker, if designed using Reddy's procedure, will need 7 ($= 2k - 1$) levels of logic and 29 ($= 2k^2 - k + 1$) gates, whereas Smith's technique requires 4 ($= k$) levels of logic and 26 ($= 2k^2 - 2k + 2$) gates as shown in Fig. 5.14(a). The number of test words derived by each method will be the same, e.g. 8 ($= 2k$) in the case of 4-out-of-8 checkers [5.7].

Crouzet *et al.* [5.9] have made a comparative study of self-checking techniques proposed by Anderson [5.1], Reddy [5.5] and Smith [5.7] for k-out-of-$2k$ codes, in terms of their ability to be integrated in MOS LSI chips. Each technique was evaluated on the basis of the number of gates, number of logic levels and number of MOS transistors (a gate in this context is a MOS gate consisting of a load transistor, and driver transistors which can be arranged in parallel or in series to perform OR and AND functions respectively). Table 5.4 shows the costs of these checkers. The curves of Fig. 5.15 give the number of MOS transistors and the number of gates required by each technique. It can be seen from Fig. 5.15 that the number of transistors for Anderson's checker increases exponentially with k. Therefore this technique is not suitable for large k. However, the important point here is that although Smith's technique is both faster and cheaper than Reddy's when SSI circuits are used, Reddy's checker is cheaper to implement in LSI circuits [5.9].

Marouf and Friedman [5.10] have also presented a procedure for designing totally self-checking checkers for any arbitrary m-out-of-n code, $m \geqslant 2$. These

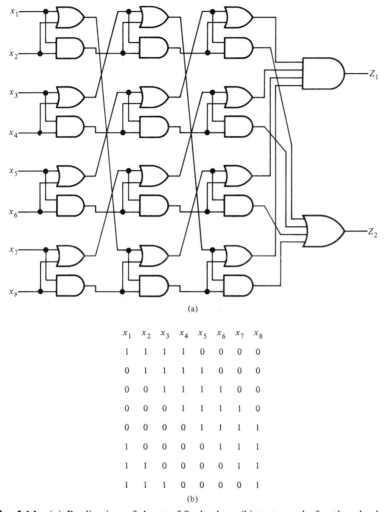

(a)

x_1	x_2	x_3	x_4	x_5	x_6	x_7	x_8
1	1	1	1	0	0	0	0
0	1	1	1	1	0	0	0
0	0	1	1	1	1	0	0
0	0	0	1	1	1	1	0
0	0	0	0	1	1	1	1
1	0	0	0	0	1	1	1
1	1	0	0	0	0	1	1
1	1	1	0	0	0	0	1

(b)

Fig. 5.14   (a) Realization of 4-out-of-8 checker; (b) test words for the checker.

	Number of gates	Number of transistors	Number of levels	AND fan-in	OR fan-in
Anderson	2	$k \cdot 2^k + 2$	1	k	2^{k-1}
Reddy	$k(k - 1)$	$4k^2 - 2k - 2$	$k - 1$	4	k
Smith	$2k^2 - 4k + 2$	$6k^2 - 8k + 2$	$k - 1$	k	k

Table 5.4   Costs of LSI implementation of checkers (*courtesy of IEEE, © 1979*)

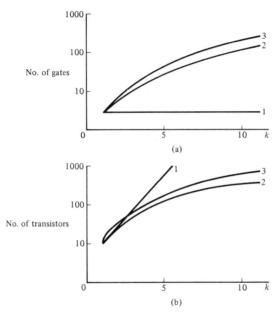

Fig. 5.15   Comparison of checkers: (1) Anderson; (2) Reddy; (3) Smith (*courtesy of IEEE, © 1979*).

checkers are also totally self-checking for single and unidirectional multiple faults. Let us first describe the procedure for the case when $2m + 2 \leqslant n \leqslant 4m$. It consists of the following steps:

1.   Partition the n bits into sets A and B such that the number of bits in set A is $n_a = \lfloor n/2 \rfloor$ and the number of bits in set B is $n_b = n - n_a = \lceil n/2 \rceil$. Define two functions f_1 and f_2 as:

$$f_1 = \sum_{i=1}^{m-1} T(a \geqslant i)T(b \geqslant m - i) \qquad (i \text{ odd})$$

$$f_2 = \sum_{i=1}^{m-1} T(a \geqslant i)T(b \geqslant m - i) \qquad (i \text{ even})$$

2.   Partition set A into two subsets A_1 and A_2 such that the number of bits in subsets A_1 and A_2 are $n_{a_1} = \lfloor n_a/2 \rfloor$ and $n_{a_2} = n_a - n_{a_1} = \lceil n_a/2 \rceil$ respectively. Define f_3 and f_4 as:

$$f_3 = \sum_{i=m-n_{a_2}}^{n_{a_1}} T(a_1 \geqslant i)T(a_2 \geqslant m - i) \qquad (i \text{ odd})$$

$$f_4 = \sum_{i=m-n_{a_2}}^{n_{a_1}} T(a_1 \geqslant i)T(a_2 \geqslant m - i) \qquad (i \text{ even})$$

3. Partition set B into two subsets B_1 and B_2 such that the number of bits in subsets B_1 and B_2 are $n_{b_1} = \lfloor n_b/2 \rfloor$ and $n_{b_2} = n_b - n_{b_1} = \lceil n_b/2 \rceil$. Define f_5 and f_6 as:

$$f_5 = \sum_{i=m-n_{b_2}}^{n_{b_1}} T(b_1 \geqslant i)T(b_2 \geqslant m - i) \qquad (i \text{ odd})$$

$$f_6 = \sum_{i=m-n_{b_2}}^{n_{b_1}} T(b_1 \geqslant i)T(b_2 \geqslant m - i) \qquad (i \text{ even})$$

4. Design a circuit with n inputs and f_i ($i = 1, 6$) outputs; realize every f_i in sum-of-products form. Call this circuit C_1, which produces a 1-out-of-6 code on its outputs.
5. Feed the outputs of circuit C_1 to the inputs of the circuit C_2, which is a totally self-checking 1-out-of-6 to 2-out-of-4 translator.
6. Feed the outputs of circuit C_2 to the inputs of circuit C_3, which is a totally self-checking checker for a 2-out-of-4 code.

The combined circuit C is a totally self-checking checker. All single and unidirectional faults in C can be detected by using T code words, where

$$T = \sum_{i=1}^{m-1} \max [C_i^{n_a}, C_{m-i}^{n_b}] + \sum_{i=m-n_{a_2}}^{n_{a_1}} \max [C_i^{n_{a_1}}, C_{m-i}^{n_{a_2}}]$$

$$+ \sum_{i=m-n_{b_2}}^{n_{b_1}} \max [C_i^{n_{b_1}}, C_{m-i}^{n_{b_2}}]$$

Let us apply the above procedure to design a checker for a 2-out-of-6 code defined by the set of inputs

$$\{x_1, x_2, x_3, x_4, x_5, x_6\}$$

Then

$$A = \{x_1, x_2, x_3\} \qquad B = \{x_4, x_5, x_6\} \qquad n_a = n_b = 3$$

$$f_1 = \sum_{i=1}^{2-1} T(a \geqslant i)T(b \geqslant 2 - i)$$

$$= (x_1 + x_2 + x_3)(x_4 + x_5 + x_6)$$

$$f_2 = \sum_{i=1}^{2-1} T(a \geqslant i)T(b \geqslant 2 - i)$$

$$= 0$$

$$A_1 = \{x_1\} \qquad A_2 = \{x_2, x_3\} \qquad n_{a_1} = 1 \qquad n_{a_2} = 2$$

$$f_3 = \sum_{i=0}^{1} T(a_1 \geqslant i) T(a_2 \geqslant 2 - i)$$

$$= x_1 (x_2 + x_3)$$

$$f_4 = \sum_{i=0}^{1} T(a_1 \geqslant i) T(a_2 \geqslant 2 - i)$$

$$= x_2 x_3$$

$$B_1 = \{x_4\} \qquad B_2 = \{x_5, x_6\} \qquad n_{b_1} = 1 \qquad n_{b_2} = 2$$

$$f_5 = \sum_{i=0}^{1} T(b_1 \geqslant i) T(b_2 \geqslant 2 - i)$$

$$= x_4 (x_5 + x_6)$$

$$f_6 = \sum_{i=0}^{1} T(b_1 \geqslant i) T(b_2 \geqslant 2 - i)$$

$$= x_5 x_6$$

Since $f_2 = 0$, C_1 will have only five outputs. Thus C_2 will be a 1-out-of-5 to 2-out-of-4 code translator. The circuit C for the checker is shown in Fig. 5.16. The number of code words required to test the checker of Fig. 5.13 is

$$T = \sum_{i=1}^{1} \max \left[C_i^3, C_{2-i}^3 \right] + 2 \sum_{i=0}^{1} \max \left[C_i^1, C_{2-i}^1 \right]$$

$$= 3 + 2(1 + 2) = 9$$

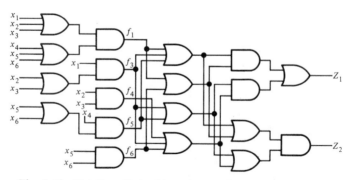

Fig. 5.16 Totally self-checking checker for a 2-out-of-6 code.

The checker design procedure for the case $n = 2m + 1, m \geqslant 2$, is as follows:

1. Partition the n-bits into two sets A and B such that the number of bits in A and B are $n_a = m$ and $n_b = m + 1$ respectively.
2. Partition set B into two subsets B_1 and B_2 such that the number of bits in B_1 and B_2 are $n_{b_1} = \lfloor n_b/2 \rfloor$ and $n_{b_2} = n_b - n_{b_1} = \lceil n_b/2 \rceil$.
3. Define the four functions f_1, f_2, f_3 and f_4 as follows:

$$f_1 = \sum_{i=1}^{m} T(a \geqslant i)T(b \geqslant m - i) \qquad (i \text{ odd})$$

$$f_2 = \sum_{i=1}^{m} T(a \geqslant i)T(b \geqslant m - i) \qquad (i \text{ even})$$

$$f_3 = \sum_{i=m-n_{b_2}}^{n_{b_1}} T(b_1 \geqslant i)T(b_2 \geqslant m - i) \qquad (i \text{ odd})$$

$$f_4 = \sum_{i=m-n_{b_2}}^{n_{b_1}} T(b_1 \geqslant i)T(b_2 \geqslant m - i) \qquad (i \text{ even})$$

4. Design a circuit with n inputs and f_i $(i = 1, 4)$ outputs. Call this circuit C_1. The output of C_1 feeds the input of circuit C_2, which is a totally self-checking 1-out-of-4 to 2-out-of-4 translator. The output of C_2 feeds the input of circuit C_3, which is a totally self-checking checker for a 2-out-of-4 code.

As an example let us design the checker for a 2-out-of-5 code defined by the set of inputs

$$\{x_1, x_2, x_3, x_4, x_5\}$$

Then

$$A = \{x_1, x_2\} \qquad B = \{x_3, x_4, x_5\} \qquad n_a = 2 \qquad n_b = 3$$
$$B_1 = \{x_3\} \qquad B_2 = \{x_4, x_5\} \qquad n_{b_1} = 1 \qquad n_{b_2} = 2$$

$$f_1 = \sum_{i=1}^{2} T(a \geqslant i)T(b \geqslant 2 - i) = (x_1 + x_2)(x_3 + x_4 + x_5)$$

$$f_2 = \sum_{i=1}^{2} T(a \geqslant i)T(b \geqslant 2 - i) = x_1 x_2$$

$$f_3 = \sum_{i=0}^{1} T(b_1 \geqslant i)T(b_2 \geqslant 2 - i) = x_3(x_4 + x_5)$$

$$f_4 = \sum_{i=0}^{1} T(b_1 \geqslant i)T(b_2 \geqslant 2 - i) = x_4 x_5$$

The combined circuit for the given m-out-of-$(2m-1)$ code is shown in Fig. 5.17. All single and unidirectional faults in the checker can be detected by using T' code words, where

$$T' = \sum_{i=1}^{m} C_{m-i}^{m-1} + \sum_{i=m-nb_2}^{nb_1} \max [C_i^{nb_1}, C_{m-i}^{nb_2}]$$

For the circuit shown in Fig. 5.17

$$T' = \sum_{i=1}^{2} C_{2-i}^{3} + \sum_{i=0}^{1} \max [C_i^1, C_{2-i}^2]$$

$$= (3+1) + (1+2) = 7 \text{ code words}$$

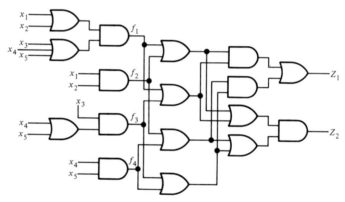

Fig. 5.17   Totally self-checking checker for a 2-out-of-5 code.

Although the method of Marouf *et al.* [5.10] is more efficient than other previously discussed methods, in terms of logic and size of test set, the resulting checker needs seven levels of gates. Halatsis [5.11] has presented a design procedure which realizes a totally self-checking checker using three levels of gates. The first step of the procedure is to partition the $(2m-1)$ input variables into m blocks, $A_1, A_2, \ldots, A_m$, so that each block contains two variables except block A_m, which contains only one variable.

As an example, let us consider the design of a totally self-checking checker for 5-out-of-9 code. Since $m = 5$, the set of input variables

$$\{x_1, x_2, x_3, x_4, x_5, x_6, x_7, x_8, x_9\}$$

is divided into 5 blocks:

$$A_1 = \{x_1, x_2\} \qquad A_2 = \{x_3, x_4\} \qquad A_3 = \{x_5, x_6\}$$

$$A_4 = \{x_7, x_8\} \qquad A_5 = \{x_9\}$$

If n_i and k_i, $i = 1, 2, \ldots, m$, are the number of variables and the number of 1's respectively in A_i, then the following "product functions" can be defined

$$P_{j_1 j_2 \ldots jm} = T(k_1 \geqslant j_1)T(k_2 \geqslant j_2) \ldots T(k_m \geqslant j_m) \qquad j_i \leqslant n_i$$

where $T(k_i \geqslant j_i)$ has the value 1 if the condition inside the brackets is true.
   For the example above,

$$P_{j_1 j_2 j_3 j_4 j_5} = T(k_1 \geqslant j_1)T(k_2 \geqslant j_2)T(k_3 \geqslant j_3)T(k_4 \geqslant j_4)T(k_5 \geqslant j_5)$$

where $j_1, j_2, j_3, j_4 \leqslant 2$ and $j_5 \leqslant 1$.
   All product functions can be grouped into a set B:

$$B = \{P_{j_1 j_2 \ldots jm} \,|\, (j_1 + j_2 + \ldots + j_m) = m\}$$

Hence for the 5-out-of-9 code,

$$\begin{aligned}
B = \{ &P_{11111}, P_{21110}, P_{21101}, P_{21011}, P_{20111}, P_{02111}, P_{12011}, P_{12101}, P_{12110}, P_{01211}, \\
&P_{10211}, P_{11201}, P_{11210}, P_{01121}, P_{10121}, P_{11021}, P_{11120}, P_{22001}, P_{22010}, P_{22100}, \\
&P_{20201}, P_{20210}, P_{21200}, P_{20021}, P_{20120}, P_{21020}, P_{02201}, P_{02210}, P_{12200}, P_{02021}, \\
&\qquad\qquad\qquad P_{02120}, P_{12020}, P_{00221}, P_{01220}, P_{10220} \}
\end{aligned}$$

Assuming $r = \lfloor m/2 \rfloor$, two sets of product functions P_r^{m-1} and P_{r+1}^{m-1} are defined as follows:

$$P_r^{m-1} = \left\{ P_{j_1 j_2 \ldots jm-1} \,\bigg|\, j_1 = 0 \text{ or } 2 \text{ so that } \sum_{i=1}^{m-1} j_i = 2r \right\}$$

$$P_{r+1}^{m-1} = \left\{ P_{j_1 j_2 \ldots jm-1} \,\bigg|\, j_1 = 0 \text{ or } 2 \text{ so that } \sum_{i=1}^{m-1} j_i = 2(r + 1) \right\}$$

The cardinality of the sets P^{m-1} and P_{r+1}^{m-1} are $^{(m-1)}C$ and $^{(m-1)}C_{(r+1)}$ respectively.
   For the example under consideration, $r = \lfloor (5 - 1)/2 \rfloor = 2$; hence

$$P_2^4 = \{P_{0022}, P_{0202}, P_{0220}, P_{2002}, P_{2020}, P_{2200}\}$$

and

$$P_3^4 = \{P_{0222}, P_{2022}, P_{2202}, P_{2220}\}$$

Next, a set B_m is formed as below:

$B_m = \{x \,|\, x$ is obtained by converting an index of an element in
$\qquad\qquad\qquad\qquad\qquad P^{m-1}(P_{r+1}^{m-1})$ from 0(2) to 1$\}$

The cardinality of the set B_m is $^{(m-1)}C_r$. Thus

$$\begin{aligned}
B_5 = \{ &P_{0122}, P_{0212}, P_{0221}, P_{1022}, P_{2012}, P_{2021}, P_{1202}, P_{2102}, \\
&\qquad\qquad\qquad P_{2201}, P_{1220}, P_{2120}, P_{2210} \}
\end{aligned}$$

A subset of B_m, defined as B_m^1, is derived next. Each member of B_m^1 is one of the S product terms obtained by changing an index of $P_{j_1 j_2 \cdots j_{m-1}} \in P_r^{m-1}$ from 0 to 1; S is obviously equal to the number of indices at 0 in $P_{j_1 j_2 \cdots j_{m-1}}$.

Alternatively, when m is odd, at most two members of B_m^1 can be selected from the product terms obtained by changing an index of $P_{j_1 j_2 \cdots j_{m-1}} \in P_{r+1}^{m-1}$ from 2 to 1. When m is odd, B_m^1 can contain only one of the converted product terms as a member. It should be noted that the members of the set B_m^1 are not unique; the cardinality of the set is $^{(m-1)}C_r$. For the example under consideration B_5^1 may be defined as

$$B_5^1 = \{P_{1022}, P_{0212}, P_{0221}, P_{2102}, P_{2120}, P_{2201}\}$$

The sets B_m^2 and B_m^3 can be derived from B_m^1 in the following manner:

$$B_m^2 = \{P_{j_1 j_2 \cdots j_m} \,|\, P_{j_1 j_2 \cdots j_{m-1}} \in B_m^1; j_m = 1 \text{ or } 0 \text{ for } m \text{ even or odd respectively}\}$$

$$B_m^3 = \begin{cases} \emptyset \text{ for } m \text{ even} \\ P_{j_1 j_2 \cdots j_m} \in B_m^1 \text{ for } m \text{ odd} \end{cases} \left| \begin{array}{l} P_{j_1 j_2 \cdots j_{m-1}} \text{ is obtained by changing the index} \\ \text{of an element in } B_m^1 \text{ from 2 to 1, and con-} \\ \text{verting the other 1 to 2; } j_m \text{ is set to 1} \end{array} \right\}$$

Hence, B_5^2 can be obtained from B_5^1 and is given by

$$B_5^2 = \{P_{10220}, P_{02120}, P_{02210}, P_{21020}, P_{21200}, P_{22010}\}$$

Let us now consider the derivation of B_5^3. The first member of B_5^1, i.e. P_{1022}, can be converted to either P_{1021} or P_{1012} by changing either of the indices from 2 to 1. P_{1021} can then be converted to P_{2021}, but P_{2021} is not a member of B_5^1 and therefore P_{1021} cannot be included in B_5^3. Similarly P_{1012} can be converted to P_{2012}, which is not in B_5^1, hence P_{1012} cannot be a member of B_5^3 either. However, the second member of B_5^1 can be changed into P_{0211}, which can be converted into P_{0221}. Since $P_{0221} \in B_5^1$, P_{0211} is a member of B_5^3. In a similar manner it can be verified that only the uncrossed product terms in B_5^3, as shown below, belong to B_5^1 and thus members of B_5^3:

$$B_5^3 = \{P_{1021}\!\!\!/, P_{1012}\!\!\!/, P_{0012}\!\!\!/, P_{0211}, P_{0021}\!\!\!/, P_{0211}, P_{1012}\!\!\!/, P_{2101},$$
$$P_{1120}\!\!\!/, P_{2010}\!\!\!/, P_{1201}\!\!\!/, P_{2101}\}$$

$$= \{P_{02111}, P_{21011}\} \text{ setting the index } j_5 \text{ to 1}$$

The set of all product functions, B, is next partitioned into two classes $\bar{B}_\mathrm{I}$ and $\bar{B}_\mathrm{II}$ so that $\bar{B}_\mathrm{I}$ and $\bar{B}_\mathrm{II}$ contain product functions with odd and even numbers of j_i $(=2)$ indices respectively. For the example above

$$\bar{B}_\mathrm{I} = \{P_{11120}, P_{21110}, P_{21101}, P_{21011}, P_{20111}, P_{02111}, P_{12011}, P_{12101}, P_{12110},$$
$$P_{01211}, P_{10211}, P_{11201}, P_{11210}, P_{01121}, P_{10121}, P_{11021}\}$$

$$\bar{B}_\mathrm{II} = \{P_{11111}, P_{22001}, P_{22010}, P_{22100}, P_{20201}, P_{20210}, P_{21200}, P_{20021}, P_{20120}, P_{21020},$$
$$P_{02201}, P_{02210}, P_{12200}, P_{02021}, P_{02120}, P_{12020}, P_{00221}, P_{01220}, P_{10220}\}$$

The next step is to define the "product separation partition" as follows:

$$\left.\begin{aligned} B_{\mathrm{I}} &= \tilde{B}_{\mathrm{I}} + B_m^2 - B_m^3 \\ B_{\mathrm{II}} &= \tilde{B}_{\mathrm{II}} - B_m^2 + B_m^3 \end{aligned}\right\} \quad r \text{ even}$$

$$\left.\begin{aligned} B_{\mathrm{I}} &= \tilde{B}_{\mathrm{I}} - B_m^2 + B_m^3 \\ B_{\mathrm{II}} &= \tilde{B}_{\mathrm{II}} + B_m^2 - B_m^3 \end{aligned}\right\} \quad r \text{ odd}$$

The output functions f and g are then defined:

$$f = \sum_{B_{\mathrm{I}}} P_{j_1 j_2 \cdots j_m}$$

$$g = \sum_{B_{\mathrm{II}}} P_{j_1 j_2 \cdots j_m}$$

Since $r \,(=2)$ is even for a 5-out-of-9 code, B_{I} and B_{II} are given by:

$$B_{\mathrm{I}} = \{P_{11120}, P_{21110}, P_{21101}, P_{20111}, P_{12011}, P_{12101}, P_{12110}, P_{01211}, P_{10211}, P_{11201},$$
$$P_{01121}, P_{10121}, P_{11021}, P_{10220}, P_{02120}, P_{02210}, P_{21020}, P_{21200}, P_{22010}, P_{11210}\}$$

$$B_{\mathrm{II}} = \{P_{11111}, P_{22001}, P_{22100}, P_{20201}, P_{20210}, P_{20021}, P_{20120}, P_{02201},$$
$$P_{12200}, P_{02021}, P_{12020}, P_{00221}, P_{01220}, P_{02111}, P_{21011}\}$$

The totally self-checking checker realization by Halatsis's procedure requires three levels of logic. The first level realizes the majority functions $T(k_i \geqslant j_i)$ using $2(m-1)$ gates. The second level of gates realizes the product terms $P_{j_1 j_2 \cdots j_m}$ using AND gates; the number of AND gates required is equal to the number of elements in set B. The third level, in the form of two OR gates, is used to realize the functions f and g; the number of inputs to the OR gates depends on the number of elements in partitions B_{I} and B_{II}. The required test code words for such a checker is equal to the number of product functions in B. This procedure results in totally self-checking checkers with fewer gates and smaller test code words as compared to Reddy's [5.2]. However, checkers designed by Reddy's procedure are faster because they have only two levels of gates.

One special case of an m-out-of-n code which is of much interest in computer systems is the 1-out-of-n code. Khakbaz [5.12] has presented a new design technique for a totally self-checking 1-out-of-n checker. This technique is oriented towards the NMOS implementation of checkers so that they can be included as parts of LSI and VLSI designs. The 1-out-of-n checker has two subcircuits C_1 and C_2. Subcircuit C_1 receives a 1-out-of-n code and produces a two-rail code. Subcircuit C_2 is a totally self-checking two-rail checker. The subcircuits are implemented using NOR logic. Subcircuit C_1 has p pairs of output lines for a 1-out-of-n input, where $p = \lceil \log_2(n) \rceil$. For example, let us design a totally self-checking checker for a 1-out-of-8 code. Figure 5.18 shows

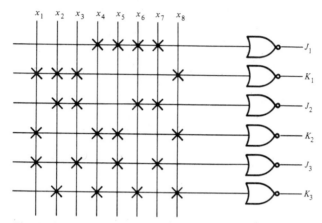

Fig. 5.18   Translator for a 1-out-of-8 code (subcircuit C_1).

the subcircuit C_1 for a 1-out-of-8 code. C_1 has 3 ($= \lceil \log_2 8 \rceil$) pairs of output lines $J_1 K_1$, $J_2 K_2$, and $J_3 K_3$; K-lines are the complements of the J-lines.

The input lines of C_1 are numbered as x_1 through x_n, as shown in Fig. 5.18; each $\times$ in the figure represents an input connection to a NOR gate. For example, the output expression for J_1 is

$$J_1 = \overline{(x_4 + x_5 + x_6 + x_7)}$$

The subscript associated with each input line, $i = 1, 2, \ldots, n$, is represented as a p-bit binary number. In this representation a 0 is interpreted as the absence and a 1 as the presence of an input connection to a NOR gate, i.e. the absence or the presence of a $\times$ on the intersection of input line x_i with the input lines to the NOR gates, from top to bottom. For example, in Fig. 5.18, where $n = 8$ and $p = 3$, the input line x_6 has no $\times$ on its intersection with the input line to J_3; this is because the 3-bit representation of 6 is 110, which means that x_6 is not connected to the input of the NOR gate associated with J_3. If there is no $\times$ on the intersection of input line x_i with the input line of the NOR gate producing J_j, then there must be a $\times$ on the intersection of the x_i line with the input line of the NOR gate producing K_j. This is because the output of the sub-circuit C_1 must be a two-rail code.

The design of a totally self-checking two-rail code checker has already been described (Sec. 5.2.1). Such a checker can also be designed using a PLA (Programmable Logic Array), implemented by two-level AND–OR, NAND–NAND, or NOR–NOR logic [5.13]. Khakbaz used NOR–NOR logic to implement the subcircuit C_2 for the two-rail code produced by subcircuit C_1. If C_1 has p-pairs of output lines, the PLA will have $2p$ input lines, two output lines and 2^p product terms. Such a PLA is self-testing for any single fault if it is inverter-free and its product terms and output lines are arranged according to the following rules [5.12]:

1. Every pair of adjacent product terms must belong to a different pattern.
2. Every pair of adjacent output lines must have different cross-point device patterns.

The PLA needed to check the two-rail code output of subcircuit C_1 is shown in Fig. 5.19. The complete circuit for the totally self-checking checker for a 1-out-of-8 code is shown in Fig. 5.20. A checker designed in this way can be tested by applying all of the n possible 1-out-of-n inputs. However, when n is not a power of 2, the two-rail checker circuit cannot be tested exhaustively by applying all possible code word inputs. For example, when $n = 5$ there are only 5 possible code inputs; however, since $p = 3$ the two-rail checker has to be tested with 8 $(= 2^3)$ two-rail code words. This problem can be overcome by rearranging the two-rail checker as shown in Fig. 5.21, when $n \neq 3$ and $n \neq 2^p$. This

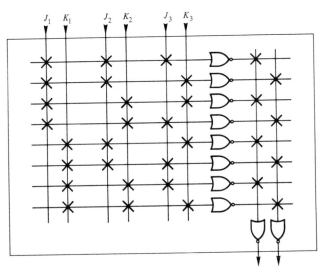

Fig. 5.19 Totally self-checking two-rail checker implemented with a PLA (subcircuit C_2).

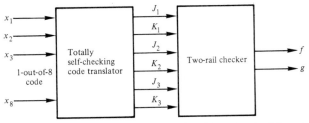

Fig. 5.20 Totally self-checking checker for a 1-out-of-8 code.

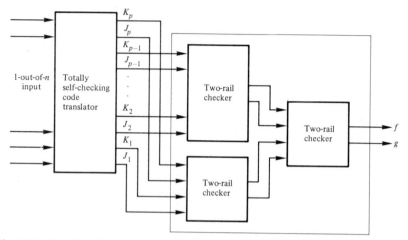

Fig. 5.21 Totally self-checking checker for a 1-out-of-n code when $n \neq 3$ and $n \neq 2^p$ (*courtesy of IEEE, © 1982*).

method is cheaper than that of Anderson [5.1] in terms of chip area for values of $n \leqslant 1024$, and faster for a few values of n (provided that n is a power of 2 and not more than 32).

5.2.3 Totally Self-checking Checker for Berger Codes

The Berger codes, like the m-out-of-n codes, detect all unidirectional faults. A Berger code of length n has I information bits and k check bits where $k = \lceil \log_2 (I + 1) \rceil$ and $n = I + k$. A code word is formed as follows: a binary number corresponding to the number of 1's in the information bits is formed and the binary complement of each digit in this number is taken; the resulting binary number forms the check bits. For example, if $I = 0101000$, $k = \lceil \log_2 (7 + 1) \rceil = 3$ and hence the Berger code must have a length of 10 ($= 7 + 3$). k check bits are derived as follows:

$$\text{Number of 1's in information bits } I = 2$$
$$\text{Binary equivalent of } 2 = 010$$

The bit by bit complement of 010 is 101, which are the k check bits. Thus

$$n = \underbrace{0101000}_{I} \underbrace{101}_{k}$$

Alternatively, the k check bits may be the binary number representing the number of 0's in I information bits.

If the number of information bits in a Berger code is $I = 2^k - 1, k \geqslant 1$, then it is called a "maximal length Berger code"; otherwise it is known as a "non-maximal-length Berger code". For example, the Berger code 0101000 101 is maximal length because $k = 3$ and $I = 7 = (2^k - 1)$, whereas 110100 011 is non-maximal length because $k = 3$ and $I = 6 \neq (2^k - 1)$.

The Berger codes have the following advantages [5.14]:

1. They are "separable" codes, i.e. no extra decoder is needed to separate the information bits.
2. They detect all unidirectional multiple faults.
3. They require the fewest number of check bits among all the separable codes.

As discussed before, the m-out-of-n codes also detect unidirectional multiple faults and they are less redundant than Berger codes. For large values of n, a Berger code requires twice the number of check bits required by an $(n/2)$-out-of-n code. However, the Berger codes are separable, whereas the m-out-of-n codes are not; consequently no extra hardware is needed to decode information bits in Berger codes.

Figure 5.22 shows the circuit for a totally self-checking checker for separable codes. C_1 is a non-redundant combinational network which generates the complements of the check bits from the information bits. The two-rail totally self-checking checker circuit compares the k check bits with the outputs of C_1.

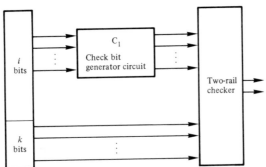

Fig. 5.22   Totally self-checking checker for separable codes.

Marouf and Friedman [5.14] have presented a procedure for designing totally self-checking checkers for maximal-length Berger codes. The combinational circuit C_1 of Fig. 5.22 generates the binary number corresponding to the number of 1's in the information bits. It is designed using a set of full-adder modules which add the information bits $(x_1, x_2, \ldots, x_{2k-1})$ in parallel and produce the binary number $g_1, g_2, \ldots, g_k$ corresponding to the number of 1's in the information bits. The number of adder modules required is

$$\sum_{a=1}^{k-1} 2^{a-1}(k - a)$$

where k is the number of check bits.

Thus for Berger codes with information bits $i = 3$ and check bits $k = 2$, the subcircuit C_1 of Fig. 5.22 is simply a full-adder module, where the sum output $s = g_1$ and the carry output $c = g_2$. Similarly for $i = 7$, $k = 3$, the number of adder modules needed to implement C_1 is 4, and for $i = 15$, $k = 4$, C_1 needs 11 modules.

The procedure to design subcircuit C_1 consists of the following steps:

1. Let $I = \{x_1, x_2, \ldots, x_i\}$ be the set of i information bits; set $m = k$ and $J = 1$.
2. Let $z = 2^{(m-1)} - 1$.
3. Partition I into three subsets A^J, B^J and E^J. A^J contains the left-most z bits, B^J contains the next z bits and E^J has the right-most bit.
4. Let $\underline{a}^J$ $(= a^J_{m-1}, a^J_{m-2}, \ldots, a^J_1)$, $\underline{b}^J$ $(= b^J_{m-1}, b^J_{m-2}, \ldots, b^J_1)$ and e^J be the binary representation of the number of 1's in subsets A^J, B^J and E^J respectively.
5. Let $\underline{g}^J$ $(= g^J_m, g^J_{m-1}, \ldots, g^J_1)$ be the binary representation of the number of 1's in set I. This is obtained from the following addition:

$$\underline{g}^J = \underline{a}^J + \underline{b}^J + e^J$$

In other words,

$$
\begin{array}{ccccccc}
 & a^J_{m-1} & a^J_{m-2} & \cdots & \cdots & a^J_1 \\
+ & b^J_{m-1} & b^J_{m-2} & \cdots & \cdots & b^J_1 \\
+ & & & & & e^J \\
\hline
g^J_m & g^J_{m-1} & g^J_{m-2} & \cdots & \cdots & g^J_1
\end{array}
$$

where g^J_m is the carry bit. $\underline{g}^J$ is generated using a ripple carry adder with $(m - 1)$ stages.

6. Go to step 8 if $m = 2$; otherwise, set $m = m - 1$, $L = J$.
7. Let $I = \{A^J\}$, $J = J + 1$; repeat steps 2-6 to generate $\underline{a}^L = \underline{g}^J$. $\underline{b}^L$ is generated in an identical manner by making $I = \{B^J\}$.
8. End.

The procedure is illustrated by designing the subcircuit C_1 for the case $i = 7$, $k = 3$, in steps:

1. $I = \{x_1, x_2, x_3, x_4, x_5, x_6, x_7\}$; $m = 3$, $J = 1$.
2. $z = 2^{(3-1)} - 1 = 3$.
3. $A^1 = \{x_1, x_2, x_3\}$, $B^1 = \{x_4, x_5, x_6\}$ and $E^1 = \{x_7\}$.
4. $\underline{a}^1 = (a^1_2, a^1_1)$, $\underline{b}^1 = (b^1_2, b^1_1)$, $e^1 = x_7$.
5. $\underline{g}^1 = (g^1_3, g^1_2, g^1_1)$ where g^1_3, g^1_2, g^1_1 are obtained from:

$$
\begin{array}{ccc}
 & a^1_2 & a^1_2 \\
+ & b^1_1 & b^1_1 \\
+ & & x_7 \\
\hline
g^1_3 & g^1_2 & g^1_1
\end{array}
$$

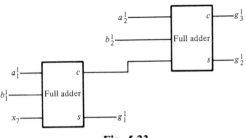

Fig. 5.23

Figure 5.23 shows the generation of $\underline{g}^1$ using a ripple carry adder with 2 $(= 3 - 1)$ stages.

6. $m > 2$, $m = 3 - 1 = 2$ and $L = 1$.
7. $I = \{A^1\} = \{x_1, x_2, x_3\}$, $J = 1 + 1 = 2$.
8. $z = 2^{(2-1)} - 1 = 1$ [Step 2].
9. $A^2 = \{x_1\}$, $B^2 = \{x_2\}$ and $E^2 = \{x_3\}$ [Step 3].
10. $\underline{a}^2 = a_1^2 = x_1$, $\underline{b}^2 = b_1^2 = x_2$, $e^2 = x_3$ [Step 4].
11. $\underline{g}^2 = (g_2^2, g_1^2)$, where g_2^2, g_1^2 are obtained from:

$$
\begin{array}{r}
x_1 \\
+ \quad x_2 \\
+ \quad x_3 \\
\hline
g_2^2 \quad g_1^2
\end{array}
\qquad \text{[Step 5]}
$$

Since $\underline{a}^L = \underline{g}^J$, we have

$$\underline{a}^1 = \underline{g}^2 \qquad \text{or} \qquad \{a_2^1, a_1^1\} = \{g_2^2, g_1^2\}$$

In other words, $g_1^2 = a_1^1$ and $g_2^2 = a_2^1$. $\underline{a}^1$ can be generated by a full adder as shown in Fig. 5.24(a). It can be shown in a similar manner by making $I = \{B^1\} = \{x_4, x_5, x_6\}$ so that

$$\underline{b}^1 = \underline{g}^2 \qquad \text{or} \qquad \{b_2^1, b_1^1\} = \{g_2^2, g_1^2\}$$

Figure 5.24(b) shows the generation of $\underline{b}^1$. Since $m = 2$ the procedure is terminated.

Figure 5.25 shows the complete design of the subcircuit C_1 for $i = 7$, $k = 3$; it is obtained by combining Fig. 5.23 and Fig. 5.24.

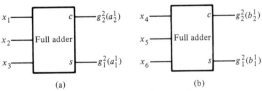

Fig. 5.24   (a) $\underline{a}^1$; (b) $\underline{b}^1$.

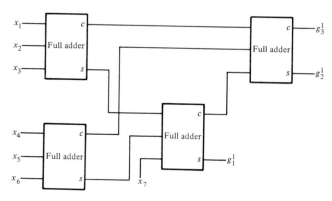

Fig. 5.25   The check bit generator circuit for $i = 7, k = 3$ (*courtesy of IEEE, © 1978*).

The check bit generator circuits designed by the above procedure can be tested for all single faults by applying only eight tests; these tests also detect all multiple faults occurring in a full-adder module. A procedure to generate four tests, none of which is identical or the complement of any other, is described below [5.14]. These four tests, together with their complements, result in the application of all eight possible input combinations to every full-adder module.

Let the set of information bits be ordered from left to right as $\{x_1, x_2, \ldots, x_j\}$, where $j = 2^k - 1$. The symbol X_i^m, $m \geqslant i$ denotes the ordered subset $\{x_1, x_2, \ldots, x_m\}$.

Steps in the procedure for generating tests:

1. Let $X_1^j(1) = 1$, $w = 1$. $X_1^j(z)$, $1 \leqslant z \leqslant 8$ denotes one of the eight input vectors associated with X_1^j.
2. Let $x_1(2) = x_1(3) = x_1(4) = 1$.
3. Go to step 8 if $w = k$.
4. Let $X_b^{(d-2)}(2) = X_1^{(b-1)}(2)$ and

$$X_{(d-1)}(2) = 0 \qquad \text{if } w \text{ is odd}$$
$$= 1 \qquad \text{if } w \text{ is even}$$

   where $b = 2^w$, $d = 2^{w+1}$.
5. Let $X_b^{(d-2)}(3) = [X_1^{(b-1)}(3)]$ and $x_{d-1}(3) = 1$; where $[\overline{X_1^{(b-1)}(3)}]$ denotes the complement of the vector $X_1^{(b-1)}(3)$.
6. Let $X_b^{(d-2)}(4) = [\overline{X_1^{(b-1)}(4)}]$ and

$$x_{(d-1)}(4) = 0 \qquad \text{if } w \text{ is odd}$$
$$= 1 \qquad \text{if } w \text{ is even}$$

7. Let $w = w + 1$; go to step 3.
8. $X_1^{(j-1)}(5) = [\overline{X_1^{(j-1)}(1)}] \qquad X_1^{(j-1)}(6) = [\overline{X_1^{(j-1)}(2)}]$

   $X_1^{(j-1)}(7) = [\overline{X_1^{(j-1)}(3)}] \qquad X_1^{(j-1)}(8) = [\overline{X_1^{(j-1)}(4)}]$

As an example let us apply the above procedure to generate tests for the circuit of Fig. 5.25. Figures 5.26(a) and (b) show the partial derivation of the tests for $w = 1$ and $w = 2$ respectively. When $w = 3 = k$, the test derivation is complete and the resulting eight tests are shown in Fig. 5.26(c).

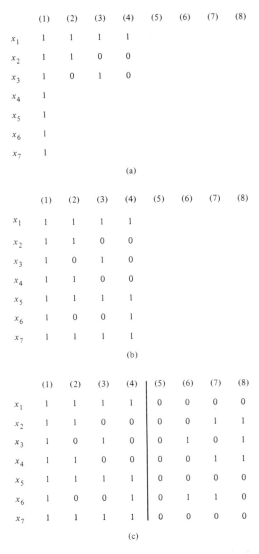

	(1)	(2)	(3)	(4)	(5)	(6)	(7)	(8)
x_1	1	1	1	1				
x_2	1	1	0	0				
x_3	1	0	1	0				
x_4	1							
x_5	1							
x_6	1							
x_7	1							

(a)

	(1)	(2)	(3)	(4)	(5)	(6)	(7)	(8)
x_1	1	1	1	1				
x_2	1	1	0	0				
x_3	1	0	1	0				
x_4	1	1	0	0				
x_5	1	1	1	1				
x_6	1	0	0	1				
x_7	1	1	1	1				

(b)

	(1)	(2)	(3)	(4)	(5)	(6)	(7)	(8)
x_1	1	1	1	1	0	0	0	0
x_2	1	1	0	0	0	0	1	1
x_3	1	0	1	0	0	1	0	1
x_4	1	1	0	0	0	0	1	1
x_5	1	1	1	1	0	0	0	0
x_6	1	0	0	1	0	1	1	0
x_7	1	1	1	1	0	0	0	0

(c)

Fig. 5.26   Test derivation for the circuit of Fig. 5.25: (a) $w = 1$; (b) $w = 2$; (c) $w = 3$.

A procedure for designing a totally self-checking checker for a non-maximal length Berger code has also been given by Marouf *et al.* [5.14]. Ashjaee and Reddy [5.15] have proved that corresponding to every non-maximal length Berger code there is an equivalent separable code, for which the checker of

Fig. 5.22 is totally self-checking. The procedure for constructing a separable code B equivalent to a given non-maximal length Berger code B_1 is as follows. Let B_1 be of length n_1 with I_1 information bits and $\lceil \log_2 (I_1 + 1) \rceil$ check bits. Let B be the maximal length Berger code with $\lceil \log_2 (I_1 + 1) \rceil$ check bits,

$$I = (2^{\lceil \log_2(I_1+1) \rceil} - 1)$$

information bits and length n.
Let C be the code defined below:

$$C = \{X : X \in B \text{ and } (I - I_1 + 1) = (n - n_1 + 1)$$
$$\text{left-most positions of } X \text{ are either all 0's or all 1's}\}$$

Then the separable code B'' is

$$B'' = \{Y : Y \text{ is obtained by deleting the left-most}$$
$$(I - I_1) = (n - n_1) \text{ positions of some code word of } C\}$$

B'' is a "complete separable" code equivalent to B_1 (a separable code is a "complete separable code", if and only if each one of the $2^{(n-I)}$ binary $(n - I)$-tuples appears in the check bits of some code word [5.15]. For example, let

$$B_1 = \{1100, 1001, 0101, 0010\} \qquad \text{with } I_1 = n_1 = 2$$

Then

$$B = \{00011, 00110, 01010, 10010, 01101, 10101, 11001, 11100\}$$
$$\text{with } I = n = 3$$

Hence

$$C = \{00011, 00110, 11001, 11100\}$$

and

$$B'' = \{0011, 0110, 1001, 1100\}$$

It can be seen that B'' is a complete separable code but B_1 is not.

The block diagram of the check bit generator is shown in Fig. 5.27. The zero counter counts the number of 0's in the information bits. The constant adder adds a 0 to the output of the zero counter if $i_1 = 1$; otherwise it adds

$$(n - n_1) = 2^{\lceil \log_2(k_1 + 1) \rceil} - k_1 - 1$$

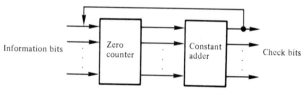

Fig. 5.27   Check bit generator for codes equivalent to Berger codes (*courtesy of IEEE, © 1977*).

5.2.4   Totally Self-checking Checker for Low-cost Residue Code

Residue codes are very useful in detecting errors in the results produced by arithmetic operations [5.16]. Like Berger codes, residue codes are also separable. This allows the data and the check bits to be handled separately. A *residue* is simply defined as the remainder after a division. The residue representation of an integer N may be obtained from

$$N = Im + r$$

where m is a check base and I is an integer, so that $0 \leqslant r < m$. The quantity r is called the *residue N modulo m* or

$$r = N \text{ modulo } m$$

In residue codes the information bits define a number $N \ [= \Sigma_{i=0}^{n} a^i (2^i)$; $a_i \in \{0, 1\}]$ and the check bits define a number $C \ (= N \text{ modulo } m)$. The number of check bits is given by $\lceil \log_2 m \rceil$.

For example, if the information bits are 1110 and $m = 3$, then $\log_2 \lceil 3 \rceil = 2$ check bits are required. Their values are given by

$$C = (14) \text{ modulo } 3$$

$$= 2, \text{ i.e. } 10 \text{ in binary}$$

One class of residue codes, known as "low-cost residue codes", has been found to be very effective in detecting unidirectional multiple errors. A low-cost residue code is obtained by making the check base m to have the form

$$m = 2^b - 1 \qquad b \geqslant 2$$

The check bits for such codes are of length b and obtained by performing a modulo-$(2^b - 1)$ addition of the information bits. This is usually done by dividing the number of information bits into k groups, each containing b bits. A modulo-$(2^b - 1)$ addition of the k b-bit groups results in the check bits. For example, let us calculate the check bits for information bits 10011110, assuming $b = 2$. The information bits must then be divided into four 2-bit groups. The groups are added together in modulo 3 $(= 2^2 - 1)$ binary adders with end-around carry. This technique is illustrated in Fig. 5.28(a). Using this technique the check bits for the given information bits are derived as follows:

$$10 + 01 + 11 + 10$$

$$= 11 + 10$$

$$= 10$$

If the number of information bits is not divisible by b, one of the adders gets less than $2b$ inputs; the missing bits are assumed to be 0's. For example, the check bits for information bits 10101100101 are generated by setting the missing bits equal to 0 as shown in Fig. 5.28(b).

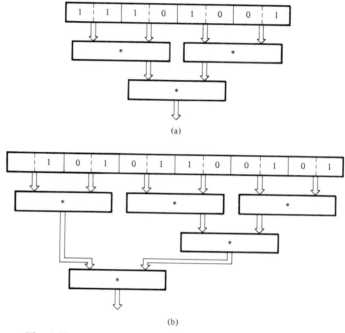

(a)

(b)

Fig. 5.28   Check bit generator for low-cost residue codes.
* Mod-3 adder.

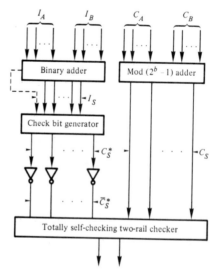

Fig. 5.29   Totally self-checking checker for low-cost residue codes. (Adapted from Ref. 5.15.)

Ashjaee and Reddy [5.15] have proposed a totally self-checking checker for low-cost residue codes. As suggested by Fig. 5.29 the checker compares the check bits of a code word with new check bits generated from the information bits of the code word. A disagreement between the two values is detected as a fault. The check bit generator is in fact a tree network of modulo-$(2^b - 1)$ adders. Under fault-free condition the check bits C_S^* are equal to C_S. The totally self-checking two-rail comparator checks whether C_S and $\overline{C_S^*}$ are bit-by-bit complements of each other or not.

However, in certain cases C_S^* may not be equal to C_S even under fault-free operation. For example, in the adder circuit of Fig. 5.29 let $I_A = 1110$ and $I_B = 0010$, then $C_A = 10$, $C_B = 10$ assuming $b = 2$. If 2's complement addition is performed, $I_S = 0000$, $C_S = 01$ and $C_S^* = 00 \neq C_S$. The reason for this is that $C_S = C_S^*$ (for all I_A and I_B) if 1's complement addition is assumed and the number of information bits is divisible by b. If 2's complement or sign-magnitude arithmetic is used, the carry-out bit of the binary adder must be included as the most significant position of the sum bits (as shown by the dotted line in Fig. 5.29). In this case $I_S = I_A + I_B = 10000$ instead of 0000 and $C_S^* = 01 = C_S$ when there is no fault.

5.3   SELF-CHECKING SEQUENTIAL MACHINES

The concepts of self-testing and fault-secureness given in Sec. 5.1 can be extended to sequential machines [5.17]. A sequential machine is self-testing if, for every fault in a fault set, there is a code space input/state pair in the circuit such that a non-code-space output is produced. A sequential machine is fault-secure if, for every fault from a faulty set, the machine never produces an incorrect code space output for code space inputs. Thus it is possible for the machine to pass through several incorrect states maintaining correct code space output, before an error indication is given. A sequential machine is totally self-checking if it is both self-testing and fault-secure.

The problem of designing totally self-checking synchronous sequential machines has been examined by Diaz [5.18] and Ozguner [5.19].

Diaz described a procedure for designing Moore-type sequential machines. The first step of the procedure is to select code words S_X, S_Y and S_Z, which are used during normal operation of the machine, by the combinations of primary inputs, state variables and outputs respectively. If the machine has m inputs, p outputs and n states, then

$$\{S_X\} \subseteq \{m\text{-out-of-}2m \text{ code words}\}$$

$$\{S_Y\} \subseteq \{n/2\text{-out-of-}n \text{ code words}\}$$

and

$$\{S_Z\} \subseteq \{p\text{-out-of-}2p \text{ code words}\}$$

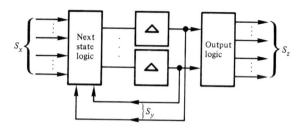

Fig. 5.30   Self-checking sequential machine model (*courtesy of IEEE,* © *1979*).

Figure 5.30 shows a model of the proposed self-checking sequential machine.

If the states of a machine are coded by using a k-out-of-n code, it is possible to express Y_i, the next state corresponding to y_i, by monotonic equations (which require only uncomplemented variables) [5.20]:

$$Y_i = \sum_j I_j(M_{j1} + \ldots + M_{jp})$$

with

$$M_{jn} = y_{n1} \ldots y_{nk}$$

where $y_{n1} \ldots y_{nk}$ are the variables having the value 1 in a present state q_n that is transferred by input I_j to a state with $Y_i = 1$. This is called an "on-set" realization.

Each output Z is represented by a pair $(Z_1, \bar{Z}_1) \in S = \{(0, 1), (1, 0)\}$, when the machine is fault-free. Then, as the machine is of the Moore type, the outputs can be expressed as functions of the states. Hence for each state q coded by $y_{n1} \ldots y_{nk}$,

$$Z = f(q) = 1 \Rightarrow \begin{cases} Z_1 = y_{n1} \ldots y_{nk} \\ \bar{Z}_1 = 0 \end{cases}$$

$$Z = f(q) = 0 \Rightarrow \begin{cases} Z_1 = 0 \\ \bar{Z}_1 = y_{n1} \ldots y_{nk} \end{cases}$$

This realization can easily be extended to the set of states and the set of outputs in a machine, and is called "on-set" realization of outputs. As an example, consider the state table of the Moore-type machine shown in Fig. 5.31(a); the encoded state table is shown in Fig. 5.31(b).

From Fig. 5.31(b), it can be derived that

$$S_x = \{01, 10\} \quad S_y = \{0011, 0101, 1010, 1001\} \quad \text{and} \quad S_z = \{01, 10\}$$

Present state	Input x = 0	x = 1	Output Z
A	C	A	1
B	D	C	1
C	B	D	0
D	C	A	0
	Next state		

(a)

$y_4\, y_3\, y_2\, y_1$	I_2 01	I_1 10	Z	$\bar{Z}$
0011	1010	0011	1	0
0101	1001	1011	1	0
1010	0101	1001	0	1
1001	1010	0011	0	1

(b)

Fig. 5.31   A Moore-type sequential machine: (a) state table; (b) input, state and output assignment.

The next state and output equations can be written in "on-set" form as follows:

$$Y_1 = I_1 \overset{\downarrow}{y_1} y_3 + \overset{\downarrow}{I_1} y_2 y_4 + I_2 \overset{\downarrow}{y_1} y_2 + \overset{\downarrow}{I_2} \overset{\downarrow}{y_2} \overset{\downarrow}{y_4} + I_2 \overset{\downarrow}{y_1} y_4$$

$$Y_2 = \overset{\downarrow}{I_1} y_1 y_2 + \overset{\downarrow}{I_1} y_1 y_4 + \overset{\downarrow}{I_2} y_1 \overset{\downarrow}{y_2} + I_2 \overset{\downarrow}{y_1} y_3 + I_2 y_1 \overset{\downarrow}{y_4}$$

$$Y_3 = I_1 y_2 y_4$$

$$Y_4 = I_1 y_1 \overset{\downarrow}{y_2} + \overset{\downarrow}{I_1} \overset{\downarrow}{y_1} \overset{\downarrow}{y_3} + I_1 y_1 \overset{\downarrow}{y_4} + \overset{\downarrow}{I_2} \overset{\downarrow}{y_1} y_3 + I_2 y_2 y_4$$

$$Z = y_1 y_2 + y_2 y_4$$

$$\bar{Z} = y_1 y_3 + y_1 y_4$$

The next state and output equations are realized using two-level AND–OR logic. Each implicant in the above expressions is a test for the corresponding AND gate and the output of the OR gate, for s-a-0 faults. The significance of the arrows is explained later.

Let M be the set of implicants, corresponding to the input vectors $(S_x \times X_y)$, applied to the next state logic and M_i be the set of implicants for Y_i $(i = 1, n)$. Then

$$M = \{I_1 y_1 y_2,\ I_1 y_1 y_3,\ I_1 y_1 y_4,\ I_2 y_1 y_3,\ I_2 y_2 y_4,\ I_2 y_1 y_2,\ I_2 y_1 y_4,\ I_1 y_2 y_4\}$$

$$M_1 = \{I_1 y_1 y_3,\ I_1 y_2 y_4,\ I_2 y_1 y_2,\ I_2 y_2 y_4,\ I_2 y_1 y_4\}$$

$$M_2 = \{I_1 y_1 y_2,\ I_1 y_1 y_4,\ I_2 y_1 y_2,\ I_2 y_1 y_3,\ I_2 y_1 y_4\}$$

$$M_3 = \{I_1 y_2 y_4\}$$

$$M_4 = \{I_1 y_1 y_2,\ I_1 y_1 y_3,\ I_1 y_1 y_4,\ I_2 y_1 y_3,\ I_2 y_2 y_4\}$$

Hence

$$M - M_1 = \{I_1 y_1 y_2, I_1 y_1 y_4, I_2 y_1 y_3\}$$

$$M - M_2 = \{I_1 y_1 y_3, I_2 y_2 y_4, I_1 y_2 y_4\}$$

$$M - M_3 = \{I_1 y_1 y_2, I_1 y_1 y_3, I_1 y_1 y_4, I_2 y_1 y_3, I_2 y_2 y_4, I_2 y_1 y_2, I_2 y_1 y_4\}$$

$$M - M_4 = \{I_2 y_2 y_4, I_2 y_1 y_2, I_2 y_1 y_4, I_1 y_2 y_4\}$$

A "divider" of an implicant, with respect to one of the variables appearing in it, is obtained by making the variable equal to 1 in the implicant. For instance, the divider of the implicant $I_1 y_2 y_4$ with respect to I_1 is $y_2 y_4$. This divider means that in order to test I_1 s-a-1, an input combination in which $y_2 = y_4 = 1$ is required.

In order to find the untested AND gate inputs, each implicant in M_i ($i = 1, n$) is considered successively. If the divider of an implicant with respect to one of its variables is not included in one implicant of $\{M - M_i\}$, the input of the AND gate corresponding to that variable is not tested. For example, the divider of implicant $I_1 y_2 y_4$ with respect to I_1, i.e. $y_2 y_4$, is not included in any implicant of $\{M - M_1\}$; therefore input I_1 of the AND gate realizing $I_1 y_2 y_4$ is not tested. The untested inputs in Y_1, Y_2, Y_3 and Y_4 can be found in this manner and are marked with arrows.

The self-testing functions $Y_{1(ST)}$, $Y_{2(ST)}$, $Y_{3(ST)}$ and $Y_{4(ST)}$ are obtained by removing the untested inputs:

$$Y_{1(ST)} = I_1 y_3 + y_2 y_4 + I_2 y_2 + I_2 y_4$$

$$Y_{2(ST)} = y_1 y_2 + y_1 y_4 + I_2$$

$$Y_{3(ST)} = I_1 y_2 y_4$$

$$Y_{4(ST)} = I_1 y_1 + I_2 y_2 y_4 + y_3$$

The untested inputs in the output logic can be found in the same manner:

$$M = \{y_1 y_2, y_2 y_4, y_1 y_3, y_1 y_4\}$$

$$M - M_1 = \{y_2 y_4, y_1 y_4\}$$

$$M - M_2 = \{y_1 y_2, y_1 y_3\}$$

Hence

$$Z = y_1 y_2 + \overset{\downarrow}{y_1} y_3 \qquad \bar{Z} = \overset{\downarrow}{y_2} y_4 + \overset{\downarrow}{y_1} y_4$$

The output logic is not self-checking, so an extra self-checking checker for 2-out-of-4 has to be added to the output logic. The totally self-checking realization of the output logic is shown in Fig. 5.32.

Ozguner presented a method for designing totally self-checking Mealy-type synchronous sequential machines. In principle her method is very similar to

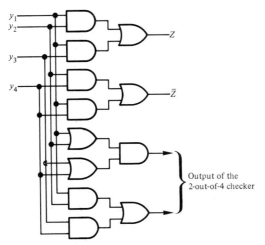

Fig. 5.32 Totally self-checking realization of the output logic of Fig. 5.31.

that of Diaz; it uses 1-out-of-n code for state assignment, and 1-out-of-p code for the input states. The outputs can be encoded with any code in which the code words have no ordering relation. As an example, let us consider the sequential machine shown in Fig. 5.33(a). It has $n = 4$ internal states, $p = 4$ input states. Hence the internal states and the input states can be encoded using 1-out-of-4 code; the outputs are encoded using 1-out-of-2 code. The encoded state table is shown in Fig. 5.33(b).

	Input			
State	$\bar{x}_1\bar{x}_2$	$\bar{x}_1 x_2$	$x_1\bar{x}_2$	$x_1 x_2$
S_1	$S_2,0$	$S_2,1$	$S_4,1$	$S_1,1$
S_2	$S_2,0$	$S_3,0$	$S_4,1$	$S_1,1$
S_3	$S_1,0$	$S_4,0$	$S_3,0$	$S_1,1$
S_4	$S_2,1$	$S_1,0$	$S_4,0$	$S_1,0$

(a)

	$I_4 I_3 I_2 I_1$, $Z\bar{Z}$			
$y_4 y_3 y_2 y_1$	0 0 0 1	0 0 1 0	0 1 0 0	1 0 0 0
0 0 0 1	0 0 1 0,0 1	0 0 1 0,1 0	1 0 0 0,1 0	0 0 0 1,1 0
0 0 1 0	0 0 1 0,0 1	0 1 0 0,0 1	1 0 0 0,1 0	0 0 0 1,1 0
0 1 0 0	0 0 0 1,0 1	1 0 0 0,0 1	0 1 0 0,0 1	0 0 0 1,1 0
1 0 0 0	0 0 1 0,1 0	0 0 0 1,0 1	1 0 0 0,0 1	0 0 0 1,0 1

(b)

Fig. 5.33 (a) State table; (b) code assignment.

The next state and output equation are written in the on-set form as follows:

$$Y_1 = I_1 y_3 + I_2 y_4 + I_4 y_1 + I_4 y_2 + I_4 y_3 + I_4 y_4$$

$$Y_2 = I_1 y_1 + I_1 y_2 + I_1 y_4 + I_2 y_1$$

$$Y_3 = I_2 y_2 + I_3 y_3$$

$$Y_4 = I_2 y_3 + I_3 y_1 + I_3 y_2 + I_3 y_4$$

$$Z = I_1 y_4 + I_2 y_1 + I_3 y_1 + I_3 y_2 + I_4 y_1 + I_4 y_2 + I_4 y_3$$

$$\overline{Z} = I_1 y_1 + I_1 y_2 + I_1 y_3 + I_4 y_4 + I_2 y_2 + I_2 y_3$$

$$+ I_2 y_4 + I_3 y_3 + I_3 y_4$$

The output circuit uses the same AND gates as the excitation circuit. Any s-a-0 fault in the excitation circuit causes the next state to be all 0's; the output will produce a non-code output at the next clock pulse. An s-a-0 fault in the OR gates of the output circuit also causes a non-code output. Any s-a-0 fault on the input connections causes the outputs to be all 0's. All single s-a-1 faults in the excitation circuit except those on AND inputs, are equivalent to single s-a-1 faults on state variables. If the state variable y_k is s-a-1, then for input I_j and any state S_i the output of the machine will be

$$Z(I_j, S_k) \lor Z(I_j, S_i)$$

This is because y_k at logic 1 corresponds to state S_k. For example, if y_4 is s-a-1 and the machine is in state S_1 (or S_2, S_3), the output in response to I_1 will be a non-code output:

$$Z(I_1, S_1) \lor Z(I_1, S_4)$$

$$= 01 \lor 10 = 11$$

Similarly, if the input I_j is s-a-1, then for state S_k and any input I_i the output will be

$$Z(S_k, I_j) \lor Z(S_k, I_i)$$

For example, if input I_1 is s-a-1 and the machine is in state S_2, the output in response to I_3 (or I_4) is

$$Z(S_2, I_1) \lor Z(S_2, I_2)$$

$$= 01 \lor 10 = 11$$

In general sequential machines designed by this method will produce non-code output in presence of faults provided the following two conditions are met:

(a) $\forall (S_k, I_j) \quad k = 1 \ldots n, \quad j = 1 \ldots p \quad \exists (S_i, I_j), \, i \neq k$
     such that $Z(S_i, I_j) \neq Z(S_k, I_j)$

(b) $\forall (S_k, I_j) \quad k = 1 \ldots n, \quad j = 1 \ldots p \quad \exists (S_k, I_i), \, i \neq j$
     such that $Z(S_k, I_i) \neq Z(S_k, I_j)$

It would be necessary to add additional outputs to machines which do not satisfy these rules. Since the output circuit is realized using the same AND gates as the excitation circuit, the additional logic will be an OR gate for each extra output.

Both the designs presented are totally self-checking for single and unidirectional multiple faults. The advantage of Ozguner's method is that it does not require the addition of a totally self-checking checker, if the sequential machine does not have a code-disjoint output.

5.4 PARTIALLY SELF-CHECKING CIRCUITS

A "partially self-checking" circuit is self-testing for a set of inputs N (which occur during normal operation of the circuit) and a fault set F_t, and it is fault-secure for a set I (a proper subset of N) and a fault set F_s [5.21]. In other words, all faults in F_t are tested in normal operation of a partially self-checking circuit. In addition, faults in F_s cannot produce incorrect code words at the output as long as the inputs lie within the subset I.

A partially self-checking circuit can operate either in "secure mode" or "insecure mode". When the inputs to a partially self-checking circuit are from the set I, the circuit is in "secure mode". When the inputs are from the set $(N - I)$, the circuit operates in "insecure mode". In the secure mode, every fault in the circuit is tested during normal operation and no fault can cause an undetectable error. In other words, a partially self-checking network operating in the secure mode is totally self-checking. On the other hand, undetected errors may occur in insecure mode and erroneous results may be transmitted to the output. If the circuit operates infrequently in the insecure mode, the probability of a fault-transmitting erroneous result is low. However, a temporary fault in the insecure mode may cause an undetectable error. Therefore, partially self-checking circuits should not be used in applications where immediate fault detection is required and undetected errors cannot be tolerated.

Wakerly [5.21] has proposed models for three types of partially self-checking networks. The simplest partially self-checking network is the Type 1 model shown in Fig. 5.34(a). Depending on whether the control lines $C_1 C_0 = 01$ or 10, the network operates in the secure or insecure mode respectively. The disadvantage of this type of network is that the output of the functional circuit may be a non-code word in insecure mode.

In Type 2 network (Fig. 5.34(b)) the output code of the functional circuit is separable, and a check symbol generator computes a new check symbol from the data output of the functional circuit. A totally self-checking equality checker compares the generated check symbol with that of the functional circuit producing the output 01 or 10 for a match. In the secure mode $(C_1 C_0 = 01)$ the error indicator is enabled, whereas in the insecure mode $(C_1 C_0 = 10)$ it is forced, to produce the "good" output 10. However, there is no guarantee that code outputs will be correct outputs during insecure mode.

The Type 3 network, illustrated in Fig. 5.34(c), causes less delay than a Type 2 network in producing functional output during the secure mode operation. This is because in a Type 2 network the check symbol is re-encoded using the check generator, whereas in a Type 3 network the delay is equal to the propagation delay of the multiplexer, which switches the check symbol to the output of the network when $C_1 C_0 = 01$ (secure mode). During the insecure mode $(C_1 C_0 = 10)$, the check symbol generator output is switched to the network output. The totally self-checking equality checker compares the generated check symbol with itself producing a "good" output. Both Type 2 and Type 3 networks have the same delay during insecure mode. The problem with the Type 3 network is that a faulty output from the functional circuit, during secure mode, may be used before the error is detected by the checker.

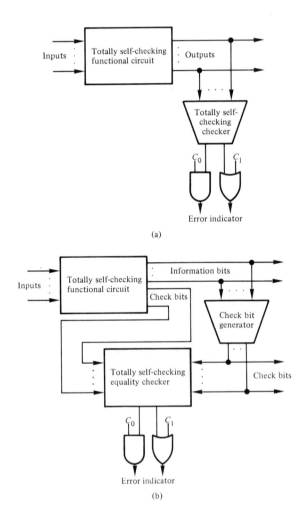

(a)

(b)

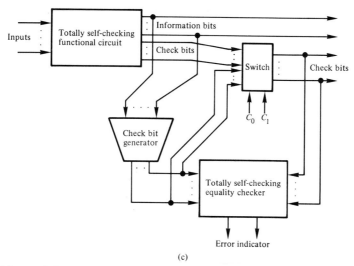

Fig. 5.34   Partially self-checking networks: (a) Type I; (b) Type II; (c) Type III
(*courtesy of IEEE*, © *1974*).

5.5   STRONGLY FAULT-SECURE CIRCUITS

The effectiveness of totally self-checking circuits is based on the assumptions
that each fault belongs to a considered fault set, and that faults occur
sequentially with the time interval between two successive faults long enough
to allow all code inputs to be applied to the circuits for testing. Thus a totally
self-checking circuit produces a non-code word as the erroneous output, if a
fault is present.

If a circuit is fault-secure but not self-testing for a fault set F, there could be
a fault $f_1 \in F$ which does not produce non-code word outputs when code
inputs are applied. In other words fault f_1 is not detectable. When a second
fault $f_2 \in F$ occurs, the circuit has a combined fault $f_1 \cup f_2$ which may not
belong to F. Therefore the circuit is not guaranteed to be fault-secure with
respect to $f_1 \cup f_2$, and an incorrect code word may be produced. On the other
hand the circuit may be fault-secure and self-testing with respect to $f_1 \cup f_2$
even though $f_1 \cup f_2 \notin F$. In general, for a fault sequence a circuit may be fault-
secure with respect to any initial subsequence, and self-testing for the combination of faults in the sequence. Let m be the smallest integer for which the
combination of faults $f_1, f_2, \ldots, f_m$ belonging to the fault sequence
$\langle f_1, f_2, \ldots, f_x \rangle$ does not produce the correct code output for at least one
input code word; if there is no such m, set $m = x$. Then the circuit is *strongly
fault secure* with respect to the fault sequence, if for any code input the output
produced by the circuit in the presence of the combination of $f_1, f_2, \ldots, f_m$ is
either correct or is a non-code word. A circuit is strongly fault-secure with

respect to a set of faults F if it is strongly fault-secure with respect to all fault sequences whose members belong to F [5.22]. It is easy to see that under the previously given fault assumptions any strongly fault-secure circuit achieves the "totally self-checking goal". However, a circuit which is fault-secure but not strongly fault-secure can produce an incorrect code output before a non-code output, while satisfying the two fault assumptions.

5.6   FAIL-SAFE DESIGN

Fail-safe realization is one approach to highly reliable system design. In a fail-safe system the output assumes one of the predetermined safe values when a fault occurs. For example, if 0 is the safe state of the output and 1 the unsafe state, then a fault could change the output from 1 to 0, but could not cause an incorrect 1 on the output. Thus a fault within a fail-safe system causes the system to produce safe-side output so that the extent of possible damage is reduced. A traffic-light which is stuck at red when faulty is an example of such a system.

5.6.1   Fail-safe Design of Synchronous Sequential Circuits using Partition Theory

A synchronous sequential circuit is $0(1)$-fail-safe if any failure in either the internal state or output logic causes only incorrect $0(1)$ and correct $1(0)$ outputs. Fail-safe synchronous sequential circuits can be designed using partition theory [5.23] as described below.

Let us consider a Mealy-type sequential machine $M(I, S, Z, \delta, \omega)$ as shown in Fig. 5.35, where

$I =$ set of input symbols
$S =$ set of states
$Z =$ set of output symbols
$\delta =$ state transition function $\delta: I \times S \to S$
$\omega =$ output function $\omega: I \times S \to Z$

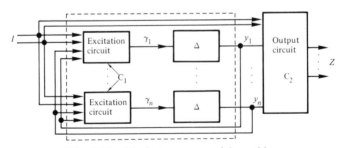

Fig. 5.35   Mealy-type sequential machine.

Since the output circuit C_2 of Fig. 5.35 is combinational, a fail-safe combinational circuit must be used for C_2 |5.24|. Let us consider only the failures that occur in the excitation circuit C_1. Furthermore, the following assumptions are made:

1. Input variables are error free.
2. There is no failure in the clock circuitry.
3. Only single and unidirectional multiple faults can occur.

Let S_R be the set of states that occur in the sequential machine under failure conditions; states of S will be called "normal" states and states of S_R will be called "erroneous" states. One condition for a fail-safe circuit is

$$S \cap S_R = \emptyset \qquad (5.1)$$

Equation (5.1) and the definition of S_R require that an erroneous state goes over to a state that must belong to S_R when an arbitrary input value is applied.

Let Δ be a completely specified state transition function such as

$$\forall x \in I, \forall q \in S \qquad \Delta(x, q) = \delta(x, q) \in S \qquad (5.2)$$

and let Δ^e be a modification of Δ by a failure condition. Then under normal conditions,

$$\forall x \in I, \forall q \in S \qquad \Delta(x, q) = \delta(x, q) = q' \in S \qquad (5.3a)$$

and under failure conditions

$$\forall x \in I, \forall q_e \in S_R \qquad \Delta^e(x, q_e) = q'_e \in S_R \qquad (5.3b)$$

A realization of sequential machine is said to be "state fail-safe" if it satisfied equations (5.1), (5.2) and (5.3) |5.25|. A "state fail-safe" machine can be made fail-safe by assigning the safe-side output to erroneous states. Figure 5.36 shows the state table of a synchronous sequential machine; also shown in Fig. 5.36 is an internal state assignment (Fig. 5.36(b)) and the next state equations (Fig. 5.36(c)), where Y_1 and Y_2 are the next state variables; y_1 and y_2 are the present state variables and $I_1 - I_2$ are the input states. Each state variable y_i

Present state	Input I_1	I_2			y_1	y_2
A	A,0	B,0		A	0	0
B	A,0	C,1		B	0	1
C	B,0	D,0		C	1	1
D	C,1	D,0		D	1	0
(a)				(b)		

$$Y_1 = I_1 y_1 \bar{y}_2 + I_2(y_1 + y_2)$$
$$Y_2 = I_1 y_1 + I_2 \bar{y}_1$$
(c)

Fig. 5.36 (a) State table of machine A; (b) a state assignment; (c) next state equations.

can be defined in terms of a "τ-partition" τ_i, which partitions those states where $y_i = 1$ in the first block from those states where $y_i = 0$ in the second block. For the state table of Fig. 5.36 the τ-partitions are:

$$\tau_1 = \{CD; AB\}$$

$$\tau_2 = \{BC; AD\}$$

A "next-state partition" η_i^p partitions those states where the next-state variable Y_i is 1 from those states where $Y_i = 0$ under input I_p. Hence, for machine A:

$$\eta_1^1 = \{D; ABC\}$$

$$\eta_2^1 = \{CD; AB\}$$

$$\eta_1^2 = \{BCD; A\}$$

$$\eta_2^2 = \{AB; CD\}$$

An "output partition", γ_j^p is a two-block partition, where elements of one block are those states where $Z_j = 1$ and the elements of the other block are those states where $Z_j = 0$ for input state I_p. For machine A

$$\gamma_1^1 = \{C; ABC\}$$

$$\gamma_1^2 = \{B; ACD\}$$

The next-state and the output equations are expressed in the following form

$$Y_i = f_{i1}(y)I_1 + f_{i2}(y)I_2 + \cdots + f_{im}(y)I_m$$
$$Z_j = g_{j1}(y)I_1 + g_{j2}(y)I_2 + \cdots + g_{jm}(y)I_m \tag{5.4}$$

where Y_i is the next-state variable, $f_{ip}(y)$ and $g_{jp}(y)$ are functions of the state variables only, I_p denotes the input state, and Z_j the output.

A "p-set" is a collection of the p states that have the same next-state entry under an input. Machine A has six p-sets as shown below:

The p-sets under I_1 are $p_1 = (AB)$, $p_2 = (C)$ and $p_3 = (D)$

The p-sets under I_2 are $p_4 = (CD)$, $p_5 = (A)$ and $p_6 = (B)$

The procedure for deriving state assignments consists of the following steps:

1. List the p-sets for each input state, deleting those contained in a trivial column. (A trivial column is one which has only one p-set.)
2. Form a τ-partition with each unique p_x in the list in the following way

$$\tau_1 = \{p_1; p_2, p_3, \ldots, p_x\}$$
$$\tau_2 = \{p_2; p_1, p_3, \ldots, p_x\}$$
$$\vdots$$
$$\tau_x = \{p_x; p_1, p_2, \ldots, p_{x-1}\} \tag{5.5}$$

3. Form the η_i^p partitions for each input I_p.
4. Find the coefficients f_{ip} in the next state equation, namely equation (5.4), using the following:

    (a) If all the elements of η_i^p are in one block, then $f_{ip} = 1$ or 0.
    (b) Let τ_i, $i = 1, 2, \ldots, x$ partition the x p-sets p_i of I_p in the form of equation (5.5).

    For all f_{ip} terms, $i = 1, 2, \ldots, x$; $f_{ip} = y_i$
    For $j \neq (1, 2, \ldots, x)$, if $\eta_j^p = \tau_i$ then $f_{jp} = y_i$
    If $\eta_j^p = \{p_1, p_2, \ldots, p_m ; p_{m+1}, \ldots, p_x\}$, $m < x$, then

    $$f_{jp} = y_1 + y_2 + \cdots + y_m .$$

The output is obtained in the following manner:

(a) List the output partitions γ_i^p.
(b) If $\gamma_i^p = \{p_1, p_2, \ldots, p_r ; p_{r+1} \cdots p_x\}$, $r < x$, the coefficient terms g_{ip} in the output equation (5.1) are:

$$g_{ip} = y_1 + y_2 + \cdots + y_r$$

The complete design of a fail-safe machine is now illustrated for the state table of Fig. 5.37.

		Input		
Present state	I_1	I_2	I_3	I_4
A	C,0	C,0	A,0	A,0
B	B,1	C,0	D,1	A,0
C	C,0	B,0	A,0	A,0
D	B,1	A,0	D,1	A,0
E	E,0	E,0	A,0	A,0

Fig. 5.37 The state table of a sequential machine.

The p-sets under each input are

I_1	I_2	I_3	I_4
(AC)	(AB)	(ACE)	(ABCDE)
(BD)	(C)	(BD)	
(E)	(D)		
	(E)		

In the above list, there are two p-sets containing state E only, two p-sets containing states B and D only, and I_4 is a trivial column. Hence the reduced list of p-sets is

$$p_1 = (AC) \qquad p_4 = (AB) \qquad p_7 = (ACE)$$

$$p_2 = (BD) \qquad p_5 = (C)$$

$$p_3 = (E) \qquad p_6 = (D)$$

The τ-partitions generated from these p-sets are

$$\tau_1 = (AC; BDE) \qquad \tau_4 = (AB; CDE) \qquad \tau_7 = (ACE; BD)$$

$$\tau_2 = (BD; ACE) \qquad \tau_5 = (C; ABDE)$$

$$\tau_3 = (E; ABCD) \qquad \tau_6 = (D; ABCE)$$

The partitioning variables for I_1, I_2 and I_3 are (τ_1, τ_2, τ_3), $(\tau_3, \tau_4, \tau_5, \tau_6)$ and (τ_2, τ_7). Therefore the fail-safe state assignment for machine is

	y_1	y_2	y_3	y_4	y_5	y_6	y_7
A	1	0	0	1	0	0	1
B	0	1	0	1	0	0	0
C	1	0	0	0	1	0	1
D	0	1	0	0	0	1	0
E	0	0	1	0	0	0	1

The next state partitions are

	I_1	I_2	I_3	I_4
η_1	$AC; BDE$	$ABD; CE$	$ACE; BD$	$ABCDE; \emptyset$
η_2	$BD; ACE$	$C; ABDE$	$BD; ACE$	$\emptyset; ABCDE$
η_3	$E; ABCD$	$E; ABCD$	$\emptyset; ABCDE$	$\emptyset; ABCDE$
η_4	$BD; ACE$	$C; ABDE$	$ACE; BD$	$\emptyset; ABCDE$
η_5	$AC; BDE$	$AB; CDE$	$\emptyset; ABCDE$	$\emptyset; ABCDE$
η_6	$\emptyset; ABCDE$	$\emptyset; ABCDE$	$BD; ACE$	$\emptyset; ABCDE$
η_7	$ACE; BD$	$ABDE; C$	$ACE; BD$	$\emptyset; ABCDE$

The resulting next-state equations appear below:

$$Y_1 = y_1 \cdot I_1 + y_4 \cdot I_2 + y_6 \cdot I_2 + y_7 \cdot I_3 + I_4$$

$$Y_2 = y_2 \cdot I_1 + y_5 \cdot I_2 + y_2 \cdot I_3$$

$$Y_3 = y_3 \cdot I_1 + y_3 \cdot I_2$$

$$Y_4 = y_2 \cdot I_1 + y_5 \cdot I_2 + y_7 \cdot I_3$$

$$Y_5 = y_1 \cdot I_1 + y_4 \cdot I_2$$

$$Y_6 = y_2 \cdot I_3$$

$$Y_7 = y_7 \cdot I_1 + y_3 \cdot I_2 + y_4 \cdot I_2 + y_6 \cdot I_2 + y_7 \cdot I_3$$

The above equations are obtained by using step 4 of the design procedure. For example, the next state equation for Y_1 is

$$Y_1 = f_{11} \cdot I_1 + f_{12} \cdot I_2 + f_{13} \cdot I_3 + f_{14} \cdot I_4$$

Since $\eta_1^1 = \{AC; BDE\}$ ($\langle y_1; y_2, y_3\rangle$), $f_{11} = y_1$ by step 4b. For the input I_2, $\eta_1^2 = \{ABD; CE\}$ ($\langle y_4, y_6; y_3, y_5\rangle$) hence $f_{12} = y_4 + y_6$. Likewise $\eta_1^3 = \{ACE; BD\}$ ($\langle y_7; y_2\rangle$), $f_{13} = y_7$. Finally, since $\eta_1^4 = \{ABDE, \varnothing\}$, $f_{14} = 1$.

The output is obtained by listing the γ_i^p partitions first.

	I_1	I_2	I_3	I_4
γ	$BD; ACE$	$\varnothing; ABCDE$	$BD; ACE$	$\varnothing; ABCD$

The output equation is

$$Z_1 = g_{11} \cdot I_1 + g_{12} \cdot I_2 + g_{13} \cdot I_3 + g_{14} \cdot I_4 \tag{5.6}$$

For each $\gamma_i^p = \{p_1, p_2 \ldots p_r; p_{r+1}, p_{r+2} \ldots p_x\}$, g_{ip} can be expressed in two ways:

$$g_{ip} = y_1 + y_2 + \cdots + y_r \quad \text{and} \quad g_{ip} = \overline{y_{r+1}} \cdot \overline{y_{r+2}} \cdots \cdots \overline{y_x}$$

Since each copy of g_{ip} is formed with different partitioning variables of input I_p, two independent copies (Z_{i1} and Z_{i2}) of Z_i can be formed. Using this concept, the two copies of output for Z_1 of equation (5.4) are:

$$Z_{11} = y_2 \cdot I_1 + y_2 \cdot I_3$$

$$Z_{12} = \bar{y}_1 \bar{y}_3 \cdot I_1 + \bar{y}_7 \cdot I_3$$

Once two copies of the output logic are generated, tying together or "dotting" the outputs of the two redundant gates which realize Z_i forms the basis for a dotted-logic error-correcting scheme. Dotting increases the network reliability since there are fewer failure possibilities for a dotted connection than for the equivalent logic structure |5.26|.

To make the output logic 1-fail-safe, two copies of Z_i, Z_{i1} and Z_{i2} are dot-ORed; a 0-fail-safe system is achieved by forming the dot-AND between Z_{i1} and Z_{i2}. A 1-fail-safe system is obtained by realizing the internal state and output logic using two-level AND–OR synthesis. An incorrect 1 on Z will cause an incorrect 1 output, but an incorrect 0 will be corrected by the dot-OR connection. A 0-fail-safe system is obtained by realizing the logic using two-level NAND synthesis. In this case an incorrect 0 output on Z will cause an incorrect 0 output, but an incorrect 1 will be corrected by the dot-AND connection.

5.6.2 Fail-safe Sequential Machine Design using Berger Codes

Chuang and Das |5.27| have proposed a procedure for designing a fail-safe synchronous sequential machine using Berger codes. The first step of the procedure is to assign a binary code to each state of the machine, as in normal sequential machine design. Every code word assigned is considered as the information bits of a Berger code with which appropriate check bits are concatenated. If the state variables of the information and the check bits are realized in the sum-of-products and product-of-sums forms respectively (or vice-versa), the machine is state fail-safe for unidirectional faults provided that the code word assigned to a state is not "$B1$"; $B1$ is a code word with all the information bits (check bits) equal to 0 and all the check bits (information bits) equal to 1. However, if certain conditions are met, the use of $B1$ in state assignment will still result in state fail-safe realization of a machine. These conditions are discussed below and hold for the case when the sum-of-products form is used for realizing the next state logic for the variables in information bits, and product-of-sums for those in check bits.

Let $B1$ be assigned to state S_0, B_S be the Berger code assigned to state S and $P_0(m)$ denote the set of predecessor states of S_0 under input I_m. Let us form two sets X and Y such that:

$$X = \{P_0(m) - S_0\} \qquad Y = \{\text{State set of the machine} - P_0(m)\}$$

The next state of any erroneous state cannot be one of the normal states of a machine, if a state assignment satisfies the following two conditions:

$$\forall I_m, \ \forall x \in X, \ \exists y \in Y \quad \text{such that}$$

(a) $0 \to 1$ faults in check bits of B_x results in a word B_e such that $B_e > B_y$; and

(b) $1 \to 0$ faults in information bits of B_x results in a word B_e such that $B_e < B_y$.

When the conditions cannot be satisfied, a dummy state variable may be added to the information bits, and the check bits are modified accordingly. This will result in a state fail-safe sequential machine.

An erroneous state in a machine designed by this procedure can be detected by using a checker circuit as shown in Fig. 5.38. Any error state due to $1 \to 0$ faults in information bits will make the output of the OR gate equal to 0; since at least one check bit is equal to 0 the output of the AND gate will also be 0. Thus the output of the checker will be 1. On the other hand any error state due to $0 \to 1$ faults has all the check bits equal to 1 and at least one data bit equal to 1. So the output of the checker will again be 1. Alternatively, the totally self-checking checkers proposed by Ashjaee et al. (Sec. 5.2.3) and Marouf et al. (Sec. 5.2.3) can also be used.

The state fail-safe machine designed by this method can also be made output fail-safe by assigning the safe-side output to each error state. The

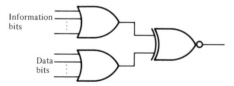

Fig. 5.38   Checker circuit (*courtesy of IEEE*, © *1978*).

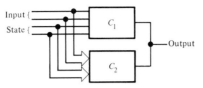

Fig. 5.39   Fail-safe output realization (*courtesy of IEEE,* © *1978*).

output fail-safe realization consists of two copies of output circuits C_1 and C_2 tied together as shown in Fig. 5.39. C_1 can be realized in either sum-of-products or product-of-sums form. C_2 is derived from C_1 by replacing a product (sum) of state variables with a product (sum) of complemented state variables missing from the replaced product (sum). When the safe-side is 0(1) the tie is a "wired-AND(OR)" and the output of C_1 is in sum-of-products (product-of-sums) form. If the machine is in an erroneous state or there is a fault in the output circuit, the outputs of C_1 and C_2 are different and the safe-side output overrides the other. However, if both outputs fail to the unsafe side, the machine is no longer fail-safe. Let us illustrate this method of designing state/output fail-safe machines by applying it to the machine of Fig. 5.40.

	Input	
Present state	$x = 0$	$x = 1$
A	$E,0$	$B,0$
B	$C,0$	$D,0$
C	$A,0$	$D,0$
D	$E,0$	$D,1$
E	$A,0$	$D,1$
	Next state/output	

Fig. 5.40

The state assignment of the machine using Berger codes is shown in Fig. 5.41(a); $y_1 \, y_2 \, y_3$ are the variables of the information bits and $y_4 \, y_5$ are those of the check bits. The excitation table is shown in Fig. 5.41(b).

	y_1	y_2	y_3	y_4	y_5
A	0	0	0	1	1
B	0	0	1	1	0
C	0	1	0	1	0
D	0	1	1	0	1
E	1	0	0	1	0

(a)

y_1	y_2	y_3	y_4	y_5		I_1					I_2				
0	0	0	1	1	1	0	0	1	0	0	0	1	1	0
0	0	1	1	0	0	1	0	1	0	0	1	1	0	1
0	1	0	1	0	0	0	0	1	1	0	1	1	0	1
0	1	1	0	1	1	0	0	1	0	0	1	1	0	1/1
1	0	0	1	0	0	0	0	1	1	0	1	1	0	1/1

(b)

Fig. 5.41   (a) State assignment; (b) excitation table for Fig. 5.40.

Let us first determine whether 00011 can be used in the state assignment. The predecessor state set of A to which 00011 has been assigned is

$$P_0(1) = \{C, E\}$$

Therefore,

$$X = \{P_0(1) - A\} = \{C, E\}$$

and

$$Y = \{\text{State set of the machine} - P_0(1)\} = \{A, B, D\}$$

States C and E need to be tested for the conditions (a) and (b) above. $0 \to 1$ faults in the check bits of B_C results in 01011, which is $> B_A$. $1 \to 0$ faults in the information bits of B_C results in 00010, which is $< B_A$ and $< B_B$. Similarly $0 \to 1$ faults in the check bits of B_E results in 10011, which is $> B_A$. $1 \to 0$ faults in the information bits of B_E results in 00010, which is $< B_A$ and $< B_B$. Hence 00011 can be used.

The next state expressions are directly obtained from the excitation table of Fig. 5.41(b) and are given below:

$$Y_1 = I_1(y_4 y_5 + y_2 y_3 y_5)$$
$$Y_2 = I_1 y_3 y_4 + I_2(y_3 y_4 + y_2 y_4 + y_2 y_3 y_5 + y_1 y_4)$$
$$Y_3 = I_2(y_4 y_5 + y_3 y_4 + y_2 y_4 + y_2 y_3 y_5 + y_1 y_4)$$
$$Y_4 = I_1(y_4 y_5 + y_3 y_4 + y_2 y_4 + y_2 y_3 y_5) + I_2 y_4 y_5$$
$$Y_5 = I_1(y_2 y_4 + y_1 y_4) + I_2(y_3 y_4 + y_2 y_4 + y_2 y_3 y_5 + y_1 y_4)$$

The output expressions C_1 and C_2 are given by

$$C_1 = I_2(y_2 y_3 y_5 + y_1 y_4)$$
$$C_2 = I_2(\bar{y}_1 \bar{y}_4 + \bar{y}_2 \bar{y}_3 \bar{y}_5)$$

C_1 and C_2 are tied together as shown in Fig. 5.42; the resulting output gives the "wired-AND" value of C_1 and C_2, and is 0 fail-safe.

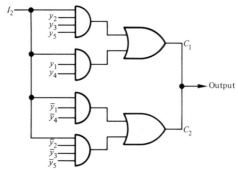

Fig. 5.42 Fail-safe output realization of the machine of Fig. 5.40.

5.7 TOTALLY SELF-CHECKING PLA DESIGN

The PLA (Programmable Logic Array) is becoming increasingly popular for the implementation of logic functions in LSI/VLSI chips. Although PLAs in general need larger chip areas than the random logic, they have the advantage of a memory-like regular structure. The PLA logic structure is shown in Fig. 5.43(a). The input lines to the AND array are called *bit lines* and the outputs of the AND array are called *word lines* or *product lines*. The input signals and their complements enter the AND array and are selectively connected to product lines in such a way that certain combinations of input variables produce a logic 1 signal on one or more product lines. The product lines are input to the OR array; hence the outputs of the OR array are the sum-of-products form of Boolean functions of the PLA inputs. A cross-point b_k, p_k is marked (●), if the product term p_k depends on b_k, and a cross-point z_j, p_k is marked if p_k is a term of z_j. Figure 5.43(b) shows an example of a PLA realizing the functions

$$z_1 = x_1 x_2 + \bar{x}_1 \bar{x}_2$$

$$z_2 = \bar{x}_1 x_2$$

Three kinds of fault can normally occur in PLAs: stuck-at faults, bridging faults and cross-point faults [5.28, 5.29, 5.30]. A cross-point or contact fault may arise due to a missing contact on the cross-point of the AND and the OR

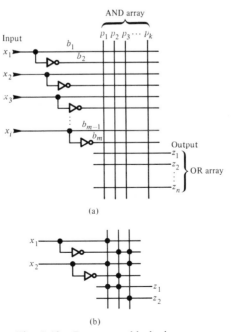

Fig. 5.43 Programmable logic array.

array where there should be a contact, or due to an additional contact at the cross-point where there should not be a contact. Much work has been done in recent years related to test generation for PLAs [5.28–5.33]. Some attempts have also been made to reduce complexity of PLA test generation by adding extra logic to PLAs so that function-independent tests of PLAs are possible [5.34–5.38]. However, very little work has been done so far to design PLAs with self-checking capabilities. Wang and Avizienis [5.13] were the first to propose an approach for designing totally self-checking PLAs. Their approach is based on the assumption that the PLA is "non-concurrent", i.e. any normal input pattern selects exactly one product term in the PLA under fault-free operation, and the output patterns of the PLA belong to a code for which a totally self-checking checker exists. However, they did not mention the effect of different types of fault. Also, if the PLAs do not produce all the possible output combinations, this approach does not guarantee that all faults in checker circuits will be detected; hence the checkers are not totally self-checking.

Mak et al. [5.39] have shown that all single faults in a PLA can cause only unidirectional errors in the output of the PLA. Consequently, codes that can detect unidirectional errors such as m-out-of-n codes, Berger codes or two-rail codes may be used for designing totally self-checking PLAs. Mak et al. [5.39] also introduce a new type of code called "modified Berger code", specifically for detecting unidirectional output errors in PLAs. The modified Berger code requires fewer check bits than the original Berger code. The check bits for the modified Berger codes are the binary encoding of the difference between the number of 0s and the minimum number of 0s in the output patterns.

A general procedure for designing strongly fault-secure (see Sec. 5.5) PLAs has also been introduced [5.39]. The first step of the procedure is to select an appropriate code to encode the outputs and to determine the assignment for check bit values. The check bit functions for the selected code are then derived. The next step is to join together the check bit function to the original output function to form a new multi-output function. The new function is then minimized by using a multi-output function minimization method to generate a minimal set of product terms. Finally, the AND and the OR arrays are implemented using the previously selected coding scheme.

The function C_i $(0 \leqslant i \leqslant m)$ of each check bit in the coding scheme is derived by summing up all the "G-functions" on which C_i is dependent. The G-functions are derived by using the following steps:

1. Let m = number of original output functions $(f_1 \ldots f_m)$
   Set $i = 1$, $G_0 = \bar{f}_1$ and $G_1 = f_1$
2. Form the product terms $G_j \bar{f}_{i+1}$ and $G_j f_{i+1}$ $(0 \leqslant j \leqslant i)$
3. Let $H_0 = G_0 \bar{f}_{i+1}$, $H_j = G_{j-1} f_{i+1} + G_j \bar{f}_{i+1}$ $(1 \leqslant j \leqslant i)$
   and $H_{i+1} = G_i f_{i+1}$
4. $i = i + 1$; set $G_j = H_j$ $(0 \leqslant j \leqslant i)$
5. If $i = m$ stop; otherwise go to step 2.

As an example, let us consider how the procedure for strongly fault secure PLA design can be applied to the following four-input, four-output function:

$$f_1(x_1, x_2, x_3, x_4) = \Sigma\,(0,\ 2,\ 3,\ 7,\ 8,\ 10,\ 12,\ 13,\ 15)$$

$$f_2(x_1, x_2, x_3, x_4) = \Sigma\,(0,\ 2,\ 3,\ 4,\ 9,\ 12,\ 13,\ 15)$$

$$f_3(x_1, x_2, x_3, x_4) = \Sigma\,(0,\ 1,\ 2,\ 4,\ 8,\ 9,\ 10,\ 14)$$

$$f_4(x_1, x_2, x_3, x_4) = \Sigma\,(0,\ 1,\ 2,\ 4,\ 5,\ 6,\ 8,\ 11,\ 14)$$

Since the number of outputs is four, the extra output bits required for Berger coding are three. The modified Berger code on the other hand requires only two extra output bits, as can be deduced from Fig. 5.44(a), (b) and (c). The assignment of check bit values for the modified Berger encoding is shown in Fig. 5.45. Since the entry in row 1 and column 1 of Fig. 5.44(c) is 0, i.e. $f_1 f_2 f_3 f_4 = 1111$, the number of check bits to be assigned is $C_1 C_2 = 00$. Hence the entries in the first row and the first column of both C_1 and C_2 are 0s.

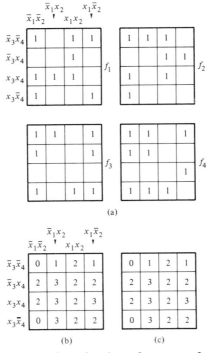

(a)

(b)   (c)

Fig. 5.44 (a) Karnaugh maps for a four-input four-output function; (b) number of zeros in the output pattern corresponding to each input combination; (c) difference of the number of zeros and the minimum number of zeros.

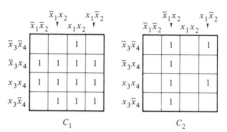

Fig. 5.45   Check bit assignment.

The G-functions are then generated using the formal approach described previously:

$$G_0 = \bar{f_1}\,\bar{f_2}\,\bar{f_3}\,\bar{f_4}$$

$$G_1 = \bar{f_1}\,\bar{f_2}\,\bar{f_3}\,f_4 + \bar{f_1}\,\bar{f_2}\,f_3\,\bar{f_4} + \bar{f_1}\,f_2\,\bar{f_3}\,\bar{f_4} + f_1\,\bar{f_2}\,\bar{f_3}\,\bar{f_4}$$

$$G_2 = \bar{f_1}\,\bar{f_2}\,f_3\,f_4 + \bar{f_1}\,f_2\,f_3\,\bar{f_4} + f_1\,f_2\,\bar{f_3}\,\bar{f_4} + f_1\,\bar{f_2}\,f_3\,\bar{f_4}$$
$$\qquad + f_1\,\bar{f_2}\,\bar{f_3}\,f_4 + \bar{f_1}\,f_2\,\bar{f_3}\,f_4$$

$$G_3 = \bar{f_1}\,f_2\,f_3\,f_4 + f_1\,\bar{f_2}\,f_3\,f_4 + f_1\,f_2\,\bar{f_3}\,f_4 + f_1\,f_2\,f_3\,\bar{f_4}$$

$$G_4 = f_1\,f_2\,f_3\,f_4$$

Hence any minterm with i 0s in the output vector will be covered only by the function $G_{(m-i)}$ where $0 \leqslant i \leqslant m$; m is the number of output lines.

It can be seen from Table 5.5 that each code assignment for C_1 and C_2 (Fig. 5.45) maps into an output vector which is covered by a G-function; for

x_1	x_2	x_3	x_4	f_1	f_2	f_3	f_4	C_1	C_2
0	0	0	0	1	1	1	1	0	0
0	0	0	1	0	0	1	1✓	1	0
0	0	1	0	1	1	1	1	0	0
0	0	1	1	1	1	0	0✓	1	0
0	1	0	0	0	1	1	1	0	1
0	1	0	1	0	0	0	1✓	1	1
0	1	1	0	0	0	0	1✓	1	1
0	1	1	1	1	0	0	0✓	1	1
1	0	0	0	1	0	1	1	0	1
1	0	0	1	0	1	1	0✓	1	0
1	0	1	0	1	0	1	0✓	1	0
1	0	1	1	0	0	0	1✓	1	1
1	1	0	0	1	1	0	0✓	1	0
1	1	0	1	1	1	0	0✓	1	0
1	1	1	0	0	0	1	1✓	1	0
1	1	1	1	1	0	0	0✓	1	0

Table 5.5   Coded truth table

example, code assignments for C_1 are covered by G_1 and G_2 (identified by ticks). Hence the check bit function can be derived by summing the appropriate G function:

$$C_1 = G_1 + G_2$$

$$C_2 = G_1 + G_3$$

The check bit functions C_1 and C_2 are added to the original functions f_1, f_2, f_3 and f_4; hence the PLA would have six output lines. Using a multi-output minimization algorithm [5.40], the functions $f_1 \ldots f_4$, C_1 and C_2 are minimized to generate a set of 14 product terms:

$P_1 = \bar{A}\bar{B}CD$ $P_5 = \bar{A}BCD$ $P_9 = A\bar{B}\bar{C}D$ $P_{13} = \bar{A}BC\bar{D}$

$P_2 = AB\bar{C}$ $P_6 = \bar{A}\bar{B}\bar{D}$ $P_{10} = \bar{A}\bar{B}CD$ $P_{14} = A\bar{B}CD$

$P_3 = ABD$ $P_7 = A\bar{B}\bar{C}\bar{D}$ $P_{11} = ABC\bar{D}$

$P_4 = A\bar{B}C\bar{D}$ $P_8 = \bar{A}B\bar{C}\bar{D}$ $P_{12} = \bar{A}B\bar{C}D$

The output functions of the PLA can now be expressed as a sum of the product terms:

$$f_1 = P_1 + P_2 + P_3 + P_4 + P_5 + P_6 + P_7$$

$$f_2 = P_1 + P_2 + P_3 + P_6 + P_8 + P_9$$

$$f_3 = P_4 + P_6 + P_7 + P_8 + P_9 + P_{10} + P_{11}$$

$$f_4 = P_6 + P_7 + P_8 + P_{10} + P_{11} + P_{12} + P_{13} + P_{14}$$

$$C_1 = P_1 + P_2 + P_3 + P_4 + P_5 + P_9 + P_{10} + P_{11} + P_{12} + P_{13} + P_{14}$$

$$C_2 = P_5 + P_7 + P_8 + P_{12} + P_{13} + P_{14}$$

The number of product terms required for implementing strongly fault secure PLAs is somewhat larger than that for conventional PLAs; in the example considered here only one extra product term was required. The PLA outputs have been encoded into the modified Berger code. Any single stuck-at fault, bridging fault or contact fault in the PLA will cause a unidirectional error at the output; an output word with a unidirectional error is a non-code word. If a fault does not cause a unidirectional error at the output, the output code word is correct and the fault is undetectable. The checker needed to detect non-code words at the PLA output must be designed so that the output produced by the PLA is sufficient to detect all faults in the checker. Hence this approach requires a new checker for each PLA to be designed. Alternatively any totally self-checking checker can be used, provided registers containing code words which are not produced by a PLA are incorporated into the circuit. During the operation of a PLA, the AND array is periodically disabled and the contents of the registers are applied to the OR array so that the checker receives all the code words required for self-testing any fault.

5.8 REFERENCES

5.1 Anderson, D. A. and G. Metze, "Design of totally self-checking check circuits for *m*-out-of-*n* codes", *IEEE Trans. Comput.*, 263–269 (March 1973).

5.2 Duke, K. A., "Detect errors in complex logic with two-rail checking technique", *Electronic Design*, 88–93 (October 1972).

5.3 Sedmak, R. S. and H. L. Liebergot, "Fault tolerance of a general purpose computer implemented by very large scale integration", *Proc. Int. Symp. Fault-tolerant Computing*, 137–143 (June 1978).

5.4 Rennels, D. A., A. Avizienis and M. Ercegovac, "A study of standard building blocks for the design of fault-tolerant distributed computer systems", *ibid.*, 144–149.

5.5 Reddy, S. M., "A note on self-checking checkers", *IEEE Trans. Comput.*, 1100–1102 (October 1974).

5.6 Reddy, S. M. and J. R. Wilson, "Easily testable cellular realizations for the (exactly *p*)-out-of-*n* and (*p* or more)-out-of-*n* logic functions", *ibid.*, 98–100 (January 1974).

5.7 Smith, J. E., "The design of totally self-checking check circuits for a class of unordered codes", *Jour. Design Automation & Fault-tolerant Computing*, 321–343 (October 1977).

5.8 Ramsey, F. P., "On a problem of formal logic", *Proc. London Math. Soc.*, 2nd Series, **30**, 264–286 (1930).

5.9 Crouzet, Y. and C. Landrault, "Design of self-checking MOS–LSI circuits, application to a four-bit microprocessor", *Proc. Int. Symp. Fault-tolerant Computing*, 189–192 (1979).

5.10 Marouf, M. A. and A. D. Friedman, "Efficient design of self-checking checker for any *m*-out-of-*n* code", *IEEE Trans. Comput.*, 482–490 (June 1978).

5.11 Halatsis, C., "Three-level totally self-checking checkers for *m*-out-of-(2*m* ± 1) codes", *Proc. IEEE Conf. Circuits and Systems*, 69–72 (1980).

5.12 Khakbaz, J., "Totally self-checking checker for 1-out-of-*n* code using two-rail codes", *IEEE Trans. Comput.*, 677–681 (July 1982).

5.13 Wang, S. L. and A. Avizienis, "The design of totally self-checking circuits using programmable logic arrays", *Proc. Int. Symp. Fault-tolerant Computing*, 173–180 (1979).

5.14 Marouf, M. A. and A. D. Friedman, "Design of self-checking checkers for Berger codes", *Proc. Int. Symp. Fault-tolerant Computing*, 179–184 (1978).

5.15 Ashjaee, M. J. and S. M. Reddy, "On totally self-checking checkers for separable codes", *IEEE Trans. Comput.*, 737–744 (August 1977).

5.16 Avizienis, A., "Arithmetic codes: cost and effectiveness studies for application in digital system design", *ibid.*, 1322–1331 (November 1971).

5.17 Wakerly, J., *Error detecting codes, self-checking circuits and applications*, Elsevier North-Holland (1978).

5.18 Diaz, M. and P. Azema, "Unified design of self-checking and fail-safe combinational circuits and sequential machines", *IEEE Trans. Comput.*, 276–281 (March 1979).

5.19 Ozguner, F., "Design of totally self-checking asynchronous and synchronous sequential machines", *Proc. Int. Symp. Fault-tolerant Computing*, 124–129 (1977).

5.20 Tohma, Y., Y. Ohyama and R. Sakai, "Realization of fail-safe sequential machines by using a *k*-out-of-*n*-code", *IEEE Trans. Comput.*, 1270–1275 (1971).

5.21 Wakerly, J., "Partially self-checking circuits and their use in performing logical operations", *IEEE Trans. Comput.*, 658–666 (July 1974).

5.22 Smith, J. E. and G. Metze, "Strongly fault secure logic networks", *ibid.*, 491–499 (June 1978).

5.23 Sawin III, D. H., "Design of reliable synchronous sequential circuits", *ibid.*, 567–569 (May 1975).

5.24 Mine, H. and Y. Koga, "Basic properties and a construction method for fail-safe logic systems", *IEEE Trans. Electron. Comput.*, 282–289 (June 1967).

5.25 Tohma, Y. and Y. Ohyama, "Realization of fail-safe sequential machines by using *k*-out-of-*n* code", *IEEE Trans. Comput.*, 1270–1275 (November 1971).

5.26 Freeman, H. A. and G. Metze, "Fault-tolerant computers using 'dotted logic' redundancy techniques", *ibid.*, 867–871 (August 1972).

5.27 Chuang, H. and S. Das, "Design of fail-safe sequential machines using separable codes", *ibid.*, 249–251 (March 1978).

5.28 Ostapko, D. L. and S. J. Hong, "Fault analysis and test generation for programmable logic arrays", *IEEE Trans. Comput.*, 617–626 (September 1979).

5.29 Cha, C. W., "A testing strategy for PLAs", *Proc. 15th Design Automation Conf.*, 326–334 (1978).

5.30 Smith, J. E., "Detection of faults in programmable logic arrays, *IEEE Trans. Comput.*, 845–853 (November 1979).

5.31 Eichelberger, E. B. and E. Lindbloom, "A heuristic test pattern generation for programmable logic arrays", *IBM Jour. Res. and Develop.*, 15–22 (March 1975).

5.32 Fujiwara, H., K. Kinoshita and H. Ozaki, "Universal test sets for programmable logic arrays", *Proc. Int. Symp. Fault-tolerant Computing*, 137–142 (1980).

5.33 Agarwal, V. K., "Multiple fault detection in programmable logic arrays", *ibid.*, 227–234 (1979).

5.34 Pradhan, D. K. and K. Son, "The effects of untestable faults in PLAs and a design for testability", *Proc. 1980 IEEE Test Conf.*, 359–367.

5.35 Son, K. and D. K. Pradhan, "Design of programmable logic arrays for testability", *ibid.*, 163–166.

5.36 Hong, S. J. and D. L. Ostapko, "FITPLA: A programmable logic array for function independent testing", *Proc. Int. Symp. Fault-tolerant Computing*, 131–136 (1980).

5.37 Fujiwara, H. and K. Kinoshita, "A design of programmable logic arrays with universal tests", *IEEE Trans. Comput.*, 823–828 (November 1981).

5.38 Ramanathan, K. S. and N. N. Biswas, "A design for complete testability of programmable logic arrays", *Proc. 1982 IEEE Test Conf.*, 67–74.

5.39 Mak, G. P., J. A. Abraham and E. S. Davidson, "The design of PLAs with concurrent error detection", *ibid.*, 303–310 (1982).

5.40 Arevalo, Z. and J. G. Bredeson, "A method to simplify a Boolean function into a near minimal sum-of-products for programmable logic arrays", *IEEE Trans. Comput.*, 1028–1039 (November 1978).

6 DESIGN FOR TESTABILITY

6.1 WHAT IS TESTABILITY?

Recent advances in LSI/VLSI technology have led to packages of increasing size and complexity. Besides the considerable problem of testing the packages by themselves (Fig. 6.1), the incorporation of these into larger designs has caused the cost of test generation to grow exponentially [6.1]. In many cases the cost of test generation and fault simulation, which is needed as a tool to determine how well the tests perform, has reached a practical limit. One of the approaches to solving the problem is to constrain the design in a way that makes test generation and diagnosis easier; this is widely known as "design for testability". Figure 6.2 shows the improvement derived from design for testability [6.2]. A testable circuit has the following properties [6.3]:

1. The circuit can be easily put in the desired initial state.
2. The internal state of the circuit can easily be controlled by the application of test patterns to the primary inputs of the circuit.
3. The internal state of the circuit can be uniquely identified through the primary outputs of the circuit or through the use of special test points.

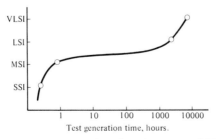

Fig. 6.1 Density vs. test generation time (*courtesy of IEEE,* © *1979*).

197

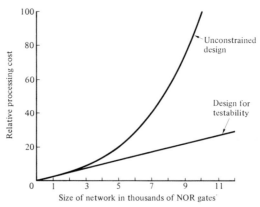

Fig. 6.2   Test pattern generation cost comparison (*courtesy of IEEE, © 1981*).

Testability is achieved by using extra logic and/or test points. The techniques for incorporating testability into circuits fall into two categories: design guidelines to be followed in order to make circuits testable; and systematic procedures or structures aimed at producing testable circuits.

6.2   CONTROLLABILITY AND OBSERVABILITY

There are two key concepts in designing for testability: controllability and observability [6.4]. *Controllability* refers to the ability to apply test patterns to the inputs of a subcircuit via the primary inputs of the circuit. For example, in Fig. 6.3(a) if the output of the equality checker circuit is always in the state of "equal", it is not possible to test whether the equality checker is operating correctly or not. If a control gate is added to the circuit (Fig. 6.3(b)), the input of the equality checker circuit and hence the operation of this circuit can be controlled. Therefore, in order to enhance the controllability of a circuit, the states which cannot be controlled directly from its primary inputs have to be reduced. *Observability* refers to the ability to observe the response of a subcircuit via the primary outputs of the circuit or at some other output point.

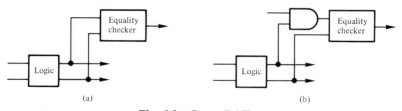

Fig. 6.3   Controllability.

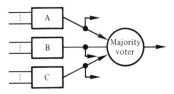

Fig. 6.4   Observability.

For example, in Fig. 6.4 the outputs of subcircuits A, B and C are connected to the inputs of the majority voter circuit and only the output of this circuit is observable. In this case it is impossible to check whether all the subcircuits are operating correctly or not. To enhance observability, it is necessary to observe the outputs of the subcircuits separately.

In general the easiest way to increase controllability/observability is to add some control gates and control terminals (controllability) or to add some output terminals (observability) for testing purposes.

6.3   DESIGN OF TESTABLE COMBINATIONAL LOGIC CIRCUITS

A number of design procedures have been proposed in recent years for the realization of easily testable combinational logic circuits. The prime objective of these design procedures is to minimize the number of fault detection tests and/or simplify the generation of such tests. Although most of these procedures are only of academic interest, and unlikely to find applications in large-variable circuits, they made major contributions to the current knowledge of designing for testability. This section discusses some of these procedures.

6.3.1   The Reed–Muller Expansion Technique

This technique can be used to realize any arbitrary n-variable Boolean function using AND and EX–OR gates only. The circuit so designed has the following properties:

(a)   If the primary input leads are fault-free then at most $(n + 4)$ tests are required to detect all single stuck-at faults in the circuit.

(b)   If there are faults on the primary input leads as well, then the number of tests required is $(n + 4) + 2n_e$, where n_e is the number of input variables that appear an even number of times in the product terms of the Reed–Muller expansion. However, by adding an extra AND gate with its output being made observable, the additional $2n_e$ tests can be removed. The input to the AND gate are those inputs appearing an even number of times in the Reed–Muller product terms.

Any combinational function of n-variables can be described by a Reed–Muller expansion of the form

$$f(x_1, x_2, \ldots, x_n) = C_0 \oplus C_1 \dot{x}_1 \oplus C_2 \dot{x}_2 \oplus \cdots \oplus C_n \dot{x}_n \oplus C_{n+1} \dot{x}_1 \dot{x}_2$$
$$\oplus C_{n+2} \dot{x}_1 \dot{x}_3 \oplus \cdots \oplus C_{2^n-1} \dot{x}_1 \dot{x}_2 \ldots \dot{x}_n$$

where $\dot{x}_i$ is either x_i or $\bar{x}_i$ but not both together, C_i is a binary constant 0 or 1 and $\oplus$ is the modulo-2 sum (exclusive-OR operation) [6.5]. If all $\dot{x}_i = x_i$, this special case is known as the "complement-free ring sum" expansion of the Boolean function.

For a three-variable function the Reed–Muller expansion is

$$f(W, X, Y) = C_0 \oplus C_1 W \oplus C_2 X \oplus C_3 Y$$
$$\oplus C_4 WX \oplus C_5 WY \oplus C_6 XY \oplus C_7 WXY$$

The constants C_i for a three-variable Reed–Muller expansion may be computed using the following rules [6.6].

$$C_0 = f_0$$
$$C_1 = f_0 \oplus f_4$$
$$C_2 = f_0 \oplus f_2$$
$$C_3 = f_0 \oplus f_1$$
$$C_4 = f_0 \oplus f_2 \oplus f_4 \oplus f_6$$
$$C_5 = f_0 \oplus f_1 \oplus f_4 \oplus f_5$$
$$C_6 = f_0 \oplus f_1 \oplus f_2 \oplus f_3$$
$$C_7 = f_0 \oplus f_1 \oplus f_2 \oplus f_3 \oplus f_4 \oplus f_5 \oplus f_6 \oplus f_7$$

where f_i are the output values of the minterms obtained from the truth table; this procedure can easily be extended for higher-order expansions.

Let us now consider the Boolean function

$$f(W, X, Y) = WX + \bar{W}Y + \bar{X}\bar{Y}$$

The Reed–Muller expansion of the function is:

$$f(W, X, Y) = 1 \oplus X \oplus WX \oplus WY \oplus XY$$

A direct implementation of the function is shown in Fig. 6.5.

It has been shown that to detect a single faulty gate in a cascade of exclusive-OR gates it is sufficient to apply a set of test inputs which will

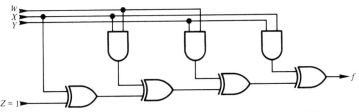

Fig. 6.5   Reed–Muller circuit for $f = WX + WY + XY$.

exercise each exclusive-OR gate for all possible input combinations. Such a test set for the circuit of Fig. 6.5 is given by

$$
T_1 = \begin{array}{cccc}
Z & W & X & Y \\
\left\{\begin{array}{cccc}
0 & 0 & 0 & 0 \\
0 & 1 & 1 & 1 \\
1 & 0 & 0 & 0 \\
1 & 1 & 1 & 1
\end{array}\right\}
\end{array}
$$

The structure of the test set is always the same independent of the number of input variables and constitutes four tests only; for example, a five-variable circuit would have the test set:

$$
\begin{array}{cccccc}
Z & U & V & W & X & Y \\
\left\{\begin{array}{cccccc}
0 & 0 & 0 & 0 & 0 & 0 \\
0 & 1 & 1 & 1 & 1 & 1 \\
1 & 0 & 0 & 0 & 0 & 0 \\
1 & 1 & 1 & 1 & 1 & 1
\end{array}\right\}
\end{array}
$$

In addition the test set T_1 will also detect:

1. Any s-a-0 fault on the input or output of an AND gate (tests 0111, 1111).
2. Any s-a-1 fault on the output of an AND gate (tests 0000, 1000).

However, an s-a-1 fault on the AND gate inputs must be detected separately using the test set

$$
T_2 = \begin{array}{cccc}
Z & W & X & Y \\
\left\{\begin{array}{cccc}
- & 0 & 1 & 1 \\
- & 1 & 0 & 1 \\
- & 1 & 1 & 0
\end{array}\right\}
\end{array}
$$

where "$-$" is a don't care condition. Thus for an n-variable function T_2 will contain n tests and the full test set will now consist of $T = T_1 + T_2$ and contain $(n + 4)$ tests.

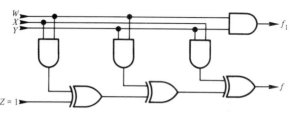

Fig. 6.6   Modified Reed–Muller circuit for $f = WX + WY + XY$.

It has already been mentioned that if the faults on the primary input lines are also considered the number of tests increases by $2n_e$. In our example $n_e = 2$, since the variables W and Y occur twice. However, by incorporating an AND gate in the circuit of Fig. 6.5, such that the inputs to the AND gate are W and Y, the original $(n + 4)$ tests can be used to detect both primary input and gate faults. The modified circuit is shown in Fig. 6.6; the output f_1 is observable.

6.3.2   Three-level OR–AND–OR Design

One of the major drawbacks of the design technique based on Reed–Muller expansion is the increased number of logic levels in a circuit. An alternative design method which results in AND–OR networks of at most three levels, and in which single s-a-1 or s-a-0 faults are locatable within certain indistinguishable classes, will now be discussed [6.7]. The method is applicable only to positive "unate" logic functions. A logic function is *unate* if it can be represented as a sum-of-products or product-of-sums expression in which each variable appears either in a complemented form or in an uncomplemented form but not in both. A positive unate function is one in which all variables are uncomplemented. The design process commences with the design of non-redundant three-level OR–AND–OR "prime trees" [6.8]. A *tree network* is a logic circuit in which the output of any gate is not fed to more than one gate, i.e. no fan-out is allowed except on primary inputs. A *restricted tree network* is a tree network comprised of AND, OR and inverter gates with the restriction that inverters are fed only from external inputs. A *restricted prime tree* is a restricted tree network satisfying the following assumptions, where f represents the output of the network.

1.   If the output gate is an OR gate and if

$$f = T_1 + T_2 + \cdots + T_p$$

where T_i is a product term, then T_i is a prime implicant of f, $1 \leqslant i \leqslant p$.

2.   If the output gate is an AND gate and if

$$f = U_1 \cdot U_2 \ldots U_q$$

where U_i is a sum term, then U_i is a prime implicant of f, $1 \leqslant i \leqslant q$.

A "prime tree" is a tree network containing AND, OR, NAND, NOR and inverter gates, which is either a restricted prime tree or whose test-equivalent network is a restricted prime tree. A way to design prime-tree networks is to start with a sum of prime implicants or a product of prime implicants for the given function and then use the following factoring techniques:

$$ab + ac = a(b + c)$$

$$(a + b)(a + c) = a + bc$$

A prime tree is non-redundant if no lead in the prime tree can be connected to a logical constant, 1 or 0, without changing the functional value of the output. In three-level tree networks, the two-level networks whose outputs are connected to the third-level gates are called "subtrees".

An OR–AND–OR tree can be formed by grouping the prime implicants according to the number of literals present in them, and then determining possible factorization within these groups. As an example, let us design an OR–AND–OR prime tree for the function

$$f(A, B, C, D, E, F) = BEF + BCF + ACF + BDE + ACDE + ABCD$$

After factorization,

$$f(A, B, C, D, E, F) = BE(D + F) + CF(A + B) + ACD(B + E)$$

The logic implementation of the function is shown in Fig. 6.7.

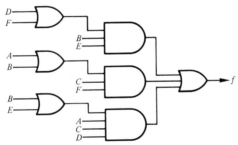

Fig. 6.7   A prime tree for the function (A, B, C, D, E, F).

The design procedure for completely fault-locatable networks for unate functions is as follows:

1. Design a non-redundant three-level OR–AND–OR prime tree.
2. Check if two subtrees can be replaced by a single subtree. Two subtrees can be replaced by a single subtree if for two resolvable stuck-at-1 faults, the same prime implicants appear in the sum-of-product expressions for both the subtrees.
3. Check if the tree network can be modified. In a non-redundant OR–AND–OR prime tree realization, if a stuck-at-1 fault at a primary input is indistinguishable from a stuck-at-1 fault at some other lead (not another

primary input or the output) and this pair of faults is resolvable, then another prime tree can be obtained in which the primary input and the other lead are inputs to the same first-level OR gate.

6.3.3   Use of Control Logic

Control logic can be used either to provide extra primary outputs (to increase observability) or to add primary input lines and gates (to enhance controllability). It has been proved that by inserting additional control logic, a combinational logic circuit can be modified so that five tests are sufficient to detect all faults in the circuit [6.9]. The design procedure is as follows:

1. Implement the given logic function using two-input NAND gates and inverters.
2. Replace all inverters by EX–OR gates; and insert additional EX–OR gates in all other NAND gate input lines. Since only one input of the EX–OR gate is used, the other inputs can be brought out as primary input lines. For normal operation the primary input lines of the EX–OR gates replacing the inverters and those inserted in the NAND input lines are set to 1 and 0 respectively.

For example, the application of the above procedure to the logic function

$$f(A, B, C) = A\bar{B} + B\bar{C}$$

is shown in Figs. 6.8 and 6.9 respectively.

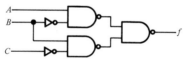

Fig. 6.8   Two-input NAND and inverter implementation of $f = A\bar{B} + B\bar{C}$.

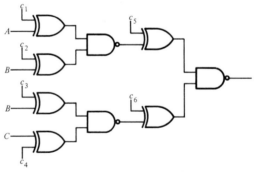

Fig. 6.9   Testable network with additional primary input lines $c_1 - c_6$.

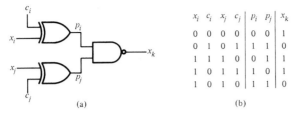

x_i	c_i	x_j	c_j	p_i	p_j	x_k
0	0	0	0	0	0	1
0	1	0	1	1	1	0
1	1	1	0	0	1	1
1	0	1	1	1	0	1
1	0	1	0	1	1	0

(a)   (b)

Fig. 6.10   Basic module and its test set.

In order to generate tests for such a circuit, let us first consider the basic module shown in Fig. 6.10(a). A two-input EX–OR gate requires all four input combinations

$$\left\{ \begin{matrix} 0 & 0 & 1 & 1 \\ 0 & 1 & 0 & 1 \end{matrix} \right\}$$

to detect all single and multiple faults. These tests produce the four different input combinations to the following NAND gate. If the NAND gate output x_k is connected to a following EX–OR gate, an additional 0 must appear at x_k, so that the EX–OR gate can have the required input combinations of two 1s and two 0s. Therefore the input combination

$$\left\{ \begin{matrix} 1 \\ 1 \end{matrix} \right\}$$

must be applied twice to the NAND gate. Each module now requires five tests as shown in Fig. 6.10(b). Thus the test set for a modified circuit must be such that each five-bit sequence on the primary and NAND gate inputs is a permutation of the sequence 00111. There are ten such sequences denoted by the set $P = \{X_0, X_1, \ldots, X_9\}$, where

$$X_0 = 00111 \qquad X_5 = 10101$$

$$X_1 = 01011 \qquad X_6 = 10110$$

$$X_2 = 01101 \qquad X_7 = 11001$$

$$X_3 = 01110 \qquad X_8 = 11010$$

$$X_4 = 10011 \qquad X_9 = 11100$$

Two sequences X_i and X_j are said to be *compatible* if their NAND function $\overline{X_i \cdot X_j}$ is also in P. For example, X_0 and X_1 are compatible since $\overline{X_0 \cdot X_1} = X_9$. X_0 and X_9 are not compatible since $\overline{X_0 \cdot X_9} = 11011$ and this is not a permutation of 00111.

The test procedure consists of assigning arbitrary sequences from P to the primary inputs and then deriving sequences on the control inputs to the first set of EX–OR gates to produce a compatible pair of sequences on the following

NAND gate inputs. Since the inputs to the NAND gates are compatible sequences from P, the outputs of the NAND gates must also be sequences from P and these become the inputs to the next set of EX–OR gates. The process is repeated until the primary outputs are reached. Applying this to the modified circuit of Fig. 6.9 the following test set is obtained

A	B	C	c_1	c_2	c_3	c_4	c_5	c_6	f
0	1	1	1	0	0	1	1	0	0
1	1	0	0	1	1	0	0	0	0
1	0	1	1	1	1	0	0	1	0
1	1	0	0	0	0	1	0	0	1
0	0	1	0	0	0	1	1	1	1

An alternative technique for designing minimally testable network produces circuits which can be tested by three tests only [6.10]. The procedure is based on the fact that any n-input AND, OR, NAND, NOR gate can be tested for single or multiple faults by $(n + 1)$ tests. Hence if a circuit is realized using two-input gates only, then each gate can be tested by three tests. For example, a three-input OR gate can be replaced with a three-level OR–AND–OR network consisting of two-input gates as shown in Fig. 6.11; a two-input AND gate has been introduced between the two-input OR gates with a control input c and observable outputs O_1 and O_2. This network can be tested by the test set $\{0010, 0101, 1010\}$ as shown in Fig. 6.11. The test sequences applied to detect any fault in the two-input AND gates belong to the set $S_1 = \{011, 101, 110\}$ and those applied to the OR gates belong to the set $S_2 = \{001, 010, 100\}$. Sets S_1 and S_2 have the following properties:

1.   If $X = (x_1 \cdot x_2 \cdot x_3)$ is a test sequence and $\overline{X} (= \bar{x}_1 \cdot \bar{x}_2 \cdot \bar{x}_3)$ is its complement, then

$$X \in S_1(S_2) \qquad \overline{X} \in S_2(S_1)$$

2.   If $X_1 = x_1^1 x_2^1 x_3^1$ and $X_2 = x_1^2 x_2^2 x_3^2$ are two test sequences, then

$$\{X_1, X_2\} \in S_1 \qquad (X_1 \cdot X_2) \in S_2 \qquad \text{where } X_1 \neq X_2$$

and

$$\{X_1, X_2\} \in S_2 \qquad (X_1 + X_2) \in S_1 \qquad \text{where } X_1 \neq X_2$$

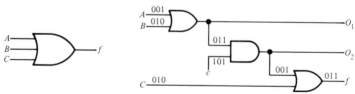

Fig. 6.11   Testable realization of three-input OR gate.

The procedure for modifying a circuit so that it consists of only two-input gates and hence testable by three tests is as follows:

Step 1.   Replace all n-input AND/OR gates, for which $n > 2$, with a tree of two-input AND/OR gates.

Step 2.   Assign arbitrary sequences from $\{S_1 \cup S_2\}$ to the primary inputs. This assignment may result in compatible or incompatible sequences to appear at the first-level gate outputs. If a gate output is incompatible with the input requirements of a successor gate, control logic is incorporated so that only compatible sequences may appear at the successor gate inputs. For example, the two-input OR gate of Fig. 6.12(a) is assumed to have the input sequences shown—these being the outputs generated by the predecessor gates. One of the sequences comes from S_2, the other one comes from S_1; hence the gate is modified as shown in Fig. 6.12(b).

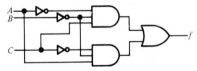

(a)   (b)

Fig. 6.12   Required modification for OR gate.

The steps of the procedure are applied to the function $f = \bar{A}\bar{B}C + A\bar{B}\bar{C}$, the two-level realization of which is shown in Fig. 6.13. The realization of the function after step 1 is shown in Fig. 6.14. The modified network after step 2 is shown in Fig. 6.15 along with the tests to be used to detect single or multiple faults. The procedure can also be applied to networks having NAND and NOR gates. Finally, it should be noted that the number of extra control inputs required cannot exceed six, since all the inputs with the same input sequence $X \in (S_1 \cup S_2)$ can be tied together (in Fig. 6.15 c_2 and c_4 are the same and

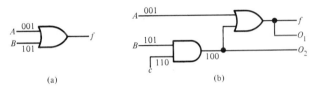

Fig. 6.13   Two-level realization of $f = \bar{A}\bar{B}C + A\bar{B}\bar{C}$.

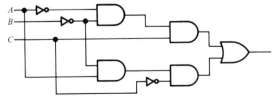

Fig. 6.14   Realization of $f = \bar{A}\bar{B}\bar{C} + A\bar{B}\bar{C}$ after step 1.

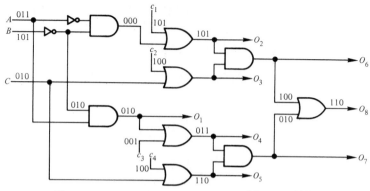

Fig. 6.15   Testable realization of $f = \bar{A}\bar{B}C + A\bar{B}\bar{C}$.

could be joined). Furthermore, the additional outputs allow fault location down to a single gate.

6.3.4   Syndrome-testable Design

Another approach to the design of testable combinational circuits is to modify a given realization by inserting extra inputs so that the final circuit becomes "syndrome testable" [6.11]. The syndrome of a Boolean function is defined as $S = K/2^n$, where K is the number of minterms realized by the function and n is the number of input lines. For example, the syndrome of a three-input AND gate is $\frac{1}{8}$ and that of a two-input OR gate is $\frac{3}{4}$. Since the syndrome is a functional property, various realizations of the same function have the same syndrome.

The input–output syndrome relation of a circuit having various interconnected blocks depends on whether the inputs to the blocks are disjoint or conjoint, as well as on the gate in which the blocks terminate. For a circuit having two blocks with unshared inputs, if S_1 and S_2 denote the syndromes of the functions realized by the blocks 1 and 2 respectively, the input–output syndrome relation S for the circuit is:

Terminating gate	*Syndrome relation* S
OR	$S_1 + S_2 - S_1 \cdot S_2$
AND	$S_1 \cdot S_2$
Exclusive-OR	$S_1 + S_2 - 2S_1 \cdot S_2$
NAND	$1 - S_1 \cdot S_2$
NOR	$1 - (S_1 + S_2 - S_1 \cdot S_2)$

If blocks 1 and 2 have shared inputs and realize the function F and G

respectively, then the following relations hold:

$$S(F + G) = S(F) + S(G) - S(FG)$$

$$S(FG) = S(F) + S(G) + S(\bar{F}\bar{G}) - 1$$

$$S(F \oplus G) = S(F\bar{G}) + S(\bar{F}G)$$

As an example let us find the syndrome and the number of minterms realized by the fan-out free circuit of Fig. 6.16. We have

$$S_1 = 3/4 \quad S_2 = 3/4 \quad S_3 = 1 - S_1 S_2 = 7/16 \quad S_4 = 1/4$$

Hence

$$S = 1 - (S_3 + S_4 - S_3 S_4) = 27/64$$

$$K = S \cdot 2^n = 27$$

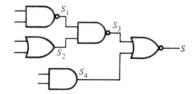

Fig. 6.16   A hypothetical circuit.

Any two-level (AND–OR) non-redundant circuit which realizes a unate function in all its variables is syndrome-testable, i.e. no fault in the circuit can cause the circuit to have the same syndrome as the fault-free circuit. However, there are two-level non-redundant circuits which have non-unate input lines, and hence are not syndrome-testable. Any two-level non-redundant network can be made syndrome-testable by adding a minimal number of control inputs. For example, let us consider the function

$$F = x_1 x_2 + x_3 \bar{x}_2$$

The fault-free syndrome of the function is $1/2$. The faulty syndrome due to the input variable x_2 being stuck-at-0 is also $1/2$. Hence F is not syndrome-testable. The function may be made syndrome-testable by inserting a control input c to realize the new function

$$F = c x_1 x_2 + x_3 \bar{x}_2$$

The input c is set to 1 during normal operation, while for testing purposes it is used as a valid input.

The test procedure of the syndrome-testable circuits is shown in Fig. 6.17. Each possible input combination is applied to the circuit under test and the number of 1s appearing on the circuit output are counted by the syndrome register which acts as a counter. The equality checker checks the register's

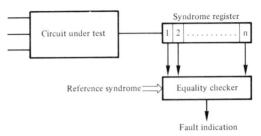

Fig. 6.17   The test procedure (*courtesy of IEEE, © 1979*).

contents with the expected syndrome. The circuit is faulty if the syndromes are unequal. The problem with this test procedure is that all possible input combinations have to be applied. However, this problem can be overcome by dividing a circuit with a large number of inputs into several subcircuits, such that each subcircuit is syndrome-testable and has a reasonably small number of inputs.

6.4   TESTABLE DESIGN OF SEQUENTIAL CIRCUITS

The use of checking experiments to determine whether a sequential machine represents the behavior specified by its state table yields good results provided that

(a)   The machine is reduced and strongly connected.
(b)   The machine has a distinguishing sequence.
(c)   The actual machine has no more states than the correctly operating machine.

For machines that do not have any distinguishing sequences the checking experiments are very long and consequently hard to apply in any practical situation. One approach to this problem is to modify a given machine by adding extra outputs so that the modified machine has a distinguishing sequence. A sequential machine which possesses one or more distinguishing sequences is said to be "diagnosable".

A procedure for modifying a sequential machine to possess a distinguishing sequence if it does not already do so, has been presented by Kohavi *et al.* [6.12]. Let us explain the procedure by considering the state table of Machine M shown in Fig. 6.18; Machine M does not have a distinguishing sequence. The procedure begins with the construction of the testing table of the machine; the testing table for Machine M is shown in Fig. 6.19. The column headings consist of all input/output combinations, where the pair X/Z corresponds to input X and output Z. The entries of the table are the "next states". For example, from state A under input 1 the machine goes to state B with an

Present state	Next state/output	
	$x = 0$	$x = 1$
A	A,0	B,0
B	A,0	C,0
C	A,1	D,0
D	A,1	A,0

Fig. 6.18　State table of Machine M.

Present state	0/0	0/1	1/0	1/1
A	A	–	B	–
B	A	–	C	–
C	–	A	D	–
D	–	A	A	–
AB	(AA)	–	BC	–
AC	–	–	BD	–
AD	–	–	AB	–
BC	–	–	CD	–
BD	–	–	AC	–
CD	–	(AA)	AD	–

Fig. 6.19　Testing table for Machine M.

output of 0. This is denoted by entering B in column 1/0 and a dash (–) in column 1/1. In a similar manner the next states of A are entered in the upper half of the table.

The lower half of the table is derived in a straightforward manner from the upper half. If the entries in rows S_i and S_j, column X_k/Z_1, of the upper half are S_p and S_q respectively, the entry in row S_iS_j, column X_k/Z_1 of the lower half, is S_pS_q. For example, since the entries in rows A and B, column 1/0, are B and C respectively, the corresponding entry in row AB, column 1/0, is BC and so on. If for a pair S_i and S_j either one or both corresponding entries in some column X_k/Z_1 are dashes, the corresponding entry in row S_iS_j, column X_k/Z_1, is a dash. For example, the entry in row BD, column 0/0 is a dash, since the entry in row D, column 0/0, is a dash. Whenever an entry in the testing table consists of a repeated state (e.g. AA in row AB), that entry is circled. A circle around AA implies that both states A and B are merged under input 0 into state A and hence are indistinguishable by any experiment starting with an input 0.

The next step of the procedure is to form the "testing graph" of the machine. The testing graph is a directed graph with each node corresponding to a row in the lower half of the testing table. A directed edge labelled X_k/Z_1 is drawn from node S_iS_j to node S_pS_q, where $p \neq q$, if there exists an entry in row S_iS_j, column X_k/Z_1 of the testing table. Figure 6.20 shows the testing graph for Machine M.

A machine is "definitely diagnosable" if and only if its testing graph has no loops and there are no repeated states, i.e. no circled entries in its testing table.

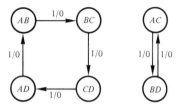

Fig. 6.20   Testing graph for Machine M.

Machine M is therefore not definitely diagnosable since $\widehat{AA}$ exists in its testing table and its testing graph contains two loops: $AB–BC–CD–AD–AB$ and $AC–BD–AC$. In order to make the machine definitely diagnosable, additional output variables are required to eliminate all repeated entries from its testing table and to open all loops in its testing graph. The maximum number of extra output terminals required to make a 2^k state machine definitely diagnosable is k; however, the addition of one output terminal is sufficient to make machine M definitely diagnosable. The modified state table of machine M is shown in Fig. 6.21; this version possesses the distinguishing sequences 0 and 11. The checking experiment for a definitely diagnosable machine can be derived as follows:

1.   Apply a homing sequence, followed by a transfer sequence (S_i, S_0) if necessary, to bring the machine into an initial state S_0.
2.   Choose a distinguishing sequence so that it is the shorter one of the sequences of all 0s or all 1s. (For the purpose of clearer presentation of the procedure, assume that the distinguishing sequence has been chosen as the all-1s sequence.)
3.   Apply the distinguishing sequence followed by a 1. (If the all-0s sequence has been chosen, apply a 0 instead of a 1.)
4.   If S_{01}, i.e. the 1-successor of S_0, is different from S_0, apply another 1 to check the transition from S_{01} under a 1 input. Similarly, if $S_{011} \neq S_{01}$ and $S_{011} \neq S_0$, apply another 1. Continue to apply 1 inputs in the same manner as long as new transitions are checked.
5.   When an additional 1 input does not yield any new transition apply an input of 0 followed by the distinguishing sequence.

Present state	Next state/output $Z_1 Z_2$	
	$X = 0$	$X = 1$
A	A,00	B,01
B	A,01	C,00
C	A,10	D,00
D	A,11	A,01

Fig. 6.21   Machine M with additional output Z_2.

6. Apply inputs of 1s as long as new transitions can be checked. Repeat steps 5 and 6 when no new transitions can be checked.
7. When steps 5 and 6 do not yield any new transitions and the machine, which is in state S_i, is not yet completely checked, apply the transfer sequence $T(S_i, S_k)$, where S_k is a state whose transition has not been checked, such that $T(S_i, S_k)$ passes through checked transitions only.
8. Repeat the last three steps until all transitions have been checked.

The checking experiment for the definitely diagnosable machine of Fig. 6.21 has been designed using the above procedure. It required only 23 symbols and is illustrated below:

```
Input      1 1 1 1 1 0 1 1 0 1 1 1 1 1 1 0 1 1 0 0 1 1
State    A B C D A B A B C A B C D A B C D A B C A A B C
Output Z₁ 0 0 0 0 0 0 0 0 1 0 0 0 0 0 0 0 1 0 0 1 0 0 0
       Z₂ 1 0 0 1 1 1 1 0 0 1 0 0 1 1 0 0 1 1 0 0 0 1 0
```

For an n-state, m-input symbol machine this procedure gives a bound on the length of checking sequences that is approximately mn^3.

As mentioned in Chap. 3 (Sec. 3.4), generation of state tables for large sequential circuits is not practicable. Hence the technique is rather academic and of little practical value in LSI/VLSI design.

6.5   THE SCAN-PATH TECHNIQUE FOR TESTABLE SEQUENTIAL CIRCUIT DESIGN

The testing of sequential circuits is complicated because of the difficulties in setting and checking the states of the memory elements. These problems can be overcome by modifying the design of a general sequential circuit so that it will have the following two properties [6.13]:

1. The circuit can easily be set to any desired internal state.
2. It is easy to find a sequence of input patterns such that the resulting output sequence will indicate the internal state of the circuit. In other words the circuit has a distinguishing sequence.

The basic idea is to add an extra input c to the memory excitation logic in order to control the mode of a circuit. When $c = 0$ the circuit operates in its normal mode but when $c = 1$ the circuit enters into a mode in which the elements are connected together to form a shift register. This facility is incorporated by inserting a double-throw switch in each input lead of every memory element. All these switches are ganged together and the circuit can operate either in its "normal" mode or "shift register" mode. Figure 6.22 shows a sequential circuit using JK flip-flops; the circuit is modified as shown

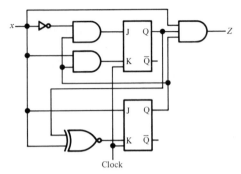

Fig. 6.22 A sequential circuit.

in Fig. 6.23. Each of the double-throw switches may be realized as indicated in Fig. 6.24. One additional input connection to the modified circuit is required to supply the signal c to control all the switches, and a few inverters will be needed to supply the complementary signal $\bar{c}$.

In the shift register mode, the first flip-flop can be set directly from the primary inputs (scan-in inputs) and the output of the last flip-flop can be directly monitored on the primary output (scan-out output). This means that the circuit can be set to any desired state via the scan-in inputs and that the

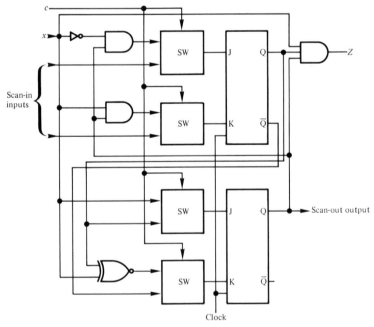

Fig. 6.23 Modified sequential circuit.

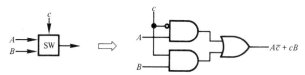

Fig. 6.24 A realization for the double-throw switch.

internal state can be determined via the scan-out output. The procedure for testing the circuit is as follows:

1. Set $c = 1$ to switch the circuit to shift register mode.
2. Check operation as a shift register by using scan-in inputs, scan-out output and the clock.
3. Set the initial state of the shift register.
4. Set $c = 0$ to return to normal mode.
5. Apply test input pattern to the combinational logic.
6. Set $c = 1$ to return to shift register mode.
7. Shift out the final state while setting the starting state for the next test.
8. Go to step 4.

With this procedure a considerable proportion of the actual testing time is spent in setting the state, an operation which requires a number of clock pulses equal to the length of the shift register. This time may be decreased by forming several short shift registers rather than a single long one; the time needed to set or read the state would then be equal to the length of the longest shift register. The extent to which the number of shift registers can be increased is determined by the number of input and output connections available to be used to drive and sense the shift registers.

The main advantage of the scan-path approach is that a sequential circuit can be transformed into a combinational circuit, thus making test generation for the circuit relatively easy. Besides, very few extra gates or pins are required for this transformation.

Another implementation of the scan-path technique has been described by Funatsu *et al.* [6.14]. The basic memory element used in this approach is known as a "raceless D-type flip-flop with scan path" [6.15]. Figure 6.25(a) shows such a memory element which consists of two latches L1 and L2. The two clock signals $C1$ and $C2$ operate exclusively. During normal operation $C2$ remains at logic 1 and $C1$ is set to logic 0 for sufficient time to latch up the data at the data input $D1$. The output of L1 is latched into L2 when $C1$ returns to logic 1.

Scan-in operation is realized by clocking the test input value at $D2$ into the latch L1 by setting $C2$ to logic 0. The output of the L1 latch is clocked into L2 when $C2$ returns to logic 1.

The configuration of the scan path approach used at logic card level is shown in Fig. 6.25(b). All the flip-flops on a logic card are connected as a shift

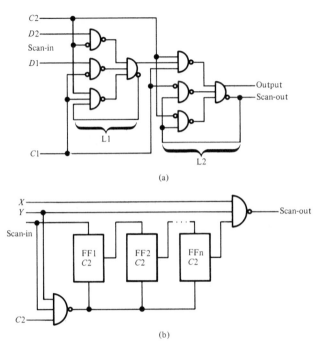

Fig. 6.25   (a) Raceless flip-flop with scan path; (b) configuration of logic card. (Adapted from Ref. 6.14.)

register, such that for each card there is one scan path. In addition there is provision for selecting a specified card in a subsystem with many cards by $X-Y$ address signals (Fig. 6.25(b)). If a card is not selected its output is blocked; thus a number of card outputs in a subsystem can be put together with only a particular card having control of the test output for that subsystem. The Nippon Electric Company in Japan has adopted this version of the scan path approach to improve the testability of their FLT–700 processor system.

6.6   LEVEL-SENSITIVE SCAN DESIGN (LSSD)

One of the best known and the most widely practiced methods for synthesizing testable circuits is the IBM LSSD (level-sensitive scan design) |6.16–6.19|. The "level sensitive" aspect of the method means that a sequential network is designed so that the steady-state response to any input state change is independent of the component and wire delays within the network. Also if an input state change involves the changing of more than one input signal, the response must be independent of the order in which they change. These conditions are ensured by the enforcement of certain design rules, particularly pertaining to the clocks that evoke state changes in the network. "Scan" refers to the ability to shift into or out of any state of the network.

6.6.1 Clocked Hazard-free Latches

In LSSD, all internal storage is implemented in hazard-free polarity-hold switches. The polarity-hold switch has two input signals as shown in Fig. 6.26(a). The latch cannot change state if $C = 0$. If C is set to 1 the internal state of the latch takes the value of the excitation input D. A flow table for this sequential network, along with an excitation table and a logic implementation, is shown in Fig. 6.26.

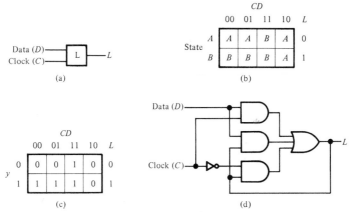

Fig. 6.26   Hazard-free polarity-hold latch: (a) Symbolic representation; (b) flow table; (c) excitation table; (d) logic implementation (*courtesy of IEEE, © 1978*).

The clock signal C will normally occur (change from 0 to 1) after the data signal D has become stable at either a 1 or a 0. The output of the latch is set to the new value of the data signal at the time the clock signal occurs. The correct changing of the latch is not dependent on the rise or fall time of the clock signal, but only on the clock signal being 1 for a period equal to or greater than the time required for the data signal to propagate through the latch and stabilize.

A shift-register latch (SRL) can be formed by adding a clocked input to the polarity hold latch L1 and including a second latch L2 to act as intermediate storage during shifting (Fig. 6.27). As long as the clock signals A and B are both 0, the L1 latch operates exactly like a polarity-hold latch. Terminal I is the scan-in input for the shift register latch and $+L2$ is the output. The logic implementation of the SRL is shown in Fig. 6.28. When the latch is operating as a shift register, data from the preceding stage are gated into the polarity-hold switch via I, through a change of the clock A from 0 to 1. After A has changed back to 0, clock B gates the data in the latch L1 into the output latch

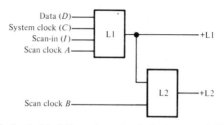

Fig. 6.27 Polarity-hold shift register latch (*courtesy of IEEE*, © *1978*).

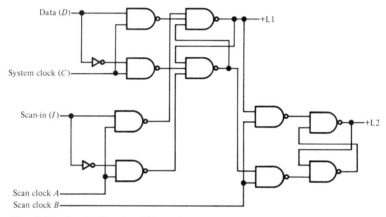

Fig. 6.28 Logic for the shift-register latch (*courtesy of IEEE*, © *1979*).

L2. Clearly, *A* and *B* can never both be 1 at the same time if the shift register latch is to operate properly.

The SRLs can be interconnected to form a shift register as shown in Fig. 6.29. The input *I* and the output +L2 are strung together in a loop and the clocks *A* and *B* are connected in parallel.

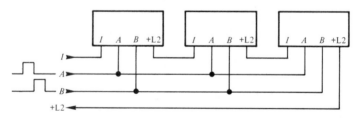

Fig. 6.29 Linkage of several SRLs (*courtesy of IEEE*, © *1979*).

6.6.2   LSSD Design Rules

A specific set of design rules has been defined to provide level-sensitive logic subsystems with a scannable design that would aid testing [5.17].

Rule 1   All internal storage is implemented in hazard-free polarity-hold latches.

Rule 2   The latches are controlled by two or more non-overlapping clocks such that:

(a)   Two latches, where one feeds the other, cannot have the same clock (see Fig. 6.30(a)).

(b)   A latch X may gate a clock C_i to produce a gated clock C_{ig} which drives another latch Y if and only if clock C_{ig} does not clock latch X, where C_{ig} is any clock derived from C_i (see Fig. 6.30(b)).

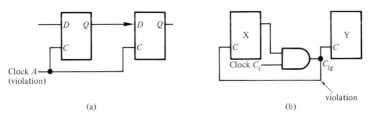

Fig. 6.30   (a) Checking rule 2a; (b) checking rule 2b.

Rule 3   It must be possible to identify a set of clock primary inputs from which the clock inputs to SRLs are controlled either through simple powering trees or through logic that is gated by SRLs and/or non-clock primary inputs (see Fig. 6.31). Given this structure the following rules must hold:

(a)   All clock inputs to all SRLs must be at their OFF states when all clock primary inputs are held to their OFF states (see Fig. 6.31(a)).

(b)   The clock signal that appears at any clock input of any SRL must be controllable from one or more clock primary inputs such that it is possible to set the clock input of the SRL to an ON state by turning any one of the corresponding clock primary inputs to its ON state and also setting the required gating condition from SRLs and/or non-clock primary inputs.

(c)   No clock can be ANDed with either the true value or the complement value of another clock (see Fig. 6.31(b)).

Rule 4   Clock primary inputs may not feed the data inputs to latches either directly or through combinational logic, but may only feed the clock input to the latches or the primary outputs.

A sequential logic network designed in accordance with Rules 1–4 would be "level-sensitive". To simplify testing and minimize the primary inputs and

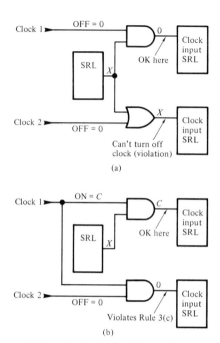

Fig. 6.31   (a) Clock OFF test; (b) clock ON test (*courtesy of IEEE, © 1977*).

outputs, it must also be possible to shift data into and out of the latches in the system. Therefore two more rules must be observed:

Rule 5   All SRLs must be interconnected into one or more shift registers, each of which has an input, an output and clocks available at the terminals of the module.

Rule 6   There must exist some primary input sensitizing condition (referred to as the scan state) such that:

(a)   Each SRL or scan-out primary output is a function of only the preceding SRL or scan-in primary input in its shift register during the shifting operation.

(b)   All clocks except the shift clocks are held OFF at the SRL inputs.

(c)   Any shift clock to an SRL may be turned ON and OFF by changing the corresponding clock primary input for each clock.

A sequential logic network that is level-sensitive and also has the scan capability as per Rules 1 to 6 is called a level-sensitive scan design (LSSD). Figure 6.32(a) depicts a general structure for an LSSD system in which all system outputs are taken from the L2 latch; hence it is called a "double latch design". In the "double-latch" configuration each SRL operates in a master–

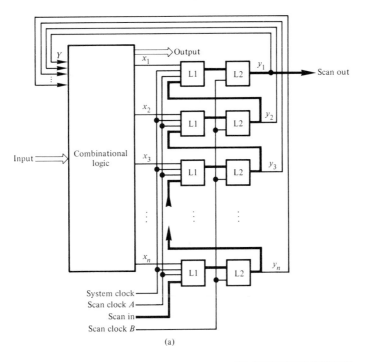

(a)

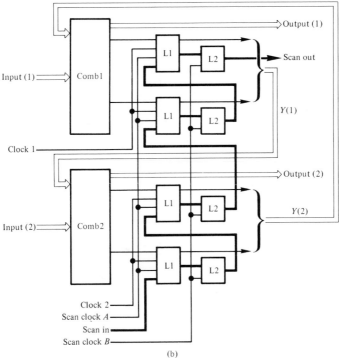

(b)

Fig. 6.32 (a) Double-latch LSSD; (b) single-latch LSSD. (Adapted from Ref. 6.16.)

slave mode. Data transfer occurs under system clock and scan clock B during normal operation, and under scan clock A and scan clock B during scan-path operation. Both latches are therefore required during system operation. In the "single-latch" configuration the combinational logic is partitioned into two disjoint sets, Comb1 and Comb2 (Fig. 6.32(b)). The system clocks used for SRLs in Comb1 and Comb2 are denoted by Clock1 and Clock2 respectively; they are non-overlapping. The outputs of the SRLs in Comb1 are fed back as secondary variable inputs to Comb2, and vice versa. This configuration uses the output of latch L1 as the system output; the L2 latch is used only for shifting. In other words the L2 latches are redundant and represent an overhead for testability. However, the basic SRL design can be modified to reduce the overhead. The modified latch called the L1/L2* SRL is shown in Fig. 6.33. The main difference between the basic SRL and the L1/L2* SRL is that L2* has an alternative system data input $D2$ clocked in by a separate system clock $C2$. The original data input D in Fig. 6.27 is also available and is now identified as $D1$ in Fig. 6.33. $D1$ is clocked in by the original system clock which is now called $C1$. Clock signals $C1$ and $C2$ are non-overlapping. The single-latch configuration of Fig. 6.32(b) can now be modified to the configuration of Fig. 6.34 in which the system output can be taken from either the L1 output or the L2* output. In other words both L1 and L2* are utilized, which means fewer latches are required in the system. As a result there is a significant reduction in the silicon cost when L1/L2* SRLs are used to implement the LSSD. Although both latches in L1/L2* SRLs can be used for system functions it is

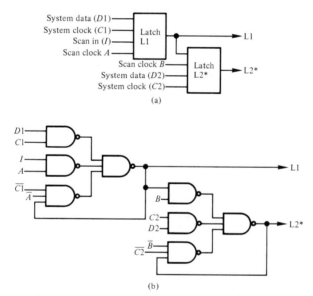

Fig. 6.33   (a) L1/L2* SRL; (b) implementation of L1/L2* SRL using NAND gates. (Adapted from Ref. 6.18.)

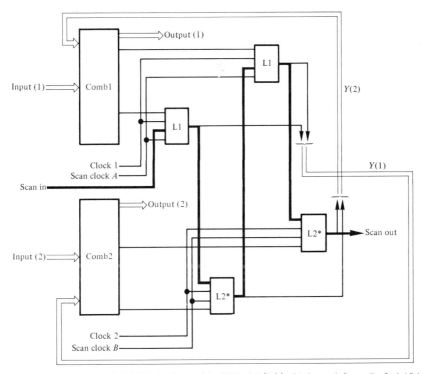

Fig. 6.34   Single-latch LSSD design using SRL L1/L2*. (Adapted from Ref. 6.18.)

absolutely essential as in conventional LSSD that both L1 and L2* outputs do not feed the same combinational logic.

6.6.3   Advantages of the LSSD Technique

The LSSD approach is very similar to the scan-path approach used by the NEC, except that it has the level-sensitive attribute and requires two separate clocks to operate latches L1 and L2. The use of LSSD alleviates the testing problems in the following ways:

1. The correct operation of the logic network is independent of a.c. characteristics such as clock edge rise time and fall time.
2. Network is combinational in nature as far as test generation and testing is concerned.
3. The elimination of all hazards and races greatly simplifies both test generation and fault simulation.

The ability to test networks as combinational logic is one of the most important benefits of the LSSD. This is done by operating the polarity-hold latches as SRLs during testing.

Any desired pattern of 1s and 0s can be shifted into the polarity-hold latches as inputs to the combinational network. For example, the combinational network of Fig. 6.32(a) is tested by shifting part of each required pattern into the SRLs, with the remainder applied through the primary inputs. Then the system clock is turned on for one cycle, the test pattern is propagated through the combinational logic and the result of the test is captured in the register and at the primary outputs. The result of the test captured in the register is then scanned out and compared with the expected response. The shift register must also be tested and this is accomplished by shifting a short sequence of 1s and 0s through the shift register latches.

In general most functions designed in an unconstrained environment can be designed using the LSSD approach with little or no impact on performance. However, the requirement of level-sensitive flip-flops demand custom-designed chips; hence the LSSD approach would be difficult to apply to a board level circuit built using off-the-shelf ICs.

6.7   RANDOM ACCESS SCAN TECHNIQUE

The design methods discussed in Secs. 6.5 and 6.6 use sequential access scan-in/scan-out techniques to improve testability, i.e. all flip-flops are connected in series during testing to form a shift-register or registers. In an alternative approach, known as "random access scan", each flip-flop in a logic network is selected individually by an address for control and observation of its state [6.20]. The basic memory element in a random access scan-in/scan-out network is an "addressable latch". The circuit diagram of an addressable latch is shown in Fig. 6.35. A latch is selected by X–Y address signals, the state of which can then be controlled and observed through scan-in/scan-out lines. When a latch is selected and its scan clock goes from 0 to 1, the scan data input is transferred through the network to the scan data output, where the inverted value of the scan data can be observed. The input on the DATA line is transferred to the latch output Q during the negative transition (1 to 0) of the

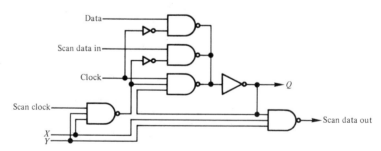

Fig. 6.35   An addressable latch (*courtesy of IEEE,* © *1980*).

clock. The scan data out lines from all latches are ANDed together to produce the chip scan out signal; the scan-out line of a latch remains at logic 1 unless the latch is selected by the X–Y signals.

A different type of addressable latch—the set/reset type—is shown in Fig. 6.36. The "clear" signal clears the latch during its negative transition. Prior to scan-in operation, all latches are cleared. Then a latch is addressed by the X–Y lines and the preset signal is applied to set the latch state.

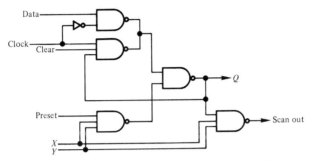

Fig. 6.36   Set/reset type addressable latch (*courtesy of IEEE,* © *1980*).

The basic model of a sequential circuit with random access scan-in/scan-out network is shown in Fig. 6.37. The X- and Y-address decoders are used to access an addressable latch—like a cell in random access memory. A tree of AND gates is used to combine all scan-out signals. Clear input of all latches are tied together to form a master reset signal. Preset inputs of all latches receive the same scan-in signal gated by the scan clock; however, only the latch which is accessed by the X–Y addresses is affected.

The test procedure of a network with random access scan-in/scan-out network is as follows:

1. Set test input to all test points.
2. Apply the master reset signal to initialize all memory elements.
3. Set scan-in address and data, and then apply the scan clock.
4. Repeat step 3 until all internal test inputs are scanned-in.
5. Clock once for normal operation.
6. Check states of the output points.
7. Read the scan-out states of all memory elements by applying appropriate X–Y signals.

The random access scan-in/scan-out technique has been proposed by the Fujitsu Co. in Japan as a systematic design method to enhance testability of VLSI chips. It has several advantages:

1. The observability and controllability of all system latches are allowed.
2. Any point in a combinational network can be observed with one additional gate and one address per observation point.

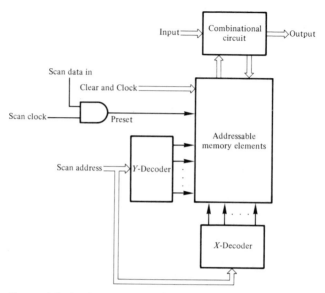

Fig. 6.37   Sequential circuit designed with addressable latches (*courtesy of IEEE,* © *1980*).

3. A memory array in a logic network can be tested through a scan-in/scan-out network. The scan address inputs are applied directly to the memory array. The data input and the write-enable input of the array receive the scan data and the scan clock respectively. The output of the memory array is ANDed into the scan-out tree to be observed.

    The technique has also a few disadvantages:

1. Extra logic in the form of two address gates for each memory element, plus the address decoders and output AND trees, result in 3–4 gates overhead per memory element.
2. Scan control, data and address pins add up to 10–20 extra pins. By using a serially loadable address counter the number of pins can be reduced to around 6.
3. Some constraints are imposed on the logic design, such as the exclusion of asynchronous latch operation.

6.8   BUILT-IN TEST

As digital circuits grow more complex and difficult to test, it becomes increasingly attractive to build some self-testing ability into the circuits under test. Built-in test may be conveniently used to detect and isolate a faulty component in a circuit and thus facilitate its replacement. An important added feature of properly designed built-in test is the ability to simplify off-line testing by taking advantage of the increased controllability and observability made possible by the incorporation of the self-testing capability.

6.8.1   Built-in Digital Circuit Observer (BIDCO)

BIDCO combines the advantages of built-in test and scan path techniques [6.21–6.22]. The test philosophy of BIDCO is to apply a set of pseudo-random test patterns to the circuit under test and determine with the help of a decoder whether the output response of the circuit is correct or not. Sequential circuits can also be tested by this technique provided that they can be set to known states, before the pseudo-random patterns are applied to the com-binational parts of the circuits. The test hardware consists of built-in-logic-block-observers (BILBO), a decoder and status indicators. Figure 6.38 shows the block diagram of the BIDCO.

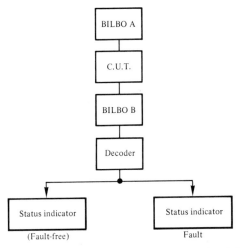

Fig. 6.38   Block diagram of BIDCO (*courtesy of IEEE, © 1980*).

A BILBO is a multi-purpose test module which can be reconfigured to func-tion as an input test pattern generator or an output signature analyzer. It is composed of a row of flip-flops and some additional gates for shift and feed-back operations. Figure 6.39 shows the logic diagram of a BILBO. The two control inputs B_1 and B_2 are used to select one of the four function modes:

Mode 1 $B_1 = 0$, $B_2 = 1$. All the flip-flops are reset.

Mode 2 $B_1 = 1$, $B_2 = 1$. The BILBO behaves as a latch. The input data $X_1 - X_n$ can be simultaneously clocked into the flip-flops and can be read from the Q and $\bar{Q}$ outputs.

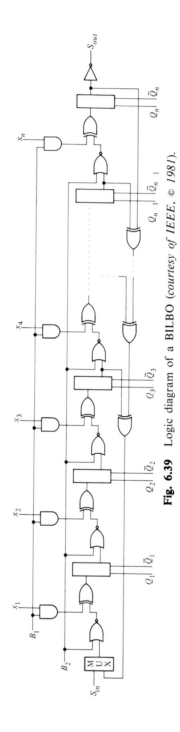

Fig. 6.39 Logic diagram of a BILBO (*courtesy of IEEE, © 1981*).

Mode 3 $B_1 = 0$, $B_2 = 0$. BILBO works as a linear shift register. Data are serially clocked into the register through I_{in}, while the register contents can be simultaneously read at the parallel Q and $\bar{Q}$ outputs, or can be clocked out through the serial output I_{out}.

Mode 4 $B_1 = 1$, $B_2 = 0$. BILBO is converted into a multiple-input signature register. In this mode BILBO may be used for performing parallel signature analysis or for issuing pseudo-random sequences. The later application is achieved by keeping $X_1 - X_n$ on fixed logical values.

BILBO A in the block diagram of Fig. 6.38 is configured as a pseudo-random pattern generator, the outputs of which are applied as test inputs to the circuit under test. BILBO B is configured as a parallel signature register and receives its input from the circuit under test. The output of BILBO B goes to the decoder. The decoder is an m-input AND gate, where m equals the number of flip-flops in BILBO B, with appropriate inverters at the input so that for the set of input combinations which correspond to that of a good circuit, the output of the decoder is a logical 1. Two LEDs (light emitting diode) can be used to indicate the fault-free and the fault status of the circuit under test.

The main advantage of the BIDCO approach is that it allows checking of logic circuits without the use of very expensive automated test equipments. In addition the test data volume is reduced very significantly; in LSSD, scan path or random access scan, a considerable amount of such data is involved with the shifting in and out. One additional advantage of the BIDCO approach is that unlike the LSSD it does not require any special flip-flops. The main limitation of this approach is that it does not provide information for isolating faults in combinational logic circuits. For sequential circuits fault isolation can be done only if the scan technique is also used [6.23].

6.8.2   Built-in Test for VLSI Chips

The built-in test strategy can be used to enhance testability of VLSI chips [6.24, 6.25]. It is based on the following principles:

1. Test patterns are generated on-chip.
2. Responses to the test patterns are also evaluated on-chip.
3. External operations are required only to initialize the built-in tests and to check the go/no-go test results from a chip.
4. Additional pins and silicon area are kept to a minimum.

The concept of a modular built-in test is illustrated in Fig. 6.40, which shows a chip composed of three functional modules A, B and C. Each module has its own built-in test pattern generator (TPG) and test answer evaluator (TAE); however, several modules can share a common TPG or TAE.

A simple test pattern generator for a functional module can be obtained by converting already existing registers in a module into a linear feedback shift

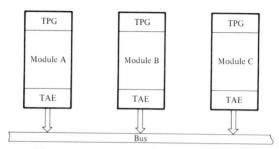

Fig. 6.40   Modular chip with built-in test.

register. The test generator produces pseudo-random test patterns. Corresponding to each test pattern the module produces a test answer. The built-in TAE compresses the complete sequence of test answers into a characteristic signature. Any difference in the actual and the known good signature, which may be stored on-chip, indicates that the module is not operating as expected; a no-go signal is obtained from the chip in this case.

A signature is usually created by feeding the data serially into the feedback line of a linear feedback register via an additional EX–OR gate. However, a signature can be obtained in a single clock cycle when a multiple input signature register (MISR) is used. Figure 6.41 shows an eight-bit MISR; the data to be coded are fed into MISR not only at the feedback line, but also at all shift lines between the register cells. The MISR too can be obtained by functional conversion of already existing registers in a module.

Both TPG and TAE can in fact be replaced by BILBOs (see Sec. 6.8.1), as shown in Fig. 6.42. In the shift mode a BILBO may be used as scan latches for shifting out signatures or shifting in deterministic test patterns if random patterns are insufficient. In the signature mode, a BILBO can also act as a pseudo-random generator when setting the inputs $Z_1 \ldots Z_n$ to fixed logical values.

The trade-offs in implementing testability at the chip level are as follows:

1. An extra pin is required to initialize the built-in tests and to read the go/no-go information. Alternatively the go/no-go information can be read from the bus.
2. Additional gates, needed to convert existing registers in a module into pattern generators and signature analyzers, may increase the overhead of silicon area by 5–15%.
3. The loss of performance is at least one gate delay. By connecting the test aids in parallel to the data paths, instead of using functional conversion this delay can be avoided. However, the overhead still increases, although the latches remain unaffected.

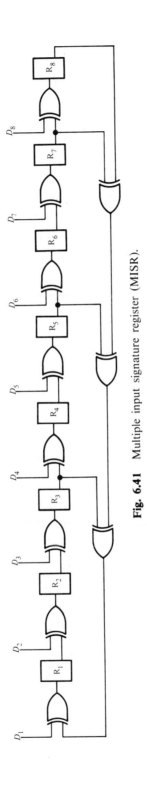

Fig. 6.41 Multiple input signature register (MISR).

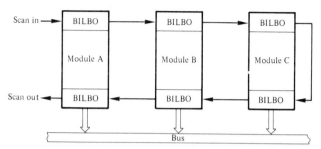

Fig. 6.42   Use of BILBOs to improve testability of chips.

6.9   DESIGN FOR AUTONOMOUS SELF-TEST

The systematic techniques for designing testable circuits, discussed in Secs. 6.5–6.7, provide substantial improvements over designs that do not include testability. However, there are a number of problems associated with these techniques, e.g.

(a)   Test generation is still necessary for the combinational part of the circuit.

(b)   Test time is substantially increased because the test pattern has to be shifted in (often serially) and the response has to be shifted out.

(c)   Tests are generated on the assumption that only stuck-at faults occur in circuits, which is not true in an LSI/VLSI environment.

Recently a new design method for digital circuits has been proposed which eliminates the need for test generation and fault modelling [6.26, 6.27]. This method is known as "autonomous design verification" and consists of:

(a)   Partitioning a circuit into subcircuits. Each subcircuit has few enough inputs so that all possible combinations of its inputs can be applied to test it.

(b)   Incorporation of additional circuits or reconfiguration of existing circuits to provide direct control of the inputs of each subcircuit and to verify its response.

A circuit, so designed, can operate either in the "normal mode" or in the "test mode". In the normal mode the circuit carries out its normal functions whereas, in the test mode, each subcircuit is tested exhaustively. Since all possible input combinations are applied to the subcircuits, test generation is not necessary and all functions of the subcircuits can be verified without any fault model assumptions. For exhaustive testing, a linear feedback shift register (LFSR) is used to generate all possible input patterns. An LFSR can also be used to compact the output response by generating a signature that can probabilistically verify the fault-free response of a circuit.

Let us consider the circuit of Fig. 6.43(a) to illustrate the use of the method for testing combinational circuits. The circuit is partitioned into two sub-circuits C_1 and C_2, as shown in Fig. 6.43(b). The functions of the two added control inputs $MC1$ and $MC2$ are as follows:

When $MC1 = 0$ and $MC2 = 1$, subcircuit C_2 is disabled. Subcircuit C_1, shown in Fig. 6.43(c), remains; this can be tested by applying all possible input combinations at x_1, x_2, x_3 and x_4.

Similarly, when $MC1 = 1$ and $MC2 = 0$, subcircuit C_1 is disabled. In this

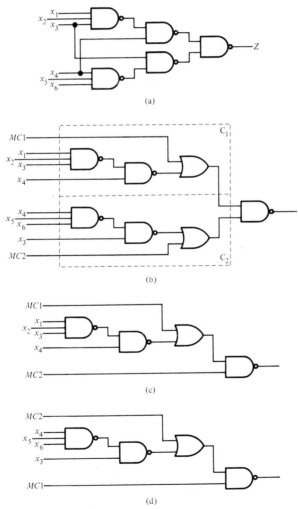

Fig. 6.43   Partitioning of a circuit for autonomous testing.

mode of testing the circuit functions as in Fig. 6.43(d), and can be tested by applying all input combinations at x_3, x_4, x_5 and x_6.

When $MC1 = MC2 = 0$ the circuit functions as the unmodified circuit, except for the added gate delay. The advantage of the design method is that any fault in the circuit itself and the testing circuit is detectable.

In general any digital circuit can be partitioned into two or more subcircuits. If the partitioning can be done so that the number of inputs to each subcircuit is reasonably small, then each subcircuit can be tested exhaustively. Figure 6.44 shows the decomposition of a circuit C with inputs $X(X_1, X_2)$ and output $Y(Y_1, Y_2)$ into two modules C_1 and C_2. The modules are connected to each other internally through buses L_{12} and L_{21}. L_{12} is the supplementary (internal) input of C_2 that is supplied by the module C_1. Similarly, L_{21} is the supplementary input of C_1 and the supplementary output of C_2. In order to test a module, it is necessary to control all the inputs, supplementary and primary, to the module and observe all its outputs directly. This can be achieved by employing multiplexers to route the primary and supplementary inputs and outputs (see Fig. 6.45(a)). In the normal mode, the supplementary input of each module is connected to the supplementary output of the other module through multiplexers 1 and 2, and the primary output of each module is routed to the output lines via multiplexers 3 and 4. In the test mode the supplementary input of the module under test is controlled by a portion of the primary input of the other module, and the supplementary output is observed directly by connecting it to the primary input lines of the other module. For example, to test module C_2, portions of X_1 can be routed via multiplexer 1 to provide control over L_{12} (Fig. 6.45(b)). Similarly, multiplexer 4 can be used to connect the supplementary output of C_2 to the output lines, so that it can be observed directly. Module C_1 can be tested in a similar way.

Autonomous testing of sequential circuits may be done in two different ways:

1. Reconfiguration of the memory elements.
2. Forced state exhaustive testing.

In the reconfiguration scheme the m flip-flops in the circuit under test are restructured into self-starting, modulus 2^m, m-stage linear feedback shift

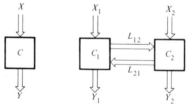

Fig. 6.44   Decomposition of a circuit into two subcircuits (*courtesy of IEEE, © 1980*).

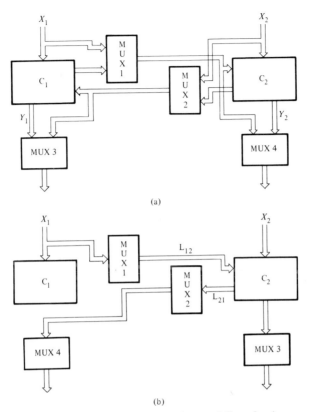

(a)

(b)

Fig. 6.45 (a) Use of multiplexers to improve the testability of a decomposed circuit; (b) test mode operation to test module 2 (*courtesy of IEEE, © 1980*).

registers which then can be used to apply all 2^m possible input patterns to the combinational parts of the circuit.

In the forced state exhaustive testing, instead of changing the configuration of the sequential machines, an input pattern generator and an output signature analyzer are built into the circuit. Both the input pattern generator and the output signature analyzer are in fact LFSRs. Figure 6.46(a) shows the configuration for the forced state exhaustive testing. In the normal operation, the input LFSR is disconnected from the circuit by resetting the multiplexers. The testing of this configuration consists of two phases:

Phase 1 Both multiplexers are set. A portion of the input LFSR is applied to the combinational part and the remaining portion is forced into the state flip-flops (Fig. 6.46(b)).

Phase 2 The lower multiplexer is reset so that the circuit changes back into the original sequential machine. Then the clock pulse is applied for the circuit to go through a state transition (Fig. 6.46(c)).

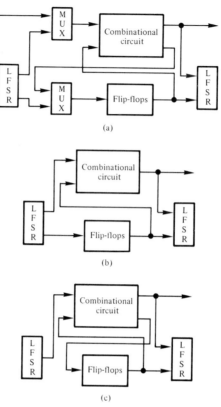

Fig. 6.46   (a) Forced state exhaustive test configuration; (b) forcing the state; (c) state transition (*courtesy of IEEE,* © *1980*).

By alternately repeating phase 1 and phase 2 the circuit can be driven into all possible states. The correct state transitions of the circuit, and its output for all possible input combinations, can be verified probabilistically by the output LFSR.

As discussed above the partitioning of a circuit into several subcircuits, and then exhaustively testing each subcircuit, definitely simplifies the testing of the overall circuit. However, partitioning of LSI/VLSI circuits could be a very complicated task, and in addition would require extra logic which needs to be tested as well. At present there are no guidelines available to indicate how efficient partitioning of a large circuit can be obtained automatically, so that each subcircuit can be exhaustively tested with the minimum number of test patterns.

A modified version of the autonomous testing, called the "verification testing" has been proposed by McCluskey [6.28]. This method is applicable to multi-output combinational circuits, provided each output depends only on a

proper subset of the inputs. The verification test set for a circuit is derived from
its "dependence matrix". The dependence matrix of a circuit has m rows and n
columns; each row represents one of the outputs and each column one of the
inputs. An entry $[(i, j); i = 1, m, j = 1, n]$ in the matrix is 1 if the output i
depends on input signal j; otherwise the entry is 0. For example, the
dependence matrix for the circuit of Fig. 6.47(a) is shown in Fig. 6.47(b). The
dependence matrix is derived by tracing paths from outputs to inputs. A
"partition dependent matrix" is then formed by partitioning the columns of a
dependence matrix into a minimum number of sets, with each row of a set
having at most one 1-entry; there may be a number of partition dependent
matrices corresponding to a "dependent matrix". The partition dependent
matrix corresponding to the dependence matrix of Fig. 6.47(b) is shown in Fig.
6.47(c).

A verification test set is obtained by assigning the same values to all input
signals belonging to the same partition of a partition dependent matrix; any
two input signals belonging to different partitions receive distinct values.
Figure 6.47(d) shows the verification test set for Fig. 6.47(a).

A "reduced" verification test set can be derived from a verification test set
by removing all repetitions of identical columns. The reduced verification test
set for the circuit of Fig. 6.47(a) is shown in Fig. 6.47(e).

This is a useful technique for testing combinational circuits, or circuits
which can be transformed into combinational forms during testing (e.g. LSSD
structure). However, the generation of the dependence matrix, which is the
most important part of this test strategy, could be a non-trivial task for circuits
of VLSI complexity.

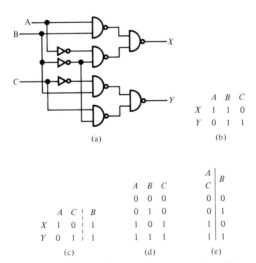

(a)

	A	B	C
X	1	1	0
Y	0	1	1

(b)

	A	C	B
X	1	0	1
Y	0	1	1

(c)

A	B	C
0	0	0
0	1	0
1	0	1
1	1	1

(d)

A C	B
0	0
0	1
1	0
1	1

(e)

Fig. 6.47   (a) Circuit under test; (b) dependence matrix; (c) partition dependent
matrix; (d) verification test set; (e) reduced verification test set.

6.10   DESIGNING TESTABILITY INTO LOGIC BOARDS

It is now widely accepted that the efficiency of testing complex logic boards on automatic test equipments (ATE) can be improved significantly by designing testability into every board. One of the simplest ways of improving testability of a board is to provide more test and control points on the board; the better they are sited the better the resolution in fault-diagnosis is [6.29–6.32]. For example, test points can be attached to:

> Points of large fan-in/fan-out.
> Outputs of memory elements.
> Internal points in feedback loops.
> Internal branches of statically redundant logic (in order to make the logic non-redundant for testing purposes).
> Data inputs of registers.

Control points can be attached to:

> Memory address lines.
> Parallel load lines of counter chains.
> Unused set/reset lines of memory elements.

Test and control points may be implemented by extra printed circuit track to spare edge connections—it is rare that all edge connections are used on a printed circuit board. This involves only a small extra cost but may contribute to the wire routing complexity of the board. If the routing test/control points to the edge connector present a problem, or if there are not enough edge pins available, test/control points can be routed to empty DIP sockets placed on the board. Even if empty DIP sockets cannot be used for test points IC clips can be attached to selected ICs to enhance observability during testing.

Frequently unused or permanently set inputs of logic devices are tied to logic 1 or 0. Instead, a pull-up resistor should be used for pins which are to be tied to logic 1 and the output of an inverter with its input pulled high, should be used for pins which are to be held at logic 0 (Fig. 6.48). This allows access to these points, via clips, if needed for testing. It also prevents a defective device from shorting power supplies to ground—a fault that can be very difficult to find. If there are separate "clear" and "preset" inputs to a device that are both tied to permanent value then two separate pull-up connections should be used, so that during testing the device can be preset or cleared using a clip. Pull-up resistors can also be used on tri-state buses. This causes a tri-state bus in the off state to go to a logic 1 so that it can be tested by an ATE.

Another way of improving testability is to insert multiplexers in order to increase the number of internal points which can be controlled or observed from the external pins. For example, in the circuit of Fig. 6.49(a) the fault α stuck-at-0 is undetectable at the primary output Z. By incorporating a multi-

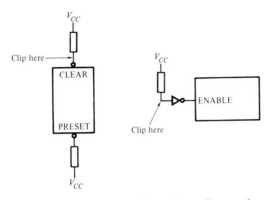

Fig. 6.48   Enhancing testability using pull-up resistors.

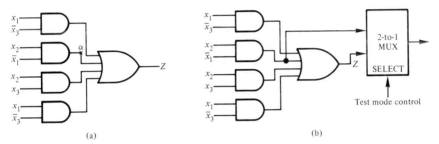

(a)   (b)

Fig. 6.49   Observation switching: (a) Circuit with fault; (b) use of multiplexer to enhance observability during testing.

plexer as shown in Fig. 6.49(b), input combination 010 can be applied to detect the fault via the multiplexer output.

A different way of achieving access to internal points is to use tri-state drivers as shown in Fig. 6.50. A test mode signal could be used to put the driver into the high impedance state. In this mode the internal point could be used as a control point. When the driver is activated the internal point becomes a test point.

Another approach to improve testability is to permit access to a subset of the logic as shown in Fig. 6.51 [6.33, 634]. Module B is physically embedded

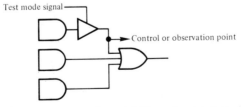

Fig. 6.50   Improvement in testability using tri-state drivers.

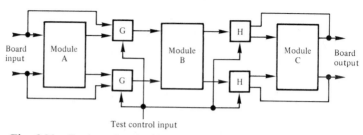

Fig. 6.51 Testing of embedded modules. (Adapted from Ref. 6.2.)

between the two modules A and C. A set of gates G and H is inserted into each of the inputs and outputs, respectively, of module B. In normal operation the test control signal is such that modules A, B and C are connected and the complete network performs its desired function. In the test mode the test control input is changed, module B is connected to the primary inputs and outputs of the board. In this mode, the control signal also causes the outputs of module C to assume a high impedance state, and hence C does not interfere with the test results generated by B. Basically this approach is similar to the previously discussed technique of using multiplexers to improve testability.

The test mode signals required by the added hardware such as multiplexers, tri-state drivers, etc. cannot always be applied via the edge pins, because there may not be enough of them. To overcome this problem, a "test state register" may be incorporated in the design. This could in fact be a shift register that is loaded and controlled by just a few signals. The various testability hardware in the circuit can then be controlled by the parallel outputs of the shift-register.

Frequently flip-flops, counters, shift registers and other memory elements assume unpredictable states when power is applied, and they must be set to known states before testing can begin. Ideally all memory elements should be reset from the external pins of the board, while in some cases additional logic may be required (Fig. 6.52(a)). Alternatively, a power-up reset may be added (Fig. 6.52(b)) to provide internal initialization, if there are no external pins on the board. With complex circuits it may be desirable to set memory elements in several known states. This not only allows independent initialization, but also simplifies generation of certain internal states required to test the board adequately.

A long counter chain presents another practical test problem. For example, the counter chain shown in Fig. 6.53 requires thousands of clock pulses to go through all the states. One way to avoid this problem is to break up the long chains into smaller ones by means of the board edge connector and by fitting jumpers to them; the jumpers can be removed during testing.

A feedback loop is difficult to test since it hides the source of a fault. The source can be located by breaking the loop physically and bringing both lines to external pins that can be short-circuited for normal operation. When not short-circuited, the separated lines provide a control point and a test point. An

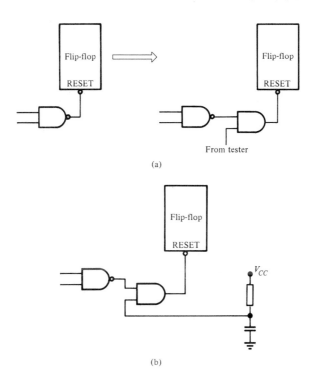

(a)

(b)

Fig. 6.52 Circuit initialization: (a) external initialization; (b) power-up reset.

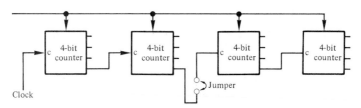

Fig. 6.53 Use of removable jumper to simplify testing of long counter chains.

alternative way of breaking a feedback loop, rather than using more costly test/control points, is to add to the feedback path a gate that can be interrupted by a signal from the tester (Fig. 6.54).

Testing timing circuits also poses a problem. On-board clock oscillators should be disconnected during tests. This can be done either by disconnecting their outputs with a test point (Fig. 6.55) or by socketing them so that they can be removed during test. One-shots should be avoided whenever possible. If one-shots must be used, slow ones (>0.5 ms) should be placed in IC sockets to facilitate their removal during testing. Fast one-shots (<0.5 ms) should have their sense lines brought out so that a latch in the tester interface can be used to observe their operation.

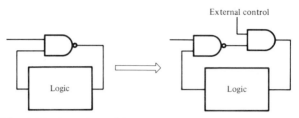

Fig. 6.54   Breaking of feedback loop using an extra gate.

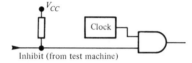

Fig. 6.55   Gated clock output.

Elements in some logic families allow a number of gate outputs to be tied together to make up wired-logic. When used, gates from the same IC package should be employed to enhance fault location.

The use of asynchronous sequential circuits should be avoided. A good practice is to use edge-triggered D-type flip-flops in preference to other types of flip-flops. Edge-connector test/control points used to improve testability of logic boards are susceptible to noise. So it is safer to use internal control points rather than edge-connector pins for initialization of noise-sensitive components such as counters.

Testing of boards containing microprocessors and other LSI devices is difficult for several reasons [6.35–6.37]:

1. LSI devices have failure modes which are more complex than the traditional stuck-at-1 or stuck-at-0 faults.
2. Access to internal logic circuits of LSI devices is severely limited by the number of I/O connections available.
3. Because of the large number of faults, a successful test requires a large number of test patterns. This causes problems because the patterns have to be stored on the tester and the test application time is increased.
4. Dynamic LSI devices must be operated within a specified range of clock frequencies in order to function. This requires that the appropriate clocks must be provided either by the tester or by the board under test. In the latter case, it is necessary to synchronize the test rate with the on-board clocks.
5. Bus structure of most LSI-based boards makes fault isolation more difficult because of the many devices on the same bus, any of which could cause the fault.

One approach to deal with microprocessors in a static testing environment is to remove or disable them so that they are essentially ignored during a board test. This can usually be accomplished by tri-stating bus buffers when they are available. The rest of the board is then tested using edge-connector and test/control points. Once the bus and most of the support circuits have been tested, the microprocessor can be single-stepped, using the READY line, to observe whether it can execute a valid microcode. Finally, the microprocessor and the entire board should be tested at normal operating speed. In order to make a microprocessor-based system testable it is necessary to provide access to the microprocessor's address, control and bidirectional data lines. These access points can be used while statically testing the board, and while single-stepping the microprocessor. The address and data lines of RAMs and ROMs should also be easily accessible.

6.11 REFERENCES

6.1 Muranaga, K., "Utilization of logic simulation and fault isolation software for practical LSI and VLSI component test program generation", *Proc. IEEE 1979 Test Conf.*, 193–202.

6.2 Muehldorf, E. I. and A. D. Savkar, "LSI logic testing—an overview", *IEEE Trans. Comput.*, 1–16 (January 1981).

6.3 Funatsu, S., N. Wakatsuki and A. Yamada, "Designing digital circuits with easily testable considerations", *Conf. Record: 1978 Semiconductor Test Conf.*, 98–102.

6.4 Goldstein, L., "Controllability/observability analysis of digital circuits", *IEEE Trans. Circuits and Systems*, 685–693 (September 1979).

6.5 Mukhopadhyay, A. and G. Schmitz, "Minimization of EXCLUSIVE–OR and LOGICAL EQUIVALENCE switching circuits", *IEEE Trans. Comput.*, 132–140 (February 1970).

6.6 Lewin, D. W., *Computer-aided Design of Digital Systems*, Chap. 5, Edward Arnold (1977).

6.7 Reddy, S. M., "A design procedure for fault-locatable switching circuits", *IEEE Trans. Comput.*, 1421–1426 (December 1972).

6.8 Dandapani, R. and S. M. Reddy, "On the design of logic networks with redundancy and testability considerations", *ibid.*, 1139–1149 (November 1974).

6.9 Hayes, J. P., "On modifying logic networks to improve their diagnosability", *ibid.*, 56–62 (January 1974).

6.10 Saluja, K. K. and S. M. Reddy, "On minimally testable logic networks", *ibid.*, 552–554 (May 1974).

6.11 Savir, J., "Syndrome-testable design of combinational circuits", *ibid.*, 442–451 (June 1980).

6.12 Kohavi, Z. and P. M. Lavelle, "Design of sequential machines with fault detection capabilities", *ibid.*, 473–484 (August 1967).

6.13 Williams, M. J. Y. and J. M. Angell, "Enhancing testability of large-scale integrated circuits via test points and additional logic", *ibid.*, 46–59 (January 1973).

6.14 Funatsu, S., N. Wakatsuki and T. Arima, "Test generation systems in Japan", *Proc. 12th Design Automation Conf.*, 114–122 (1975).

6.15 Yamada, A., *et al.*, "Automatic system level test generation and fault location for large digital systems", *Proc. 14th Design Automation Conf.*, 347–352 (1978).

6.16 Eichelberger, E. B. and T. W. Williams, "A logic design structure for LSI testability", *ibid.*, 462–468.

6.17 Godoy, H. C., G. B. Franklin and P. S. Bottorff, "Automatic checking of logic design structure for compliance with testability ground rules", *ibid.*, 469–478.

6.18 Dasgupta, S., P. Goel, R. G. Walther and T. W. Williams, "A variation of LSSD and its implications on design and test pattern generation in VLSI", *Proc. 1982 IEEE Test Conf.*, 63–66.

6.19 Williams, T. W. and K. P. Parker, "Design for testability—a survey", *IEEE Trans. Comput.*, 2–15 (January 1982).

6.20 Ando, H., "Testing VLSI with random access scan", *Proc. COMPCON Spring 1980*, 50–52.

6.21 Fasang, P. P., "BIDCO, Built-in digital circuit observer", *Proc. 1980 IEEE Test Conf.*, 261–266.

6.22 Koenamann, B., J. Mucha and G. Zwiehoff, "Built-in logic block observation technique", *Proc. 1979 IEEE Test Conf.*, 37–41.

6.23 Fasang, P. P., "Circuit module implements practical self-testing", *Electronics International*, 164–167 (May 1982).

6.24 Koenamann, B., J. Mucha and G. Zwiehoff, "Built-in test for complex integrated circuits", *IEEE Jour. Solid-state Circuits*, 315–321 (June 1980).

6.25 Mucha, J., "Hardware techniques for testing VLSI circuit based on built-in test", *Proc. COMPCON*, 366–369 (1981).

6.26 Nesbet, S. B. and E. J. McCluskey, "Structured design for testability to eliminate test pattern generation", *Proc. Int. Symp. Fault-tolerant Computing*, 158–163 (1980).

6.27 McCluskey, E. J. and S. B. Nesbet, "Design for autonomous test", *Proc. 1980 IEEE Test Conf.*, 15–21.

6.28 McCluskey, E. J., "Verification testing", *Proc. 19th Design Automation Conf.*, 495–500 (1982).

6.29 Mittelbach, J., "Put testability into PC boards", *Electronic Design*, 128–131 (June 1978).

6.30 Davidson, R. P., "Some straightforward guidelines help improve board testability", *EDN*, 127–129 (May 1979).

6.31 Grason, J. and A. W. Nagle, "Digital test generation and design for testability", *Proc. 17th Design Automation Conf.*, 175–189 (1980).

6.32 "Designing digital circuits for testability", Hewlett–Packard Application Note 210–214 (1977).

6.33 Muehldorf, E. I., "Designing LSI logic for testability", *Proc. 1976 Semicond. Test. Symp.*, 45–49.

6.34 Oberly, R. P., "How to beat the card test game", *Proc. 1977 Semicond. Test. Symp.*, 16–18.

6.35 Hayes, J. P. and E. J. McCluskey, "Testability considerations in microprocessor-based design", *IEEE Computer*, 17–26 (March 1980).

6.36 Anderson, R. E., "Microprocessor board testing—review tutorial", *Proc. 1978 IEEE Test Conf.*, 118–123.

6.37 Foley, G., "Designing microprocessor boards for testability", *ibid.*, 176–179.

7 CONCLUSION

The growth in the performance of LSI/VLSI in recent years has resulted in the development of highly complex computing systems. This, coupled with the fact that many applications now demand error-free computation over long periods of time, has significantly increased the required level of reliability and availability. The reliability of a computing system can be enhanced by employing two complementary approaches: fault tolerance and design for testability. The fault tolerance approach aims to prevent system failures despite the presence of faults, while design for testability uses component and system design techniques to facilitate repair. Considerable research has been done in recent years to improve the reliability of computing systems (Chaps. 2–6). This chapter discusses the current research issues.

Test generation has become one of the most costly, complicated and time-consuming problems in VLSI system design. Most of the current work in testing logic networks is based on classical (stuck-at) fault assumption, which does not accurately represent the failure mechanisms in currently popular technologies, e.g. NMOS, CMOS. It has been estimated that one-third of the faults in NMOS and CMOS structures are of non-classical nature; new fault models which supplement the classical model and permit automatic test pattern generation for high density LSI/VLSI chips must therefore be developed [7.1]. A recent approach in this direction is the introduction of the "conductance fault model" for CMOS integrated circuits [7.2]. This can represent both open and short transistor failure modes and leakage faults (excessive leakage current). A test generation procedure for detecting conductance faults is also given in Ref. [7.2]. Galiay et al. [7.3] identified the failure modes of MOS circuits and suggested that the layout of a circuit be submitted to a set of rules so that all defects could be covered by the stuck-at fault model. However, this requires an increase in chip area. Chiang and Vranesic [7.4] considered the test generation problem for networks composed of NMOS "complex gates". A complex gate is modelled as a pair of dual connection graphs; opens and shorts on branches in connection graphs are used to

246

represent faults in the network. Tests for such networks are generated by activating paths in the connection graphs. El-Ziq [7.5] introduced a new technique for generating tests for stuck-open faults in CMOS networks. First a test procedure based on a stuck-at fault model is used to detect some stuck-open faults. Tests needed to specifically detect the remaining stuck-open faults are then generated.

It is widely accepted now that the gate level approach of test generation is no longer feasible for LSI/VLSI circuits. Although several algorithms were developed for generating tests from circuit structures, they are primarily applicable to combinational circuits. The computation time needed to generate tests using these algorithms is an exponential function of the logical depth of a circuit. For sequential circuits the number of internal states is also an exponential function, which makes automatic test pattern generation for sequential circuits an almost impossible task.

In the structural testing approach, fault coverage provided by a set of tests is usually determined by conducting fault simulation at the gate level. As more and more LSI/VLSI chips are employed in systems, it is no longer feasible nor economical to use gate level simulation for the following reasons:

(a) The gate level representations of most LSI/VLSI chips are not available.
(b) The time and the memory required to simulate LSI/VLSI chips containing thousands of gates can be excessive.
(c) Some faults in LSI/VLSI chips cannot be represented by gate models.

Because of these difficulties the current trend in simulating LSI/VLSI circuits appears to be towards the functional level. Functional models are based upon the state diagram or data-transfer descriptions of LSI/VLSI chips. Several approaches for implementing fault simulation capabilities using functional models have been proposed in recent years [7.6–7.10]. However, as the complexity of circuits increases with the associated increase in the number of fault modes, the use of fault simulation may soon be unrealistic [7.11].

A new approach—functional testing—has been proposed in recent years to solve the complexity of testing LSI/VLSI chips comprehensively. This way of testing accepts a unit as being fault-free if the functions of the unit are executed correctly. Functional testing of memory chips is relatively easy because of their regular structures. Such testing verifies the correct operation of a memory chip by checking that:

(a) Each memory cell can be addressed.
(b) Each cell can be written into or read from with a 0 or 1.
(c) Data stored in a cell is not affected by addressing, writing into or reading from other cells.
(d) The access time and other specified timing parameters of the device are satisfactory.
(e) The device is not subject to pattern sensitivity problems.

Several functional testing procedures have been developed in recent years to detect faults in memory chips [7.12–7.16]. However, the memory chip dimensions are continuously on the increase; testing algorithms which can deal with memory chips of large dimensions in an acceptable period of time will be needed in the very near future. Functional test generation for LSI/VLSI chips of irregular structure has received relatively little attention in the past. Recent research has produced techniques for generating tests for microprocessors on the basis of information contained in the user's manual, e.g.

(a)   The set of instructions.
(b)   The set of operators.
(c)   The interfacing signals.

The popular approach to test microprocessors has been to subdivide the microprocessor into several functional modules whose behavior and interactions can be verified by executing appropriate test patterns [7.18, 7.19]. The main disadvantage of this approach is that testing is focused only on modules in the data processing section (e.g. ALU, program counter, stack pointer, etc.); the control section is assumed to operate correctly if the data processing functions are satisfactory. Besides there is no fault model, so it is difficult to determine which faults have actually been detected. Thatte and Abraham [7.19] proposed a graph-theoretic approach for functional testing of microprocessors. In this approach the microprocessor is modelled as a directed graph (S-graph) in which each register in the microprocessor is represented by a node; the main memory and the I/O devices are represented by two additional nodes named IN and OUT. The edges connecting the nodes are associated with instructions which transfer information between the nodes. The various functions of a microprocessor are partitioned into five sets: data storage, data transfer, data manipulation, register decoding and instruction decoding and control. Functional level fault models quite independent of the implementation details have also been proposed; some of these were later modified by Abraham and Parker [7.20]. The faults specified for the data storage and transfer functions are conventional stuck-at faults. No specific fault model is proposed for the data manipulation function because of the wide variety in existing designs for functional units. Register decoding faults result in the wrong register being written into or read out. In the case of a fault in the instruction decoding and control function either or both of the following faulty behaviors may result:

(a)   The instruction will not be executed.
(b)   The information stored in the microprocessor will be incorrectly modified.

By analyzing the microprocessor behavior in the present of these faults, a number of test procedures are determined; each procedure is designed for detecting a particular class of faults. The generated test sequences consist of a set of valid instructions which can be assembled to produce the test program. For an eight-bit Hewlett–Packard microprocessor the coverage of the single stuck-at faults by this technique was of the order of 96%. A major problem associated with this technique is the assumption that faults in the instruction decoding and control circuitry may lead to the execution of a wrong instruction, execution of multiple instructions or execution of no instruction at all. These assumptions may not be valid for microprocessors with micro-programmed control units, where faults may result in the incomplete execution or execution of instructions not in the valid instruction set of the microprocessor [7.21].

Functional level fault models have also been developed for bit-sliced ALU/register devices. Sridhar and Hayes [7.22] have modelled bit-slice devices as iterative logic arrays, which require a constant number of tests independent of array size; such arrays have been called "C-testable", where C stands for a constant [7.23]. For testing purposes C is considered as a network of small register-level modules whose input–output behavior is completely defined; the internal structures of these modules are ignored. These modules are either combinational or sequential. It is assumed that faults in a combinational module cannot convert it into a sequential circuit, and the faults in a sequential module can cause changes in its state table without increasing the number of states. Combinational modules are tested by applying all possible input combinations to the modules. The sequential modules are tested using the checking sequence approach (Sec. 3.4.2). El-Litty and Husson [7.24] proposed a test procedure for one of the recent bit-sliced ALU/register devices (AMD 2903 Superslice). The fault model is formulated at a functional level which treats the device as an interconnection of smaller functional modules and provides a complete coverage for the most likely hardware faults in such devices.

The fundamental problem associated with the functional testing approach is how to represent the functional description of a device. Truth tables and state tables grow exponentially with the number of variables, and hence are not practicable for LSI/VLSI circuits. New methods of specifying large digital functions, which can be handled efficiently, are needed if tests are to be generated directly from functional descriptions. Akers [7.25] has introduced such a functional description tool called the "binary decision diagram". The main feature of this technique is that the behavior of a circuit in any of its operation modes can be clearly defined by the decision diagrams. These diagrams are amenable to extensive logical analysis, and can be stored and processed easily in a computer.

The difficulty and expense of testing LSI/VLSI chips have become so great that it is now imperative to incorporate testability features into the chips. Various approaches have been suggested in recent years to improve testability of circuits; however there is no general agreement on how to design for testability. The main problem in testable chip design is that extra I/O pins are required to increase the controllability and observability of internal circuits, which is a significant overhead. Clearly any approach to improve testability of an LSI/VLSI circuit must take into consideration the impact of additional pins and additional logic (chip area) on the original design [7.26].

Another approach which can be used to enhance the testability of a circuit is the testability measure analysis. Whereas the design for testability ensures that the generation of tests for a circuit is considerably simplified, testability measure analysis is used to identify sections of a circuit which are difficult to control and to observe via the I/O pins. This information allows estimation of a circuit's testability before the test generation is attempted. Hence any potential testing problem can be located early in the design phase, allowing modifications to be introduced to improve the final testability of the circuit.

A testability analysis procedure must satisfy two basic requirements before it can be useful:

1. It should use less computer resources than the test generation process.
2. It must accurately identify the sections of a circuit for which test generation is difficult.

Several testability measure programs are currently in use: SCOAP [7.27], TMEAS [7.28], TESTSCREEN [7.29], CAMELOT [7.30], VICTOR [7.31], COMET [7.32] and ITTAP [7.33]. These programs are useful only for analyzing circuits with gates and flip-flops as the primitive elements. As the complexity of circuits increases these programs become less practicable. Hence it is becoming increasingly important to develop efficient techniques in order to perform testability analysis at the functional level [7.34].

As the internal complexity of the integrated circuit chip increases, the idea of built-in tests (BIT) becomes more and more attractive. BIT has many advantages:

(a) Test patterns are generated automatically inside chips.
(b) Responses to test patterns need not be stored.
(c) Use of expensive test equipment is not necessary.

BIT approaches are grouped into two categories: off-line (non-concurrent) or on-line (concurrent).

The off-line test techniques use either resident software or hardware approaches. The resident software used for testing is invoked by a computer operating system during times when normal functional processing is not being done. Examples are syndrome testing and transition count testing. In the off-line resident hardware, the system is reconfigured and tested when normal functional processing does not occur. The example of this approach is BILBO. The off-line test techniques suffer from the disadvantage of not being able to detect temporary faults, which are likely to be more important in VLSI systems.

The on-line testing techniques may be classified as information-redundant or hardware-redundant. Information redundancies such as parity, cyclic redundancy check, residue codes, Hamming codes, etc., increases the width of data. Hardware-redundant schemes use duplication at the module level with a comparator, to check for faults. Totally self-checking circuits employ both information and hardware redundancies to check the validity of their inputs and their own operation. As more and more digital systems in future will be built using complex VLSI chips, concurrent fault detection at the chip level could be one way of implementing fault tolerance in such systems.

Although structured testability approaches such as scan-path and LSSD have significantly lessened the difficulty of testing sequential circuits, the problem of testing large combinational circuits containing both multiple stuck-at and non-stuck-at faults still remains to be solved [7.35]. The ability to put extra logic into chips without incurring high cost clearly favors the use of on-chip concurrent testing techniques for VLSI. It has been found that if current LSI technology is used, the increase in hardware needed to convert a conventionally checked computer design to a fully checked design (100% single-fault coverage) is only of the order of 5–7% [7.36]. Therefore, design techniques which use extra hardware in order to achieve greater levels of automatic fault detection inside VLSI chips seems to be quite practicable. Such testing technique must be applicable to both stuck-at and non-stuck-at faults, and provide high fault coverage. Little research has been done in this area apart from that reported in Refs. [7.37–7.39].

Further investigation is also necessary to establish whether some form of "exception handling" mechanism can be built into chips so that faults detected during normal operation can be masked. The traditional fault-masking techniques which incorporate double or triple redundancy increase the complexity of circuitry, and therefore require a large area on chips. Hence alternative redundancy strategies such as the use of error-correcting codes should be considered for masking faults, as they are detected. It is important that circuits used for this purpose are totally self-checking; otherwise the overall reliability of chips will be seriously compromised. The impact of additional logic and I/O pins on the performance should also be taken into account. A major problem in designing a self-checking chip architecture is to determine at what level concurrent fault detection becomes practicable. One possible approach is to partition the logic into clearly defined functional units; appropriate concurrent test techniques can then be selected. More work is necessary in order to develop methods for appropriate partitioning of logic of VLSI complexity.

7.1 REFERENCES

7.1 Siewiorek, D., "Workshop report: fault-tolerant VLSI design", *IEEE Computer*, 51–53 (December 1980).

7.2 Malaiya, Y. K. and S. Y. H. Su, "A new fault model and testing technique for CMOS devices", *Proc. 1982 IEEE Test Conf.*, 25–34.

7.3 Galiay, J., *et al.*, "Physical versus logical fault models MOS LSI: impact on their testability", *IEEE Trans. Comput.*, 527–531 (June 1980).

7.4 Chiang, K. and Z. Vranesic, "Test generation for MOS complex gate networks", *Proc. Int. Symp. Fault-tolerant Computing*, 149–157 (1982).

7.5 El-Ziq, Y. M., "Automatic test generation for stuck-open faults", *Proc. 18th Design Automation Conf.*, 347–354 (1981).

7.6 Abramovici, M., *et al.*, "Concurrent fault simulation and functional level modelling", *Proc. 14th Design Automation Conf.*, 128–137 (1977).

7.7 Alia, G., *et al.*, "LSI components modelling in a three valued functional simulation", *Proc. 15th Design Automation Conf.*, 428–438 (1978).

7.8 Wilcox, P., "Digital logic simulation at the gate and functional level", *Proc. 16th Design Automation Conf.*, 242–248 (1979).

7.9 Thomson, E. W., *et al.*, "The incorporation of functional level element routines into an existing digital simulation system", *Proc. 17th Design Automation Conf.*, 394–401 (1980).

7.10 Menon, P. R. and S. G. Chappell, "Deductive fault simulation with functional blocks", *IEEE Trans. Comput.*, 689–695 (August 1978).

7.11 Breuer, M. A. and A. C. Parker, "Digital system simulation: current status and future trends", *Proc. 18th Design Automation Conf.*, 269–275 (1981).

7.12 Nair, R., *et al.*, "Efficient algorithms for testing semi-conductor random access memories", *IEEE Trans. Comput.*, 572–576 (June 1978).

7.13 Hayes, J. P., "Testing memories for single cell pattern sensitive faults", *ibid.*, 249–254 (March 1980).

7.14 Suk, D. S. and S. M. Reddy, "Test procedures for a class of pattern sensitive faults in semi-conductor random access memories", *ibid.*, 419–429 (June 1980).

7.15 Suk, D. S. and S. M. Reddy, "A march test for functional faults in semi-conductor random access memories", *ibid.*, 982–985 (December 1981).

7.16 Marinescu, M., "Simple and efficient algorithms for functional RAM testing", *Proc. 1982 IEEE Test Conf.*, 236–239.

7.17 Chiang, A. C. L. and R. McCaskill, "Two new approaches to simplify testing of microprocessors", *Electronics*, 100 (January 1976).

7.18 Smith, D. H., "Exercising the functional structure gives microprocessors a real workout", *Electronics*, 109–112 (February 1977).

7.19 Thatte, S. M. and J. A. Abraham, "Test generation for microprocessors", *IEEE Trans. Comput.*, 429–441 (June 1980).

7.20 Abraham, J. A. and K. P. Parker, "Practical microprocessor testing: open and closed loop approaches", *Proc. IEEE COMPCON*, 308–311 (1981).

7.21 Parthasarsthy, S., *et al.*, "A testable design of general purpose microprocessors", *Proc. Int. Symp. Fault-tolerant Computing*, 117–124 (1982).

7.22 Sridhar, T. and J. P. Hayes, "A functional approach to testing bit-sliced microprocessors", *IEEE Trans. Comput.*, 563–571 (August 1981).

7.23 Friedman, A. D., "Easily testable iterative system", *ibid.*, 1061–1064 (December 1973).

7.24 El-Litty, M. and R. Husson, "Bit-sliced microprocess testing—a case study", *Proc. Int. Symp. Fault-tolerant Computing,* 126–128 (1980).

7.25 Akers, S. B., "Binary decision diagrams", *IEEE Trans. Comput.,* 509–515 (June 1978).

7.26 Renésegers, M. T. M., "The impact of testing on VLSI design methods", *IEEE Jour. Solid-state Circuits,* 481–486 (June 1982).

7.27 Goldstein, L. H. and E. L. Thigpen, "SCOAP: Sandia controllability and observability analysis program", *Proc. 17th Design Automation Conf.,* 190–196 (1980).

7.28 Grason, J., "TMEAS: a testability measurement program", *Proc. 16th Design Automation Conf.,* 156–161 (1979).

7.29 Koviganic, P. G., "Testability analysis", *Proc. IEEE 1979 Test Conf.,* 310–316.

7.30 Bennetts, R. G., *et al.,* "CAMELOT: a computer-aided measure for logic testability", *Proc. IEE,* 177–189 (September 1981).

7.31 Ratiu, I. M., *et al.,* "VICTOR: a fast VLSI testability analysis program", *Proc. 1982 IEEE Test Conf.,* 397–401.

7.32 Berg, W. C. and R. D. Hess, "COMET: a testability analysis and design modifications package", *ibid.,* 364–378.

7.33 Goel, D. K. and R. M. McDermott, "An interactive testability analysis program—ITTAP", *Proc. 19th Design Automation Conf.,* 581–586 (1982).

7.34 Fong, J. Y. O., "On functional controllability and observability analysis", *Proc. IEEE 1982 Test Conf.,* 170–175.

7.35 Sedmak, R. M., "Implementation techniques for self-verification", *Proc. IEEE 1980 Test Conf.,* 267–278.

7.36 Carter, W. C., *et al.,* "Cost-effectiveness of self-checking computer design", *Proc. Int. Symp. Fault-tolerant Computing,* 117–123 (1977).

7.37 Sedmak, R. M. and H. L. Liebergot, "Fault-tolerance of a general purpose computer implemented by very large scale integration", *ibid.,* 137–143 (1978).

7.38 Sridhar, T. and S. M. Thatte, "Concurrent checking of program flow in VLSI processors", *Proc. 1982 IEEE Test Conf.,* 191–199.

7.39 Iyenger, S. V. and L. L. Kinney, "Concurrent testing of flow of control in simple microprogrammed control units", *ibid.,* 469–475.

APPENDIX   MARKOV MODELS

Markov models are used to analyze probabilistic systems [A.1]. The two key concepts of such models are state and state transition. A system can be in any one of a finite number of states at any instant of time, and move successively from one state to another as time passes. The changes of state are called *state transitions*. In general the probability that a system will be in a particular state at time $t + 1$ depends on the state of the system at time $t, t - 1, t - 2$ and so on. However, if the state of the system at time $t + 1$ only depends on the state at time t, and not on the sequence of transitions through which the state at t was arrived at, the system corresponds to a "first order" Markov model. If the state at time $t + 1$ is independent of the previous state, i.e. the state at time t, then the system corresponds to a Markov model of "zero order".

The probability that the system will, when in state i, make a transition to state j is known as the *transition probability*. A system with S states has S^2 transition probabilities, which can be denoted by p_{ij}, $1 \leqslant i \leqslant S$, $1 \leqslant j \leqslant S$. For computational purposes the transition probabilities are organized into a square matrix P, called the *transition probability matrix*, as shown below; the (i, j) entry in P is the probability of transition from state i to state j.

$$P = \begin{bmatrix} p_{11} & p_{12} & \cdots & p_{1S} \\ p_{21} & p_{22} & \cdots & p_{2S} \\ \vdots & \vdots & & \vdots \\ p_{S1} & p_{S2} & \cdots & p_{SS} \end{bmatrix}$$

In any particular situation, the transition probabilities p_{ij}, and consequently the transition matrix P, depend upon what is assumed about the behavior of the system.

The Markov models discussed so far are "discrete time" models. These models require all state transitions to occur at fixed intervals; each transition is assigned with a certain probability. On the other hand "continuous-time"

Markov models are characterized by the fact that state transitions can occur at any point in time; the amount of time spent in each state, before proceeding to the next state, is exponentially distributed.

REFERENCE

A.1 Shooman, M. L., *Probabilistic Reliability: An Engineering Approach*, McGraw-Hill (1968).

ANNOTATED BIBLIOGRAPHY

This annotated bibliography references the books, journals and conference proceedings that contain high quality research papers.

JOURNALS

1 *IEEE Transactions on Computers*—the main source of references for current work in reliable hardware design.
2 *IEEE Computer*—occasionally contains survey and tutorial articles on fault tolerant design and test generation.

CONFERENCES

1 *International Test Conference*—held annually; this is the prime source for the state-of-the-art information on test generation, design for testability and built-in tests.
2 *Design Automation Conference*—held annually; design, simulation and test generation issues make up a significant portion of the topics covered.
3 *International Symposium on Fault-tolerant Computing*—held annually; contains the latest research ideas on all aspects of computer system reliability including the software.
4 *Symposium on Computer Architecture*—held annually; usually contains papers on reliable computer system design.

BOOKS

1 *Computer-aided Design of Digital Systems* by D. Lewin (Crane Russak, 1977). This book deals with various CAD techniques that can be applied in logic network synthesis, logic simulation and testing. System specification by means of hardware description languages and by using Petri nets is also discussed. It also contains a number of helpful worked examples. The book can be recommended to those interested in most aspects of CAD techniques in digital system design.
2 *Diagnosis and Reliable Design of Digital Systems* by M. A. Breuer and A. D. Friedman (Pitman, 1977).

This book provides a useful guide to the various techniques of test generation for combinational and sequential circuits, with many examples to help the reader in understanding these techniques. It contains an excellent chapter on logic simulation which provides useful general material on simulators and also describes their application to fault simulation. Although the section on reliable design is rather thin, the book can be recommended as a useful reference volume.

3   *Error Detecting Codes, Self-checking Circuits and Applications* by J. Wakerly (Elsevier North-Holland Inc., 1978).
This book deals with the applications of various error detecting codes to digital system design. It gives a good introduction to the basics of coding theory and examines the general properties of self-checking circuits. It also describes checking techniques for arithmetical and logical operations, data paths, memory and microprogrammed control units. A valuable list of references is also included.

4   *Computer Logic, Testing and Verification* by J. Paul Roth (Computer Science Press, 1980).
The book presents several original methods for the design and testing of switching functions. The two major methods discussed, the cubical calculus and the D-algorithm were published by the author during the 1960s and have become standard topics in many text books on switching theory. Although the abbreviated presentation and peculiar syntax make it a difficult text to follow, nevertheless it would make a useful back-up reference for research students in Computer Science/Engineering.

5   *Microprogrammed Control and Reliable Design of Small Computers* by G. D. Kraft and W. N. Toy (Prentice-Hall, 1981).
The book describes in detail the methods and philosophies adopted by Bell Laboratories in designing fault tolerant ESS processors. It is divided into two parts: microprogrammed design and fault tolerant design. The first part presents a detailed and comprehensive treatment of microprogramming techniques. The second part begins with the basic concepts of redundancy, reliability and maintainability. It also deals with fault characteristics and basic approaches to improving reliability, before continuing with the consideration of a large collection of existing and proposed fault detection techniques, e.g. data path checking, totally self-checking circuits, control store checking, error detection in arithmetic and logic operations and hardware checks for software bugs. In addition the use of microdiagnostics is explored. The book should be useful to those interested in the design of highly reliable microprogrammed computer systems.

6   *The Theory and Practice of Reliable System Design*, edited by D. P. Siewiorek and R. S. Swarz (Digital Press, 1982).
The book is divided into two parts. Part 1 deals with the disciplines required to construct a reliable computing system. Part 2 is a collection of papers on some of the existing fault tolerant architectures. Part 1 commences with an introductory chapter covering the philosophy of reliable systems. This is followed by chapters on faults in a computer system, reliability techniques, maintainability techniques, evaluation criteria for computing structures and modelling such structures, and finally financial considerations involved in the development, purchase and operation of a computer system.

7   *Design of Testable Logic Circuits* by R. G. Bennetts (Addison-Wesley, 1984).
The book presents various techniques for designing testable logic circuits such as scan-path, LSSD, random access scan and BILBO. It includes a chapter on testability measures with a detailed discussion of the CAMELOT approach. The problem of testing scan-designed circuits is discussed and test generation algorithm PODEM is presented with worked examples. The final chapter of the book provides a series of guidelines for improving the testability of digital boards and chips.

INDEX